She Professed Herself Pupil of the Wise Man

Art by
dicca*suemitsu
Story by
Ryusen Hirotsugu
Character Design by
fuzichoco

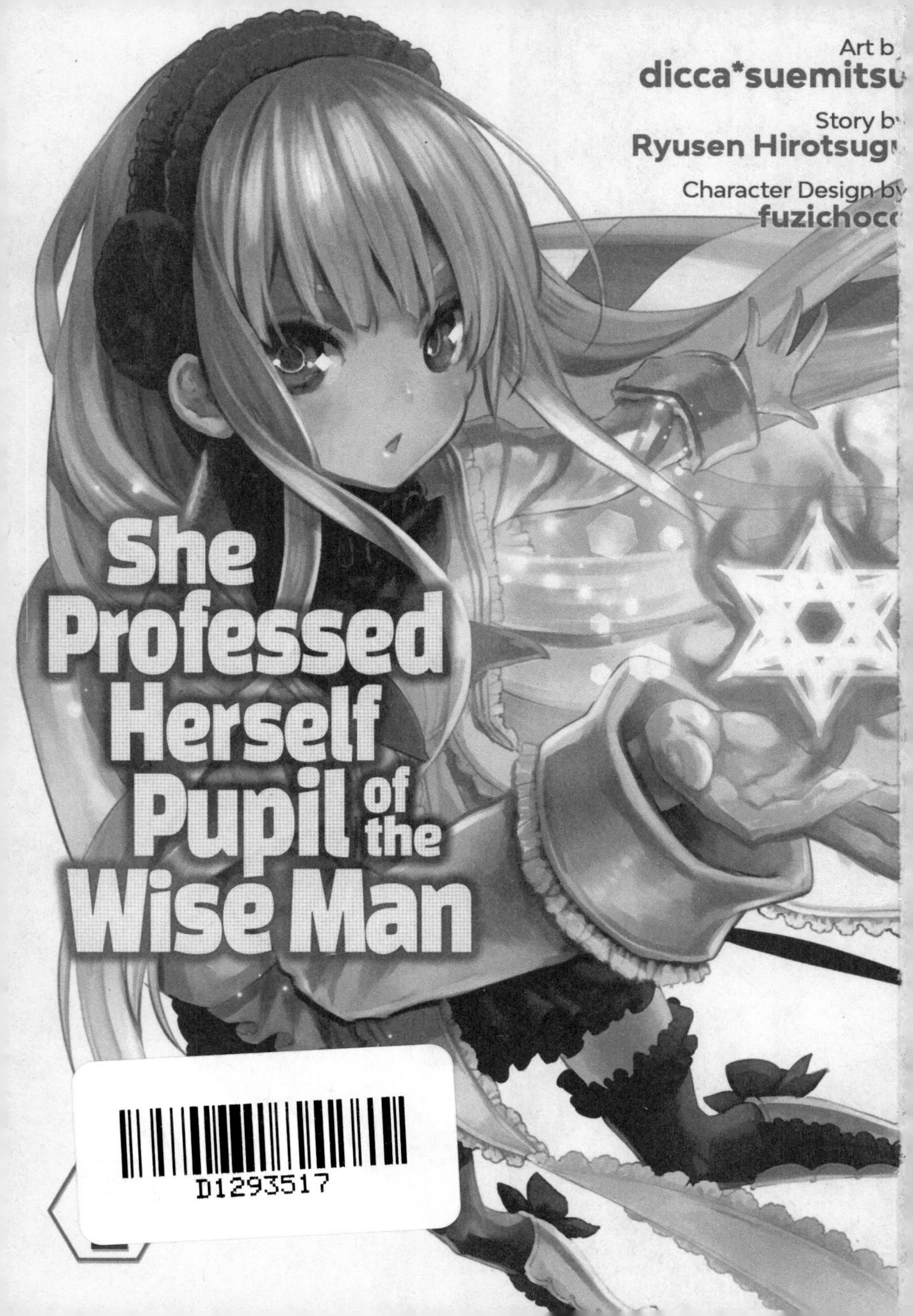

CONTENTS

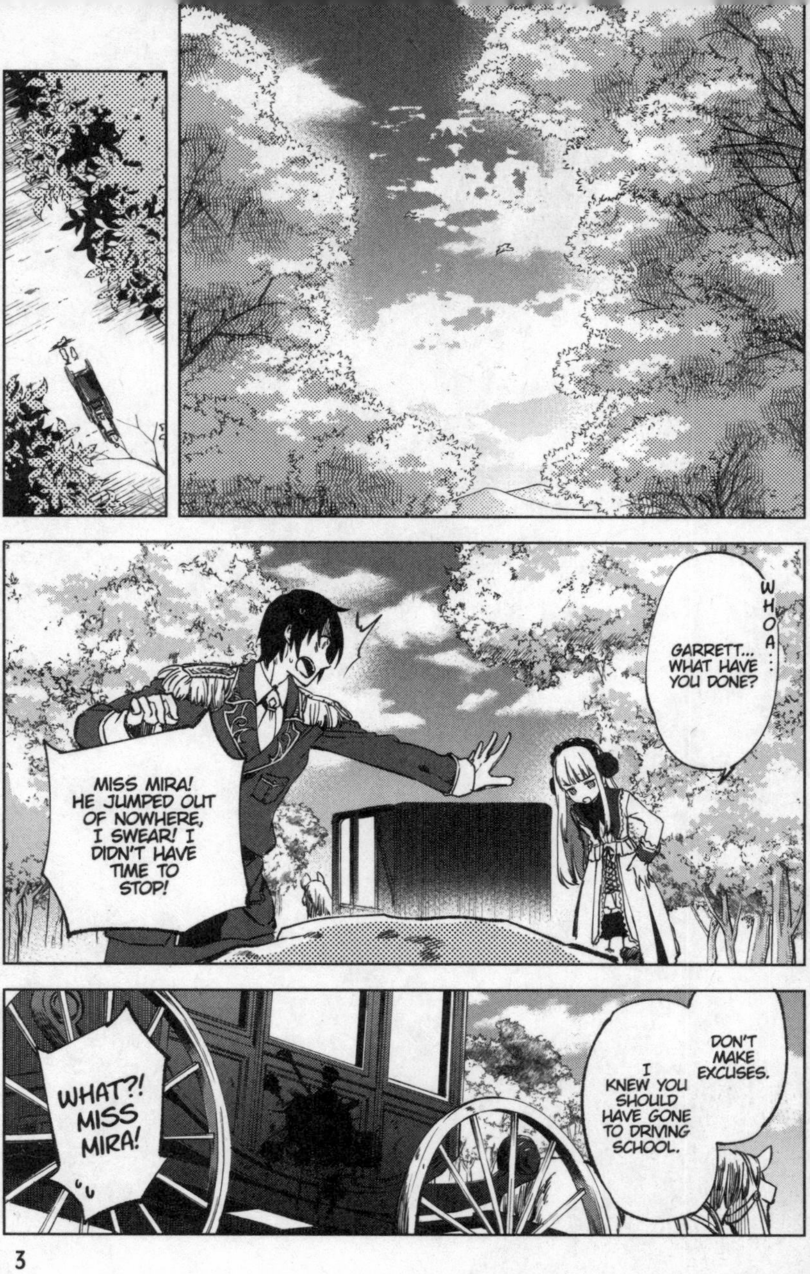
WHOA...
GARRETT... WHAT HAVE YOU DONE?
MISS MIRA! HE JUMPED OUT OF NOWHERE, I SWEAR! I DIDN'T HAVE TIME TO STOP!
DON'T MAKE EXCUSES.
I KNEW YOU SHOULD HAVE GONE TO DRIVING SCHOOL.
WHAT?! MISS MIRA!

Summon 8: [Karanak]

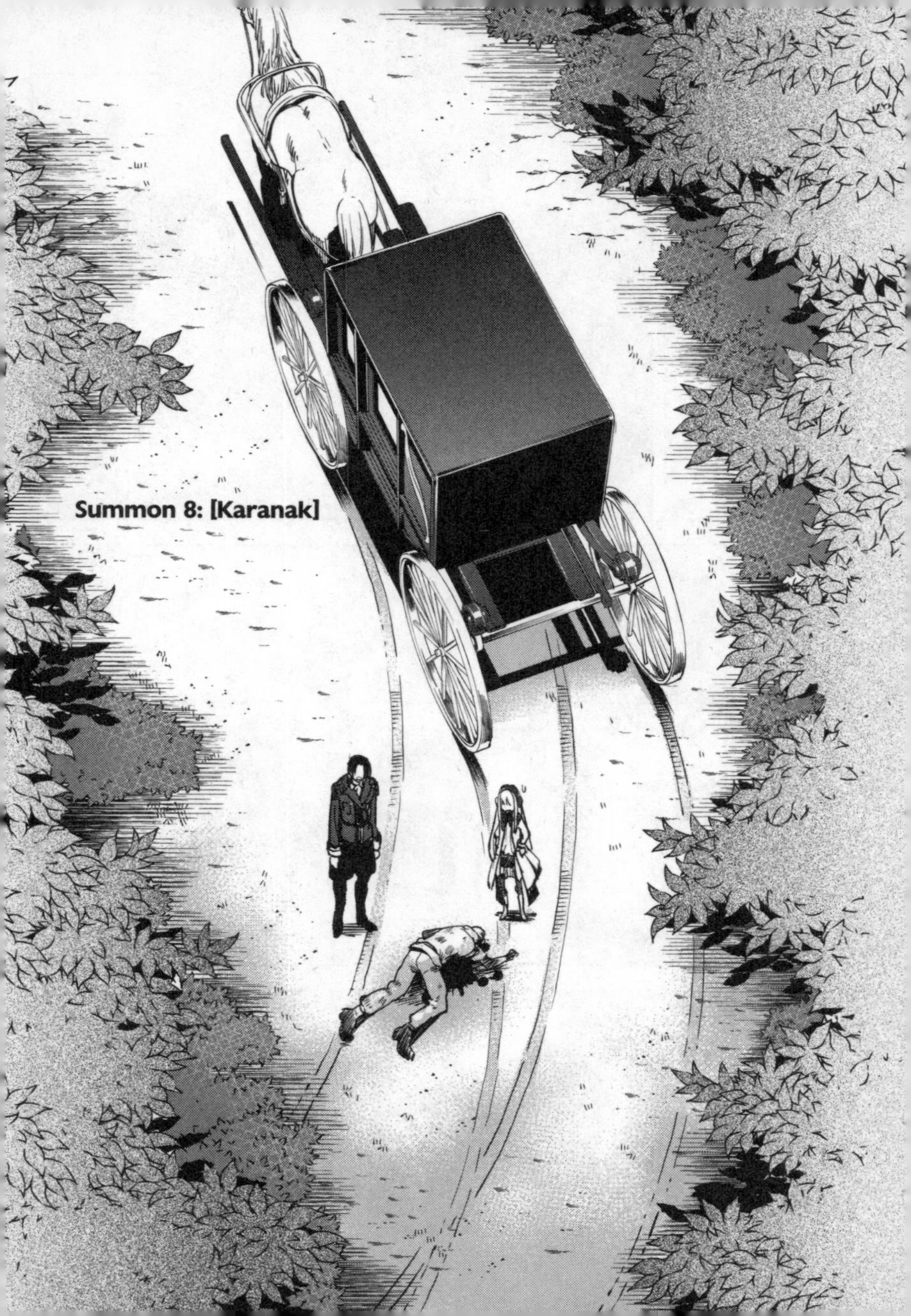

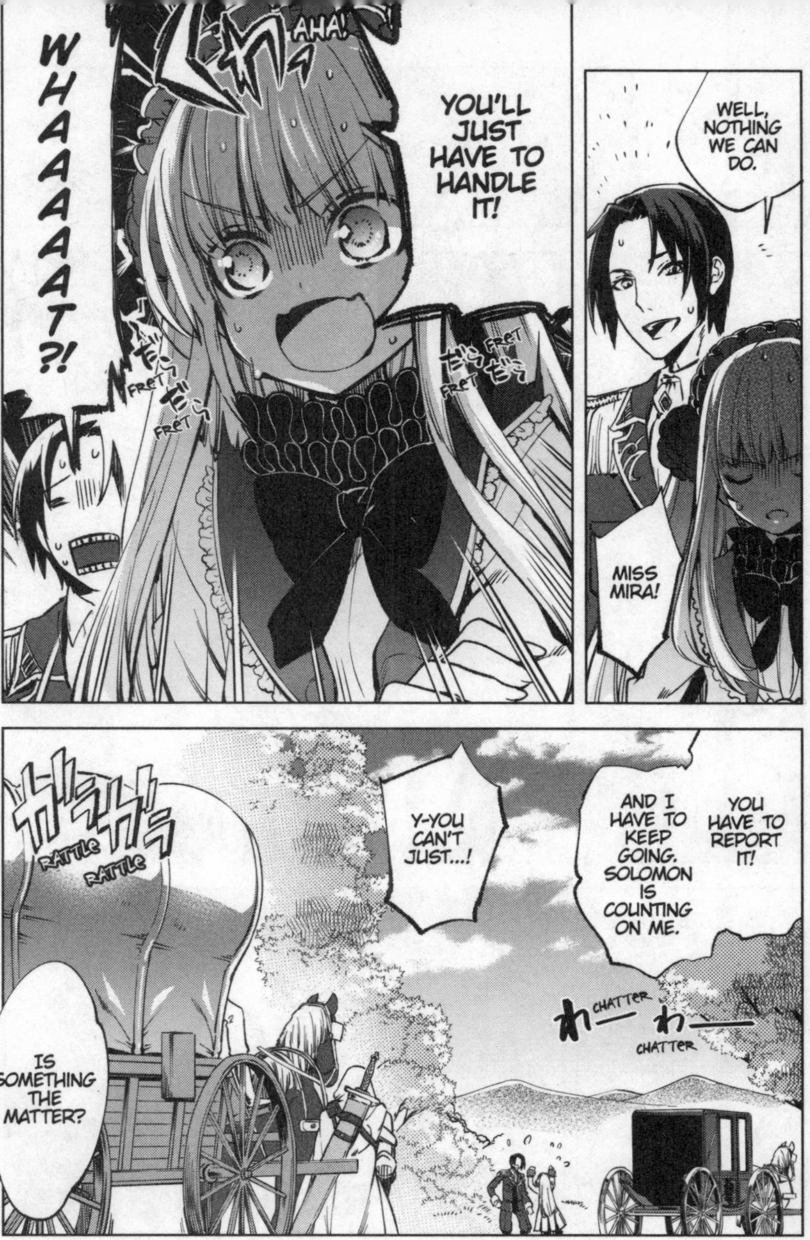
WELL, NOTHING WE CAN DO.
MISS MIRA!
AHA!
YOU'LL JUST HAVE TO HANDLE IT!
FRET FRET
FRET FRET
WHAAAAAAAT?!
YOU HAVE TO REPORT IT!
AND I HAVE TO KEEP GOING. SOLOMON IS COUNTING ON ME.
Y-YOU CAN'T JUST...!
CHATTER CHATTER
RATTLE RATTLE
IS SOMETHING THE MATTER?

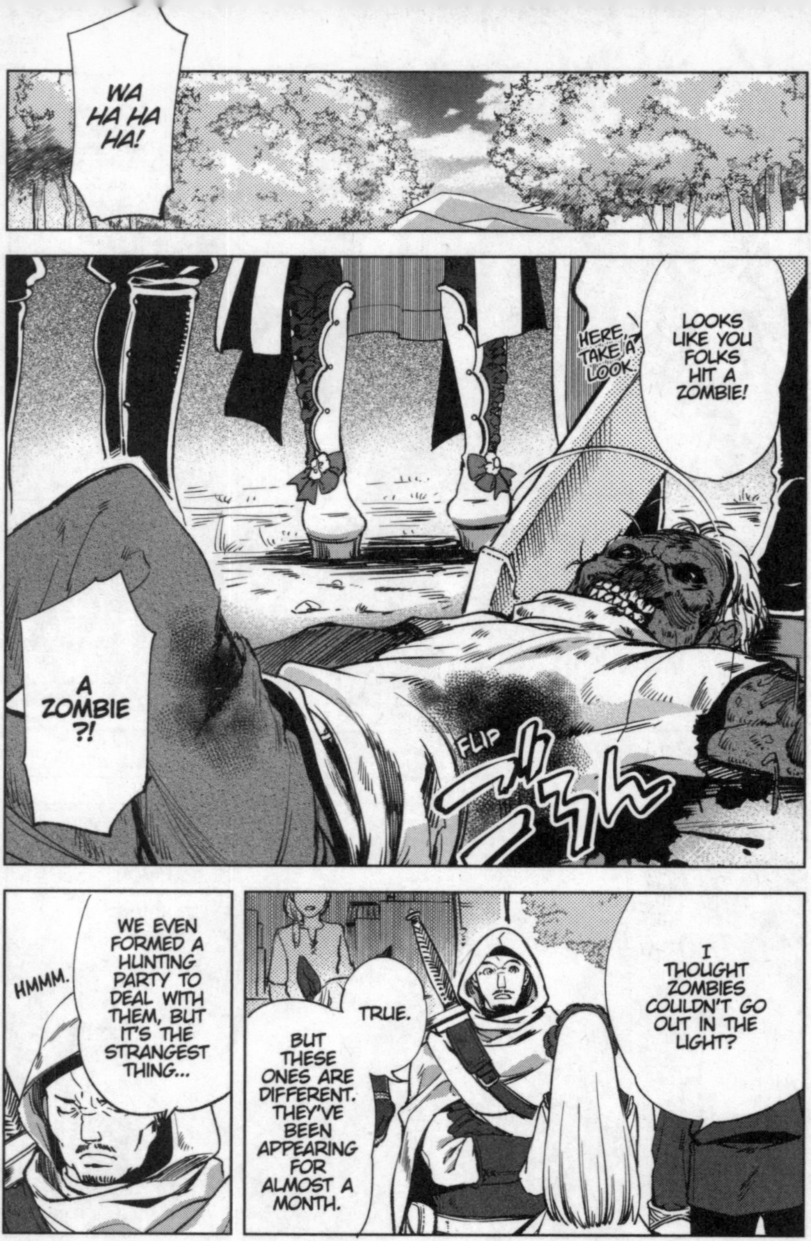
WA HA HA HA!
LOOKS LIKE YOU FOLKS HIT A ZOMBIE!
HERE, TAKE A LOOK
FLIP
A ZOMBIE?!
I THOUGHT ZOMBIES COULDN'T GO OUT IN THE LIGHT?
TRUE.
BUT THESE ONES ARE DIFFERENT. THEY'VE BEEN APPEARING FOR ALMOST A MONTH.
WE EVEN FORMED A HUNTING PARTY TO DEAL WITH THEM, BUT IT'S THE STRANGEST THING...
HMMM.

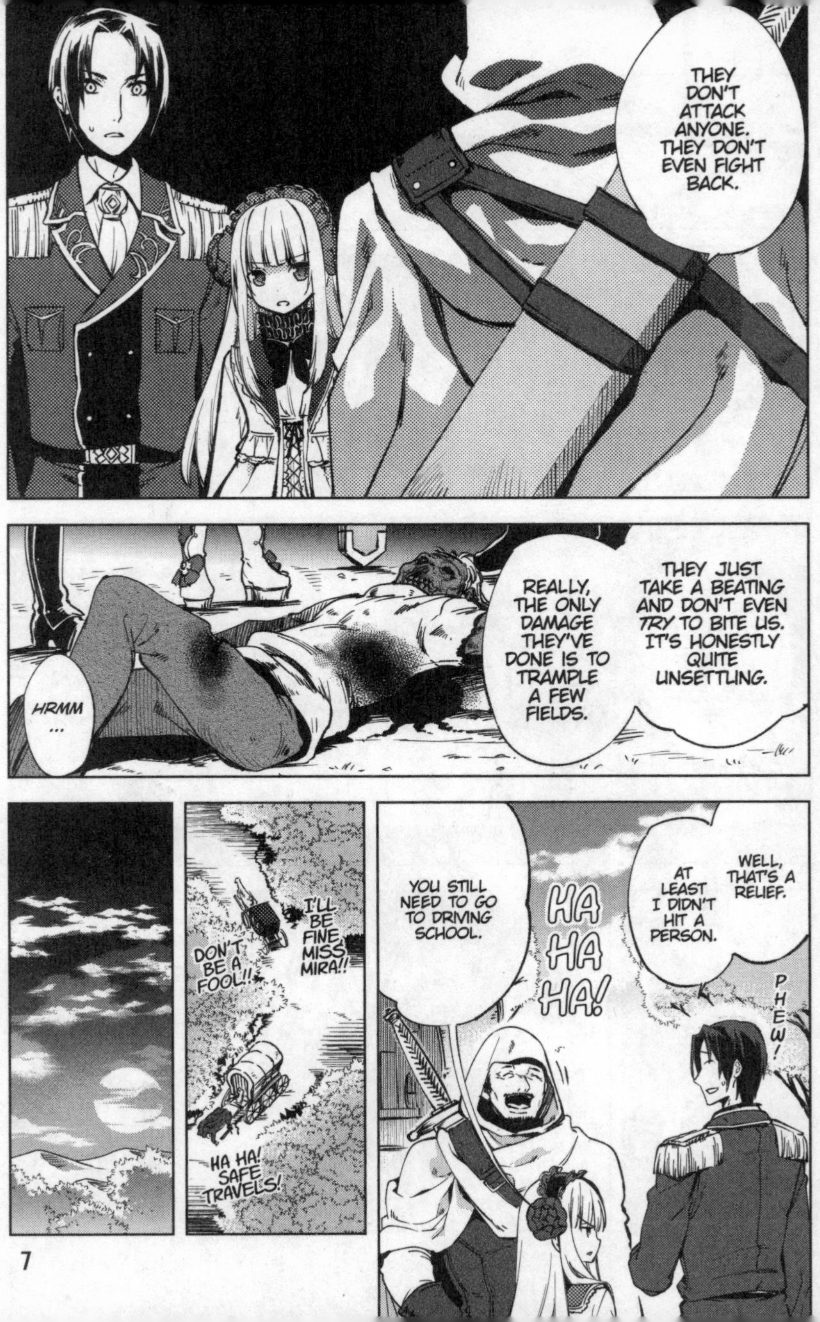
THEY DON'T ATTACK ANYONE. THEY DON'T EVEN FIGHT BACK.
THEY JUST TAKE A BEATING AND DON'T EVEN *TRY* TO BITE US. IT'S HONESTLY QUITE UNSETTLING.
REALLY, THE ONLY DAMAGE THEY'VE DONE IS TO TRAMPLE A FEW FIELDS.
HRMM...
WELL, THAT'S A RELIEF.
AT LEAST I DIDN'T HIT A PERSON.
PHEW!
HA HA HA!
YOU STILL NEED TO GO TO DRIVING SCHOOL.
I'LL BE FINE, MISS MIRA!!
DON'T BE A FOOL!!
HA HA! SAFE TRAVELS!

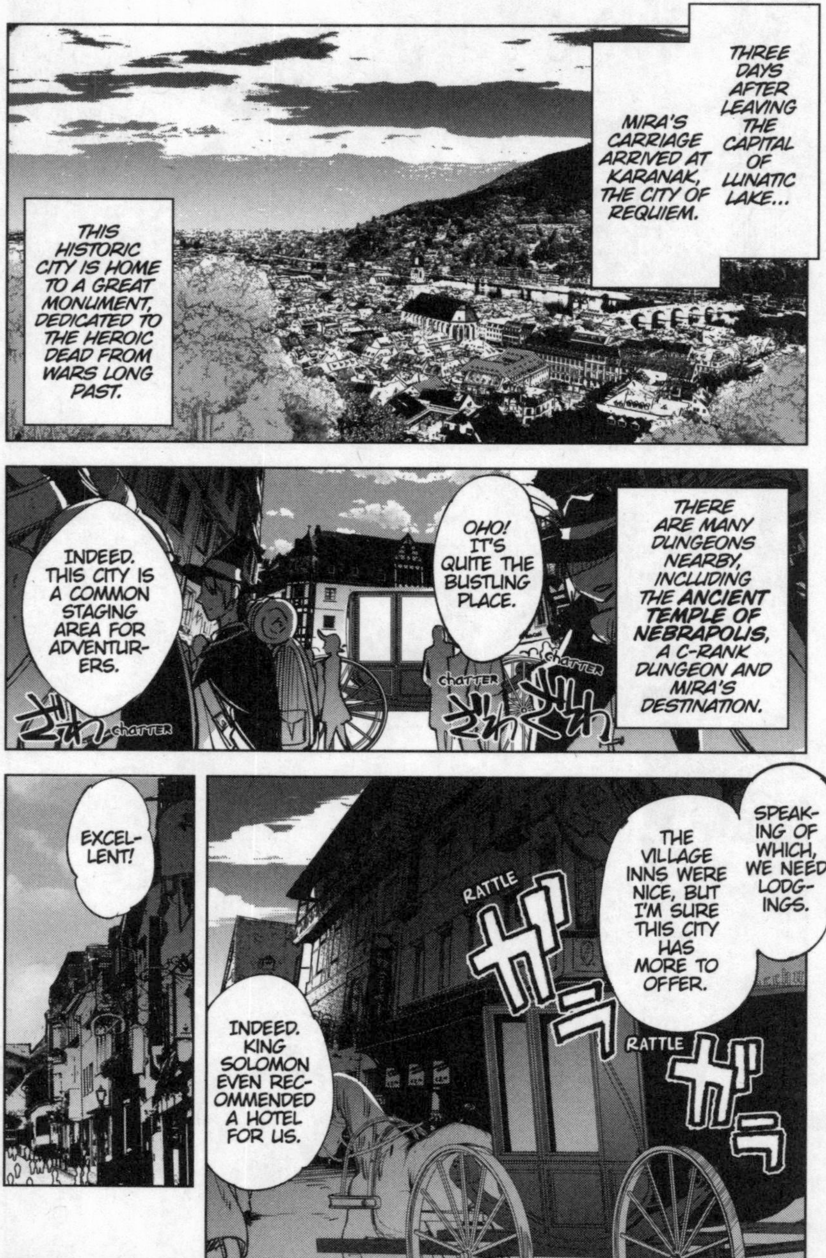
THREE DAYS AFTER LEAVING THE CAPITAL OF LUNATIC LAKE...
MIRA'S CARRIAGE ARRIVED AT KARANAK, THE CITY OF REQUIEM.
THIS HISTORIC CITY IS HOME TO A GREAT MONUMENT, DEDICATED TO THE HEROIC DEAD FROM WARS LONG PAST.
THERE ARE MANY DUNGEONS NEARBY, INCLUDING THE ANCIENT TEMPLE OF NEBRAPOLIS, A C-RANK DUNGEON AND MIRA'S DESTINATION.
OHO! IT'S QUITE THE BUSTLING PLACE.
ざわ ざわ
chatter chatter
INDEED. THIS CITY IS A COMMON STAGING AREA FOR ADVENTURERS.
ざわ
chatter
SPEAKING OF WHICH, WE NEED LODGINGS.
THE VILLAGE INNS WERE NICE, BUT I'M SURE THIS CITY HAS MORE TO OFFER.
ガラ ガラ
RATTLE RATTLE
INDEED. KING SOLOMON EVEN RECOMMENDED A HOTEL FOR US.
EXCELLENT!

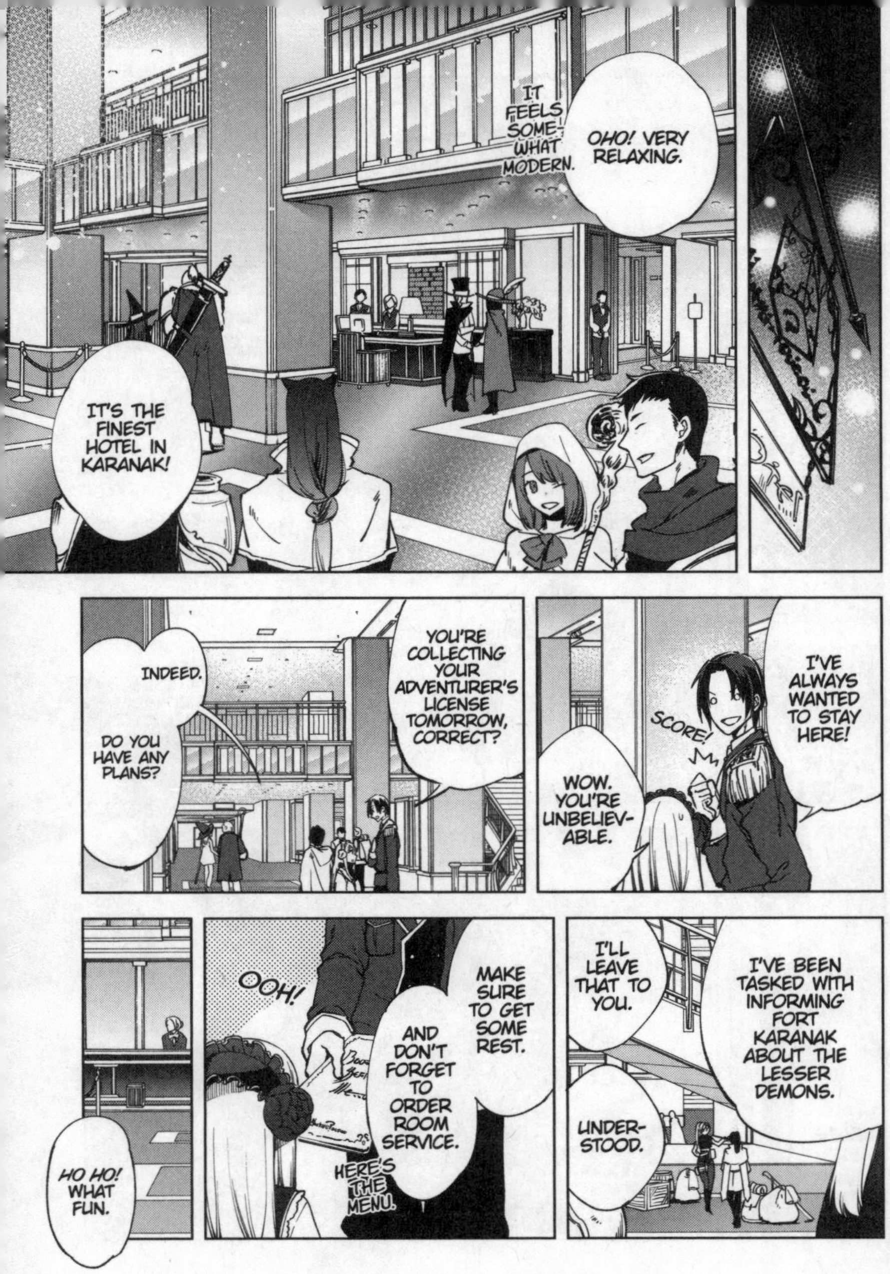
OHO! VERY RELAXING.
IT FEELS SOME-WHAT MODERN.
IT'S THE FINEST HOTEL IN KARANAK!
I'VE ALWAYS WANTED TO STAY HERE!
SCORE!
WOW. YOU'RE UNBELIEV-ABLE.
YOU'RE COLLECTING YOUR ADVENTURER'S LICENSE TOMORROW, CORRECT?
INDEED.
DO YOU HAVE ANY PLANS?
I'VE BEEN TASKED WITH INFORMING FORT KARANAK ABOUT THE LESSER DEMONS.
I'LL LEAVE THAT TO YOU.
UNDER-STOOD.
MAKE SURE TO GET SOME REST.
OOH!
AND DON'T FORGET TO ORDER ROOM SERVICE.
HERE'S THE MENU.
HO HO! WHAT FUN.

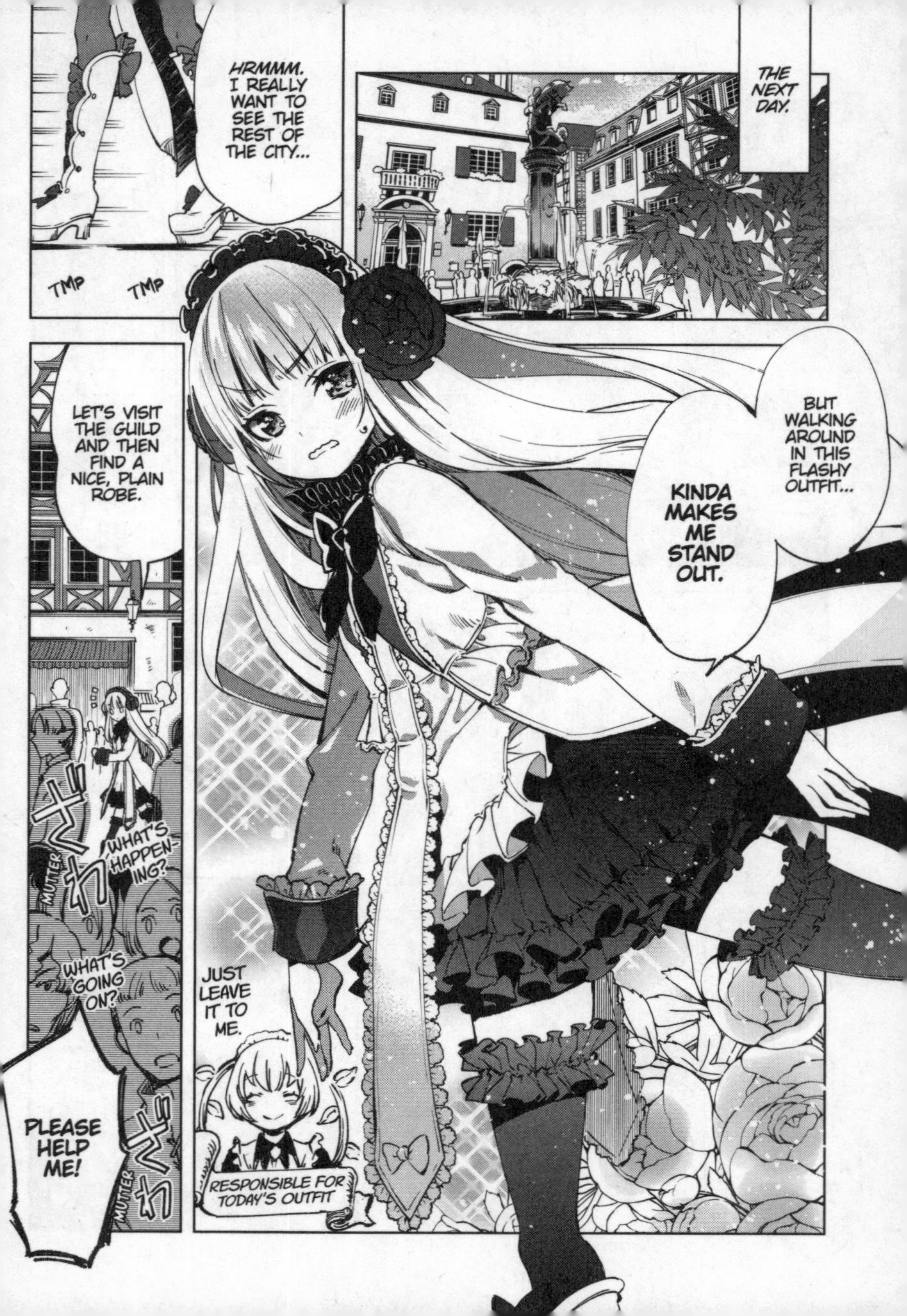
THE NEXT DAY.
HRMMM. I REALLY WANT TO SEE THE REST OF THE CITY...
TMP TMP
BUT WALKING AROUND IN THIS FLASHY OUTFIT...
KINDA MAKES ME STAND OUT.
JUST LEAVE IT TO ME.
RESPONSIBLE FOR TODAY'S OUTFIT
LET'S VISIT THE GUILD AND THEN FIND A NICE, PLAIN ROBE.
WHAT'S HAPPENING?
MUTTER
WHAT'S GOING ON?
PLEASE HELP ME!
MUTTER

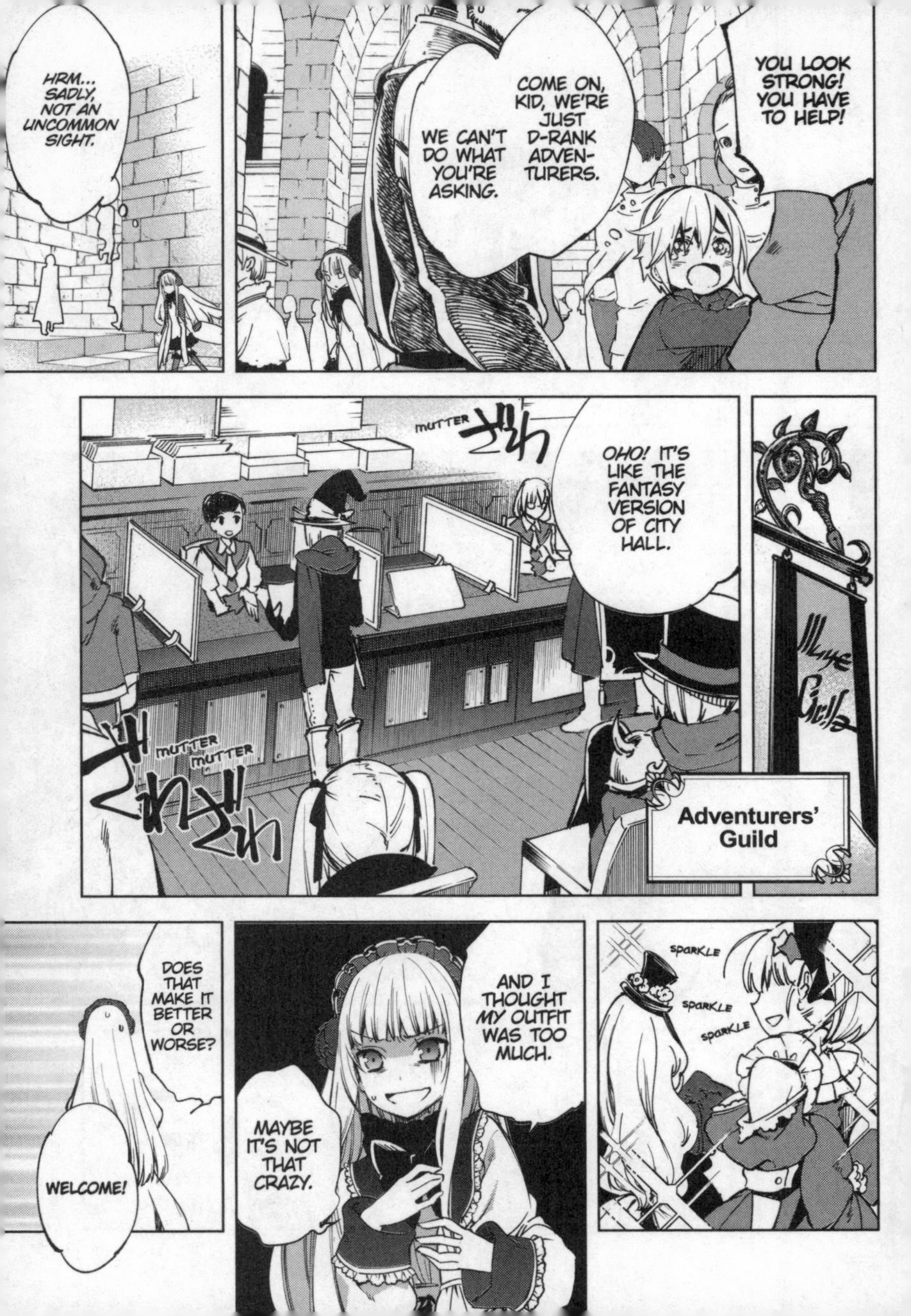
YOU LOOK STRONG! YOU HAVE TO HELP!
COME ON, KID, WE'RE JUST D-RANK ADVEN-TURERS.
WE CAN'T DO WHAT YOU'RE ASKING.
HRM... SADLY, NOT AN UNCOMMON SIGHT.
OHO! IT'S LIKE THE FANTASY VERSION OF CITY HALL.
mutter
Adventurers' Guild
mutter mutter
sparkle
sparkle
sparkle
AND I THOUGHT MY OUTFIT WAS TOO MUCH.
MAYBE IT'S NOT THAT CRAZY.
DOES THAT MAKE IT BETTER OR WORSE?
WELCOME!

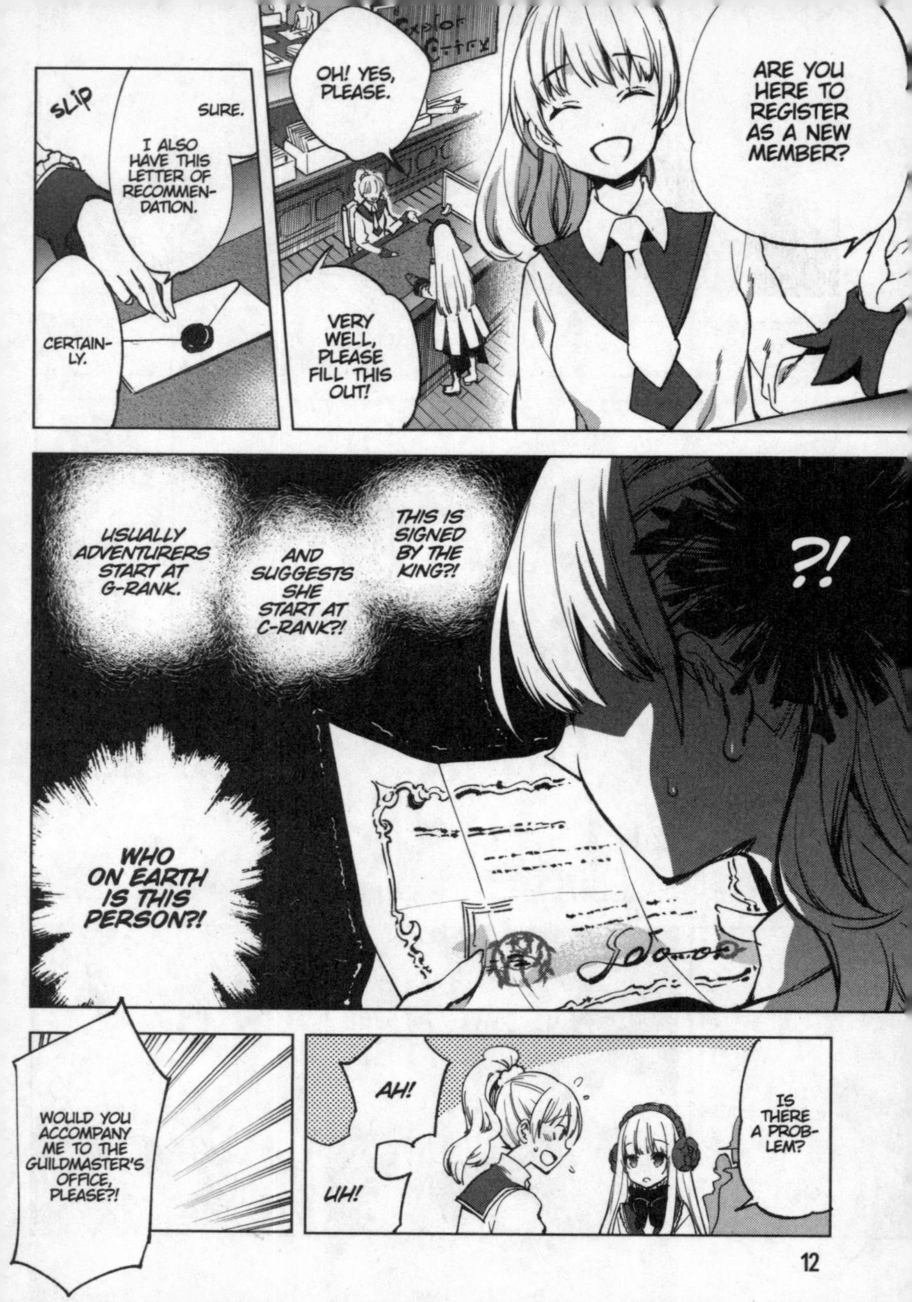
ARE YOU HERE TO REGISTER AS A NEW MEMBER?
OH! YES, PLEASE.
VERY WELL, PLEASE FILL THIS OUT!
SURE.
I ALSO HAVE THIS LETTER OF RECOMMEN-DATION.
SLIP
CERTAIN-LY.
?!
THIS IS SIGNED BY THE KING?!
AND SUGGESTS SHE START AT C-RANK?!
USUALLY ADVENTURERS START AT G-RANK.
WHO ON EARTH IS THIS PERSON?!
IS THERE A PROB-LEM?
AH!
UH!
WOULD YOU ACCOMPANY ME TO THE GUILDMASTER'S OFFICE, PLEASE?!

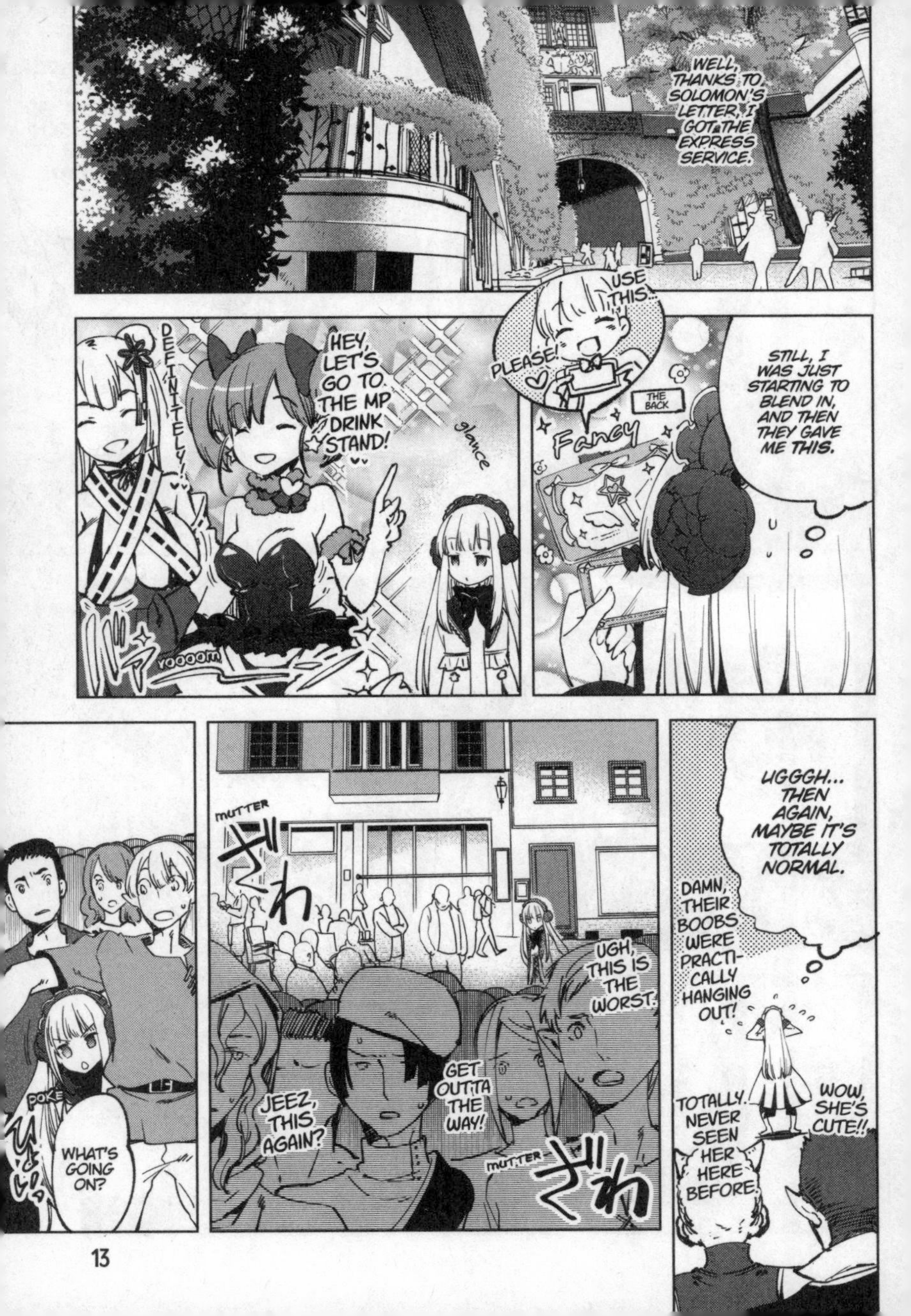
WELL, THANKS TO SOLOMON'S LETTER, I GOT THE EXPRESS SERVICE.
STILL, I WAS JUST STARTING TO BLEND IN, AND THEN THEY GAVE ME THIS.
USE THIS...
PLEASE!
THE BACK
Fancy
HEY, LET'S GO TO THE MP DRINK STAND!
DEFINITELY!
glance
yoooom
UGGGH... THEN AGAIN, MAYBE IT'S TOTALLY NORMAL.
DAMN, THEIR BOOBS WERE PRACTICALLY HANGING OUT!
WOW, SHE'S CUTE!!
TOTALLY NEVER SEEN HER HERE BEFORE.
mutter
UGH, THIS IS THE WORST.
GET OUTTA THE WAY!
JEEZ, THIS AGAIN?
mutter
POKE
WHAT'S GOING ON?

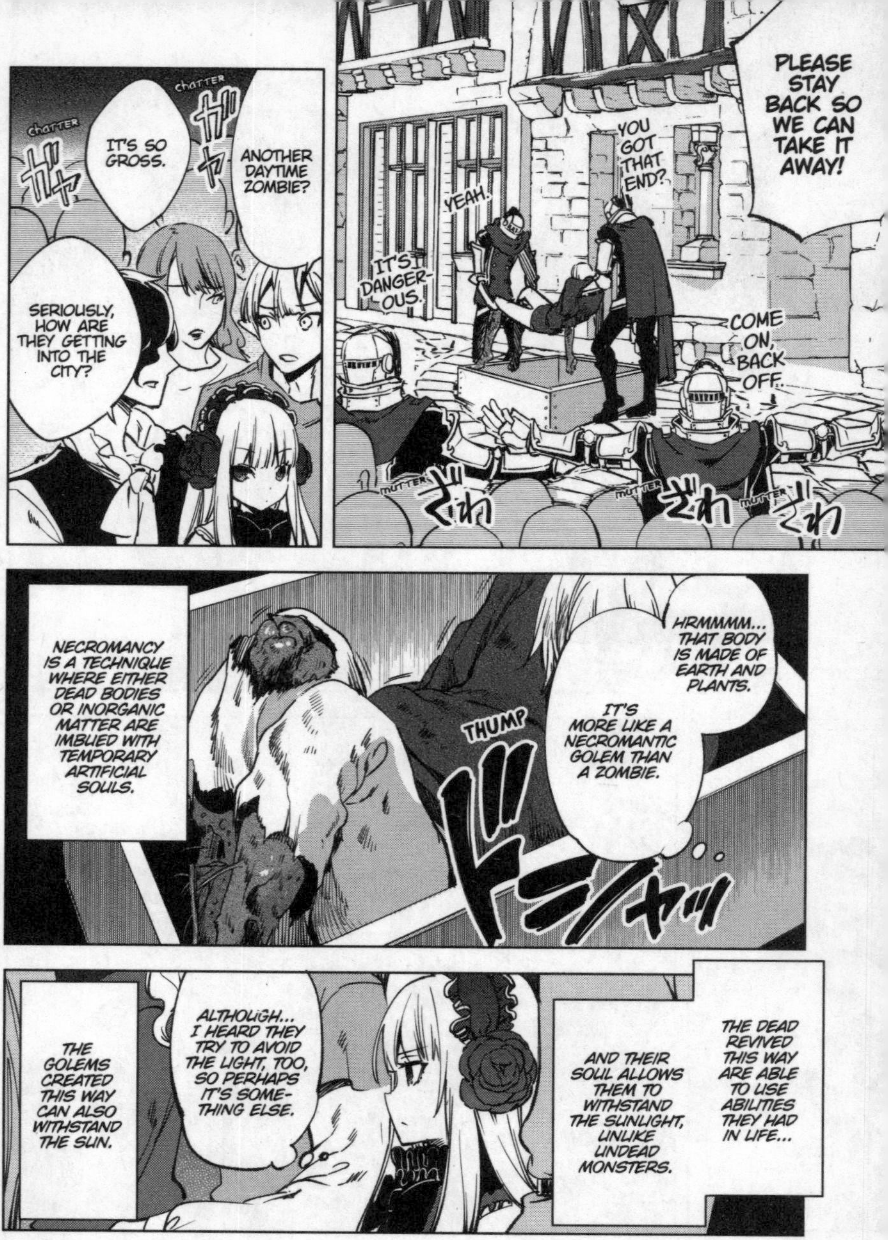
PLEASE STAY BACK SO WE CAN TAKE IT AWAY!
YOU GOT THAT END?
YEAH.
IT'S DANGER-OUS.
COME ON, BACK OFF.
MUTTER ざわ
MUTTER ざわ
MUTTER ざわ
ANOTHER DAYTIME ZOMBIE?
CHATTER ガヤ
IT'S SO GROSS.
CHATTER ガヤ
SERIOUSLY, HOW ARE THEY GETTING INTO THE CITY?
HRMMMM... THAT BODY IS MADE OF EARTH AND PLANTS.
IT'S MORE LIKE A NECROMANTIC GOLEM THAN A ZOMBIE.
THUMP ドシャッ
NECROMANCY IS A TECHNIQUE WHERE EITHER DEAD BODIES OR INORGANIC MATTER ARE IMBUED WITH TEMPORARY ARTIFICIAL SOULS.
THE DEAD REVIVED THIS WAY ARE ABLE TO USE ABILITIES THEY HAD IN LIFE...
AND THEIR SOUL ALLOWS THEM TO WITHSTAND THE SUNLIGHT, UNLIKE UNDEAD MONSTERS.
ALTHOUGH... I HEARD THEY TRY TO AVOID THE LIGHT, TOO, SO PERHAPS IT'S SOME-THING ELSE.
THE GOLEMS CREATED THIS WAY CAN ALSO WITHSTAND THE SUN.

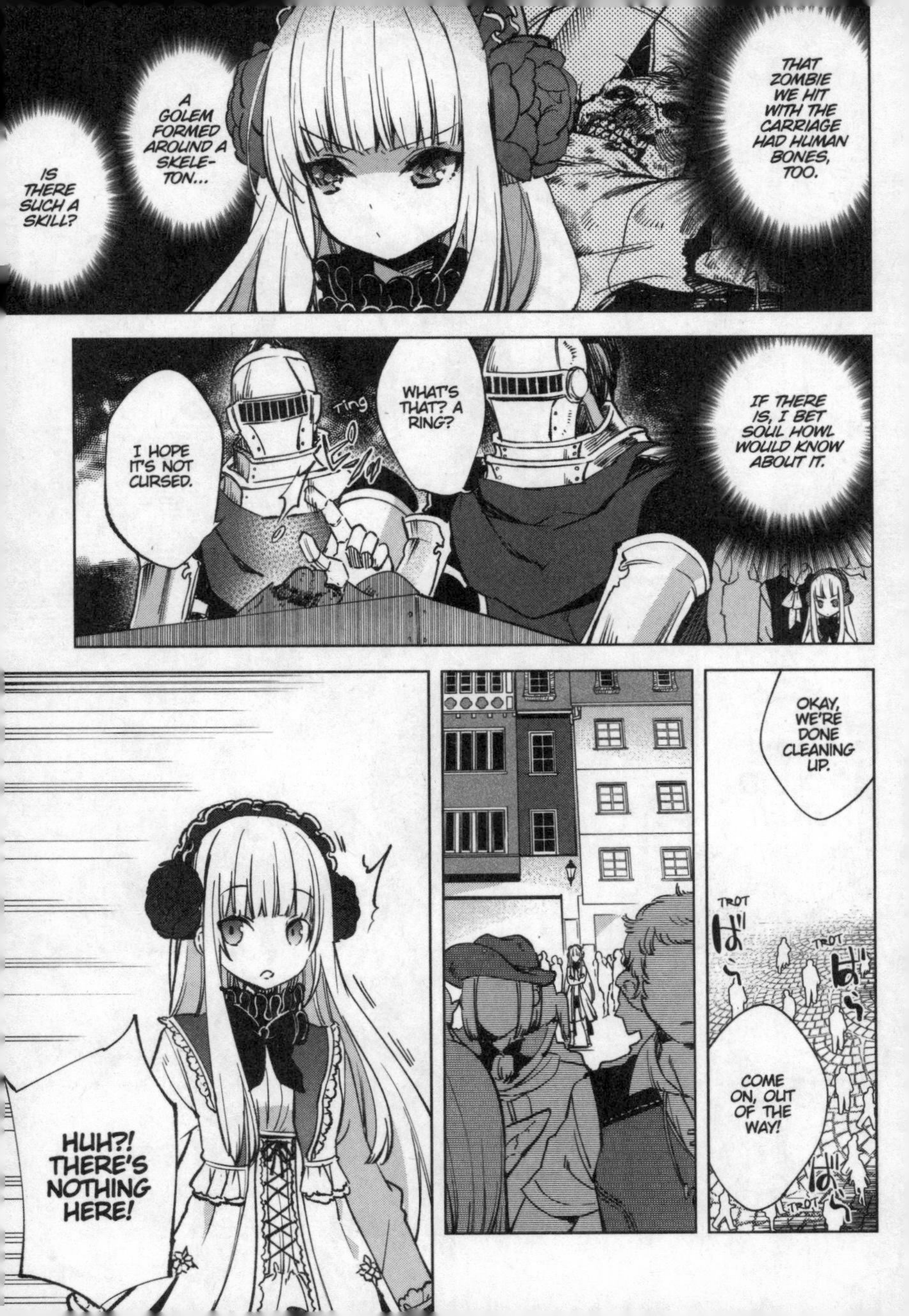
THAT ZOMBIE WE HIT WITH THE CARRIAGE HAD HUMAN BONES, TOO.
A GOLEM FORMED AROUND A SKELE-TON...
IS THERE SUCH A SKILL?
IF THERE IS, I BET SOUL HOWL WOULD KNOW ABOUT IT.
WHAT'S THAT? A RING?
Ting
I HOPE IT'S NOT CURSED.
OKAY, WE'RE DONE CLEANING UP.
TROT
TROT
COME ON, OUT OF THE WAY!
TROT
HUH?! THERE'S NOTHING HERE!

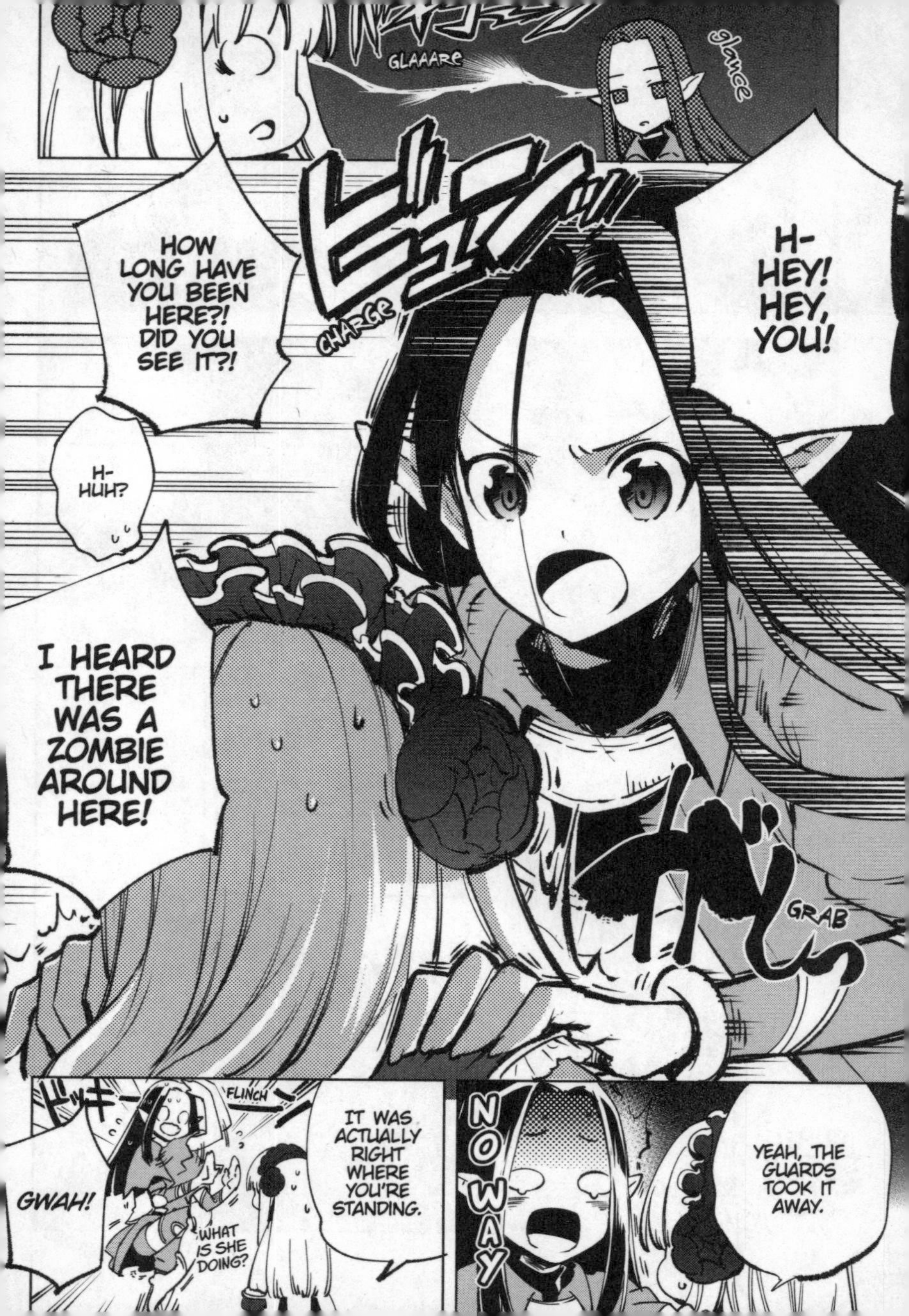
glance
GLAAARE
H- HEY! HEY, YOU!
CHARGE
HOW LONG HAVE YOU BEEN HERE?! DID YOU SEE IT?!
H- HUH?
I HEARD THERE WAS A ZOMBIE AROUND HERE!
GRAB
YEAH, THE GUARDS TOOK IT AWAY.
NO WAY
IT WAS ACTUALLY RIGHT WHERE YOU'RE STANDING.
FLINCH
GWAH!
WHAT IS SHE DOING?

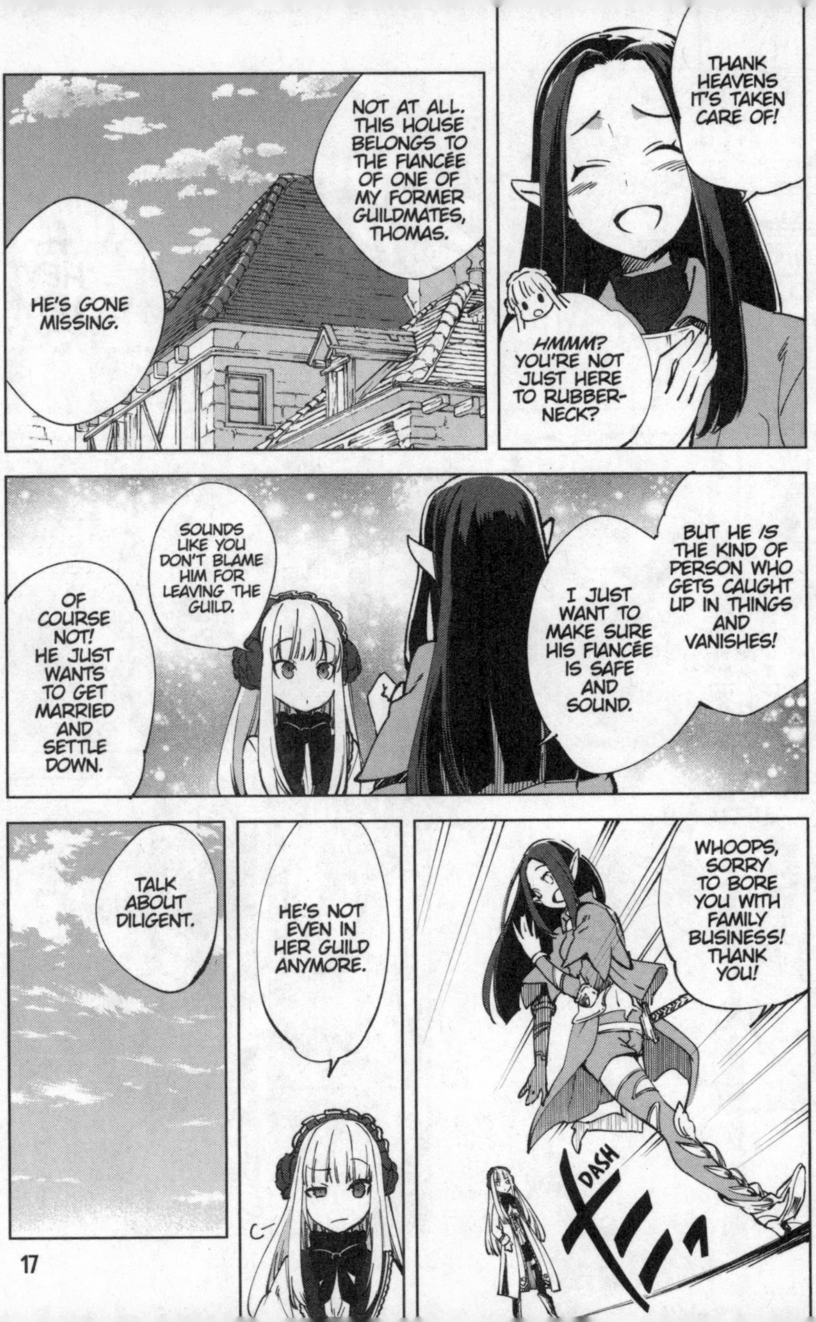
THANK HEAVENS IT'S TAKEN CARE OF!
HMMM? YOU'RE NOT JUST HERE TO RUBBERNECK?
NOT AT ALL. THIS HOUSE BELONGS TO THE FIANCÉE OF ONE OF MY FORMER GUILDMATES, THOMAS.
HE'S GONE MISSING.
BUT HE *IS* THE KIND OF PERSON WHO GETS CAUGHT UP IN THINGS AND VANISHES!
I JUST WANT TO MAKE SURE HIS FIANCÉE IS SAFE AND SOUND.
SOUNDS LIKE YOU DON'T BLAME HIM FOR LEAVING THE GUILD.
OF COURSE NOT! HE JUST WANTS TO GET MARRIED AND SETTLE DOWN.
WHOOPS, SORRY TO BORE YOU WITH FAMILY BUSINESS! THANK YOU!
DASH
HE'S NOT EVEN IN HER GUILD ANYMORE.
TALK ABOUT DILIGENT.

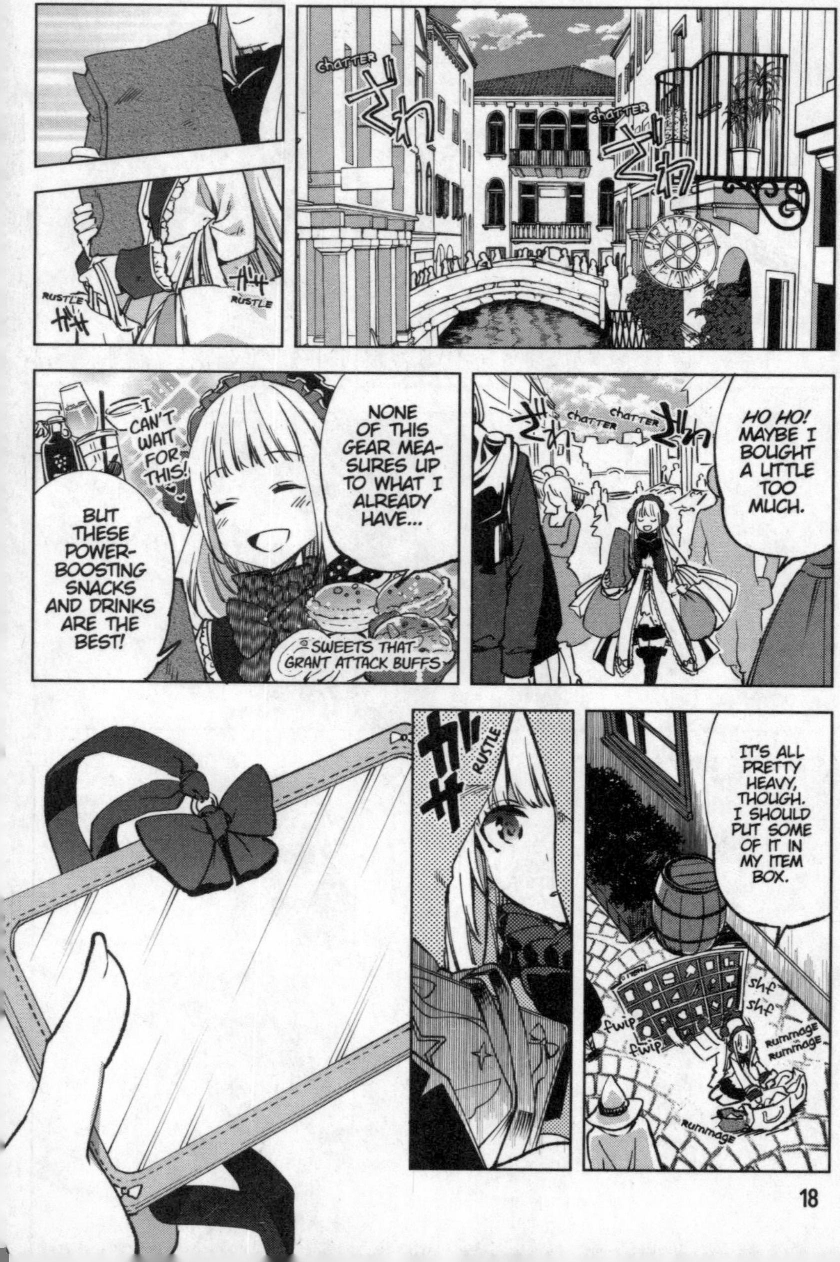

CHATTER
CHATTER
RUSTLE
RUSTLE
HO HO! MAYBE I BOUGHT A LITTLE TOO MUCH.
CHATTER
CHATTER
NONE OF THIS GEAR MEASURES UP TO WHAT I ALREADY HAVE...
I CAN'T WAIT FOR THIS!
BUT THESE POWER-BOOSTING SNACKS AND DRINKS ARE THE BEST!
SWEETS THAT GRANT ATTACK BUFFS
IT'S ALL PRETTY HEAVY, THOUGH. I SHOULD PUT SOME OF IT IN MY ITEM BOX.
shf shf
fwip fwip
rummage rummage
rummage
RUSTLE

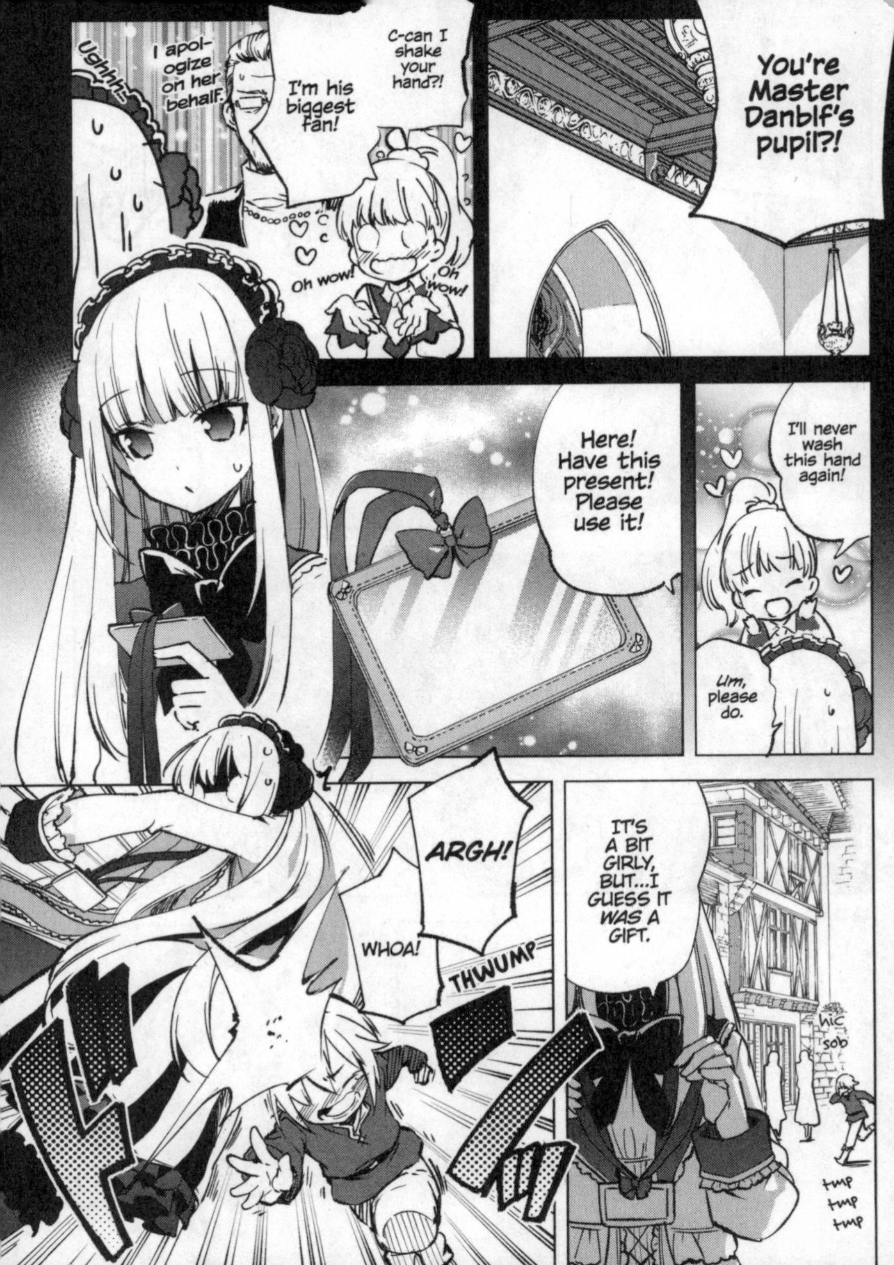

You're Master Danblf's pupil?!
C-can I shake your hand?!
I'm his biggest fan!
I apologize on her behalf.
Ughhh...
Oh wow!
Oh wow!
I'll never wash this hand again!
Um, please do.
Here! Have this present! Please use it!
IT'S A BIT GIRLY, BUT...I GUESS IT WAS A GIFT.
hic
sob
tmp
tmp
tmp
ARGH!
WHOA!
THWUMP

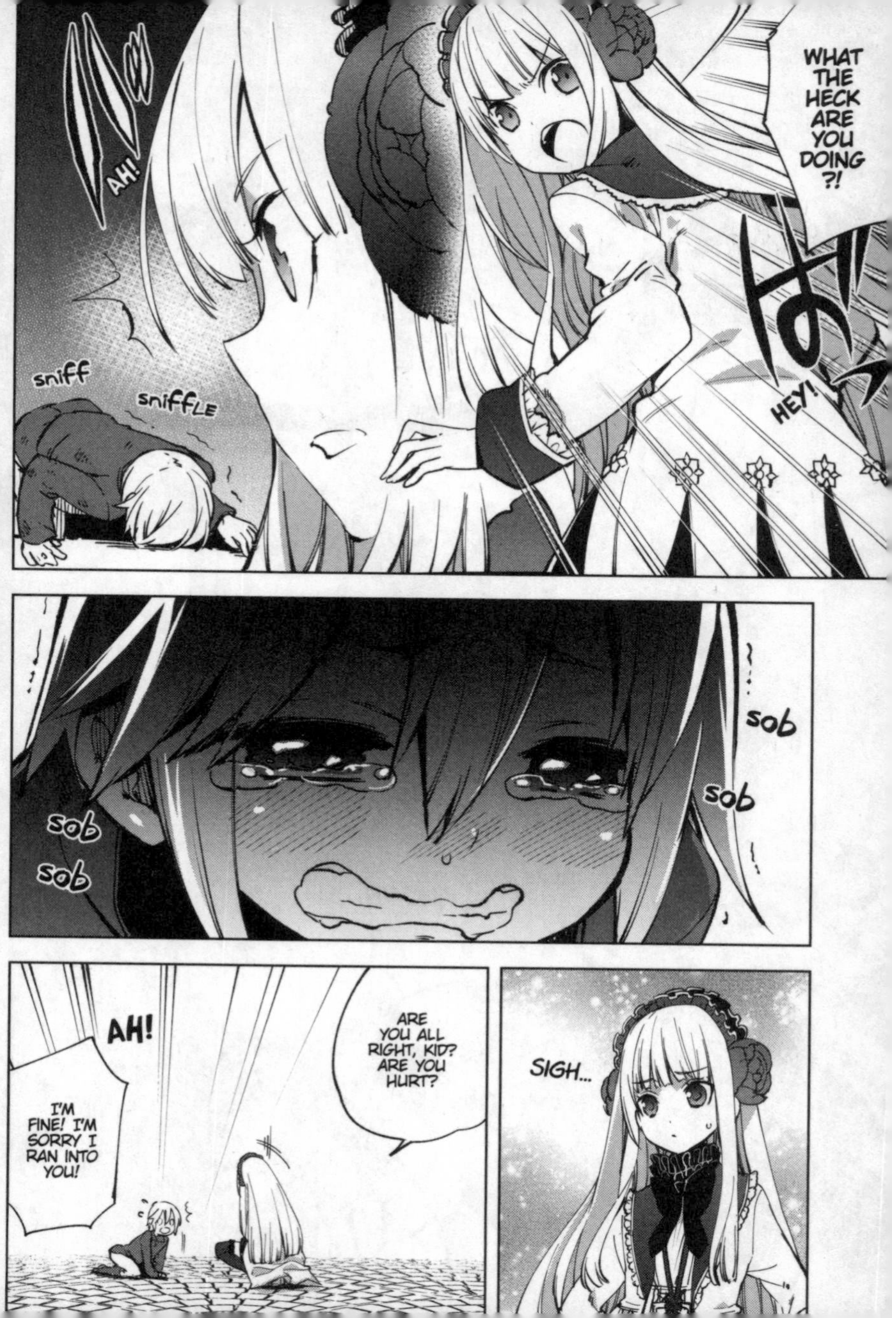
WHAT THE HECK ARE YOU DOING?!
HEY!
AH!
sniff
sniffLE
sob
sob
sob
sob
SIGH...
ARE YOU ALL RIGHT, KID? ARE YOU HURT?
AH!
I'M FINE! I'M SORRY I RAN INTO YOU!

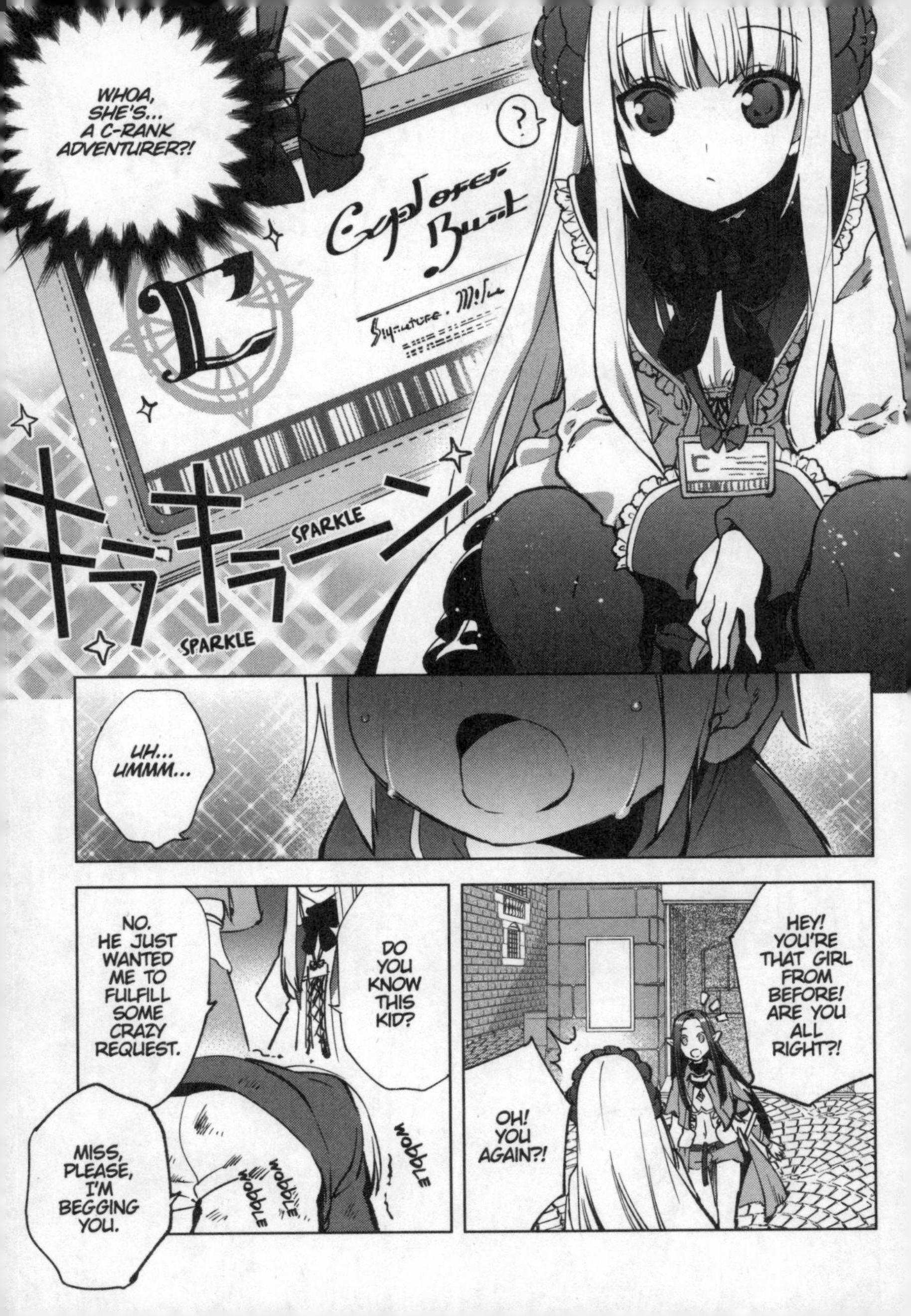
?
WHOA, SHE'S... A C-RANK ADVENTURER?!
SPARKLE
SPARKLE
UH... UMMM...
HEY! YOU'RE THAT GIRL FROM BEFORE! ARE YOU ALL RIGHT?!
OH! YOU AGAIN?!
DO YOU KNOW THIS KID?
NO. HE JUST WANTED ME TO FULFILL SOME CRAZY REQUEST.
WOBBLE
WOBBLE
WOBBLE
MISS, PLEASE, I'M BEGGING YOU.

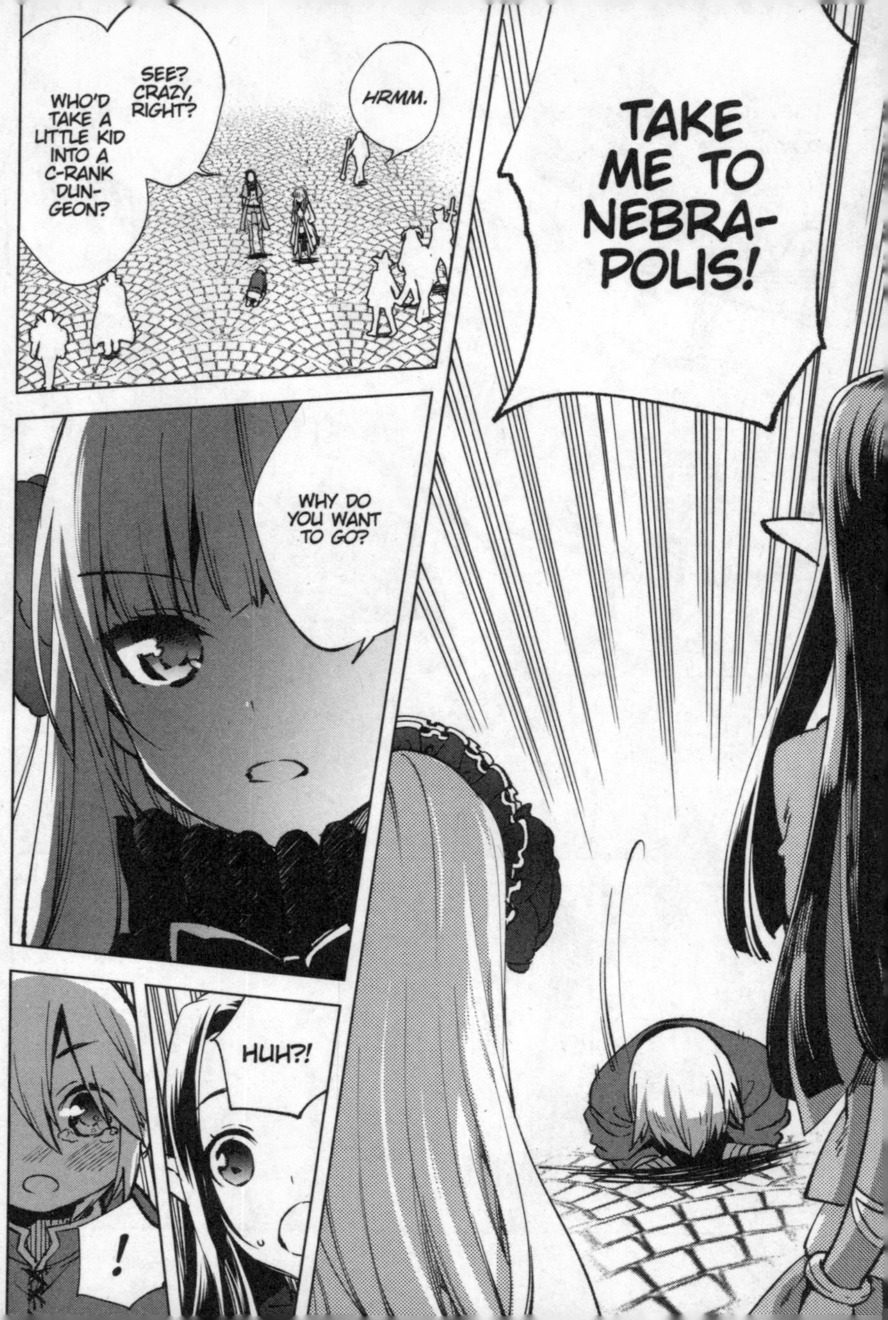
TAKE ME TO NEBRA-POLIS!
HRMM.
SEE? CRAZY, RIGHT?
WHO'D TAKE A LITTLE KID INTO A C-RANK DUN-GEON?
WHY DO YOU WANT TO GO?
HUH?!
!

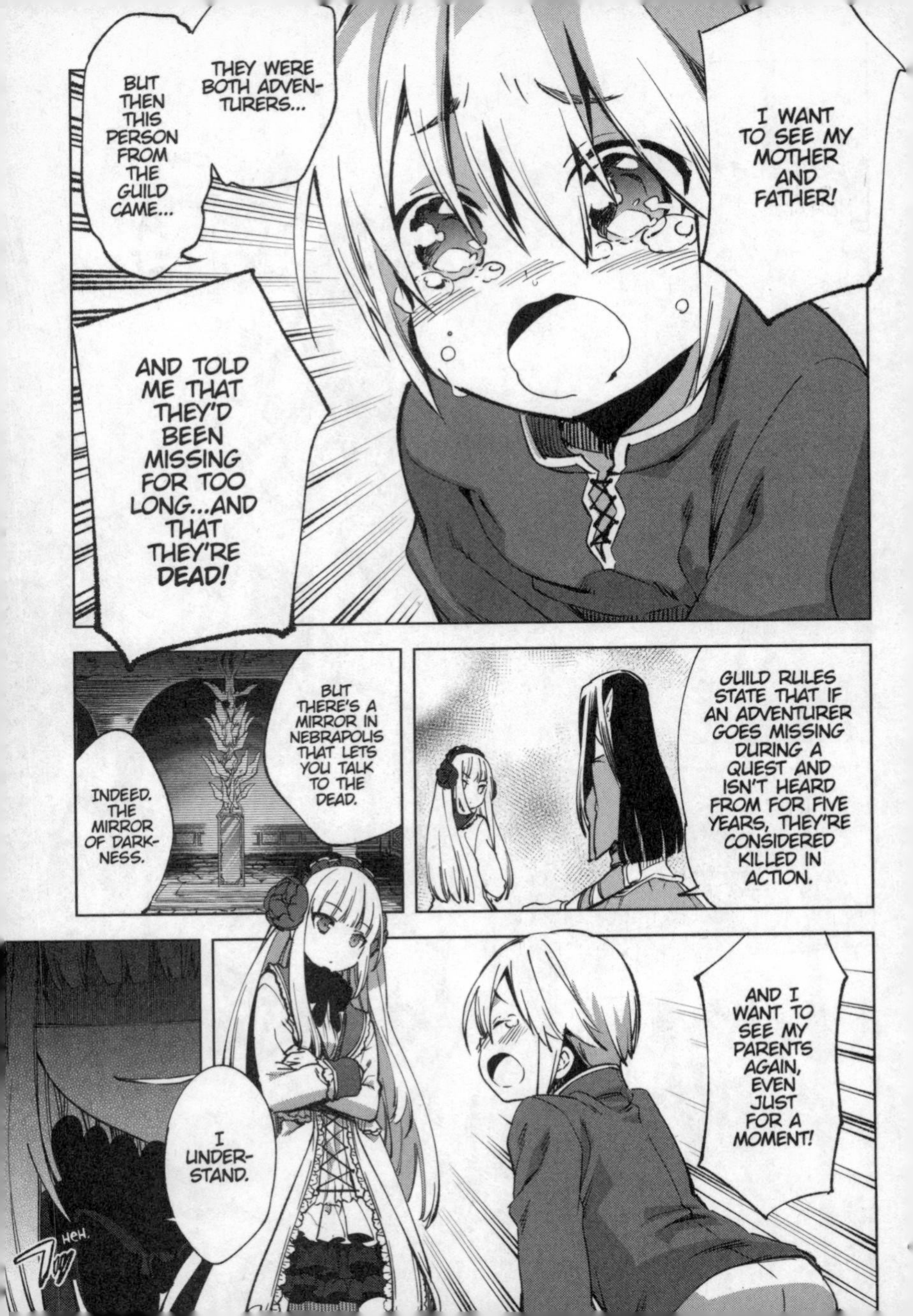
I WANT TO SEE MY MOTHER AND FATHER!
THEY WERE BOTH ADVEN-TURERS...
BUT THEN THIS PERSON FROM THE GUILD CAME...
AND TOLD ME THAT THEY'D BEEN MISSING FOR TOO LONG...AND THAT THEY'RE DEAD!
GUILD RULES STATE THAT IF AN ADVENTURER GOES MISSING DURING A QUEST AND ISN'T HEARD FROM FOR FIVE YEARS, THEY'RE CONSIDERED KILLED IN ACTION.
BUT THERE'S A MIRROR IN NEBRAPOLIS THAT LETS YOU TALK TO THE DEAD.
INDEED. THE MIRROR OF DARK-NESS.
AND I WANT TO SEE MY PARENTS AGAIN, EVEN JUST FOR A MOMENT!
I UNDER-STAND.
HEH.

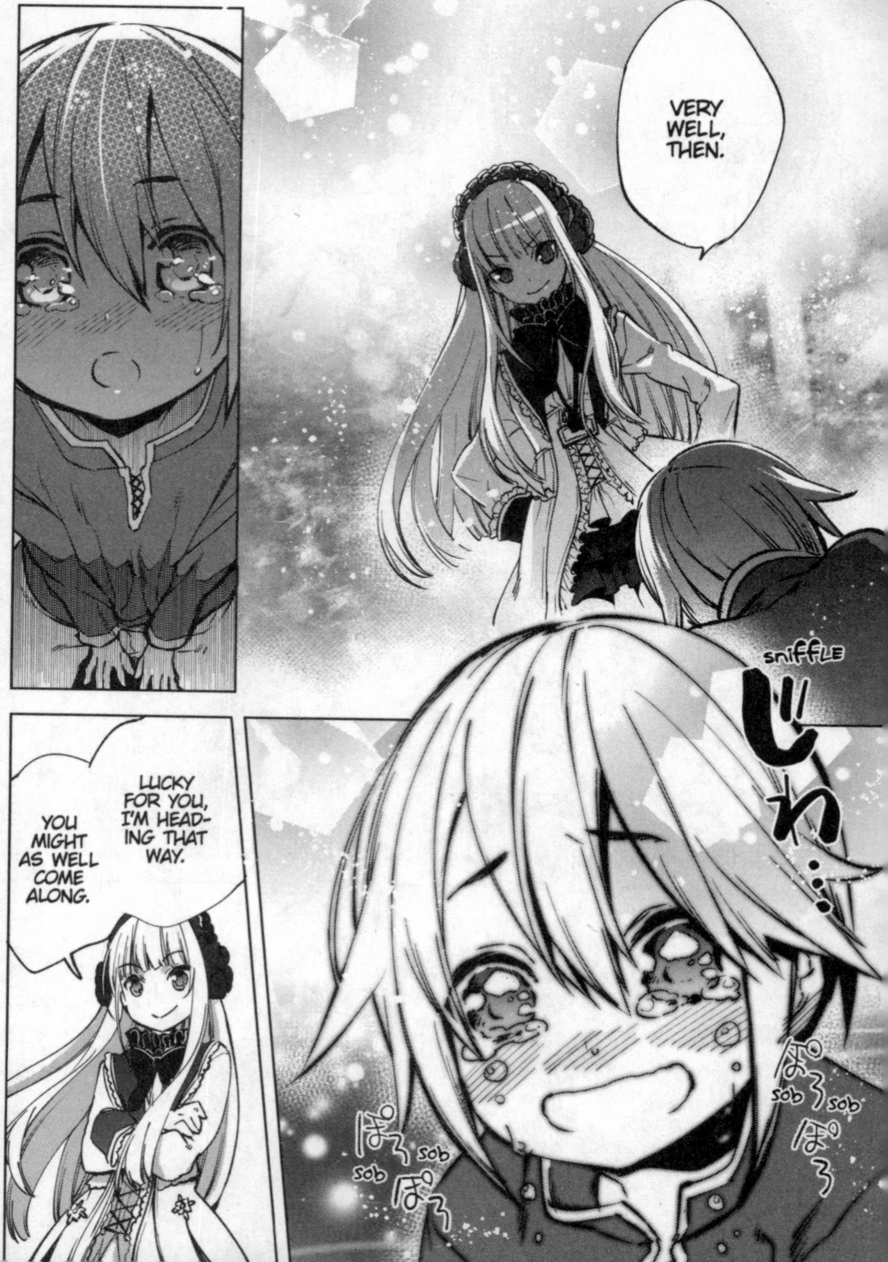
VERY WELL, THEN.
sniffle
じわ…
sob sob
ぽろぽろ
sob sob
ぽろぽろ
LUCKY FOR YOU, I'M HEADING THAT WAY.
YOU MIGHT AS WELL COME ALONG.

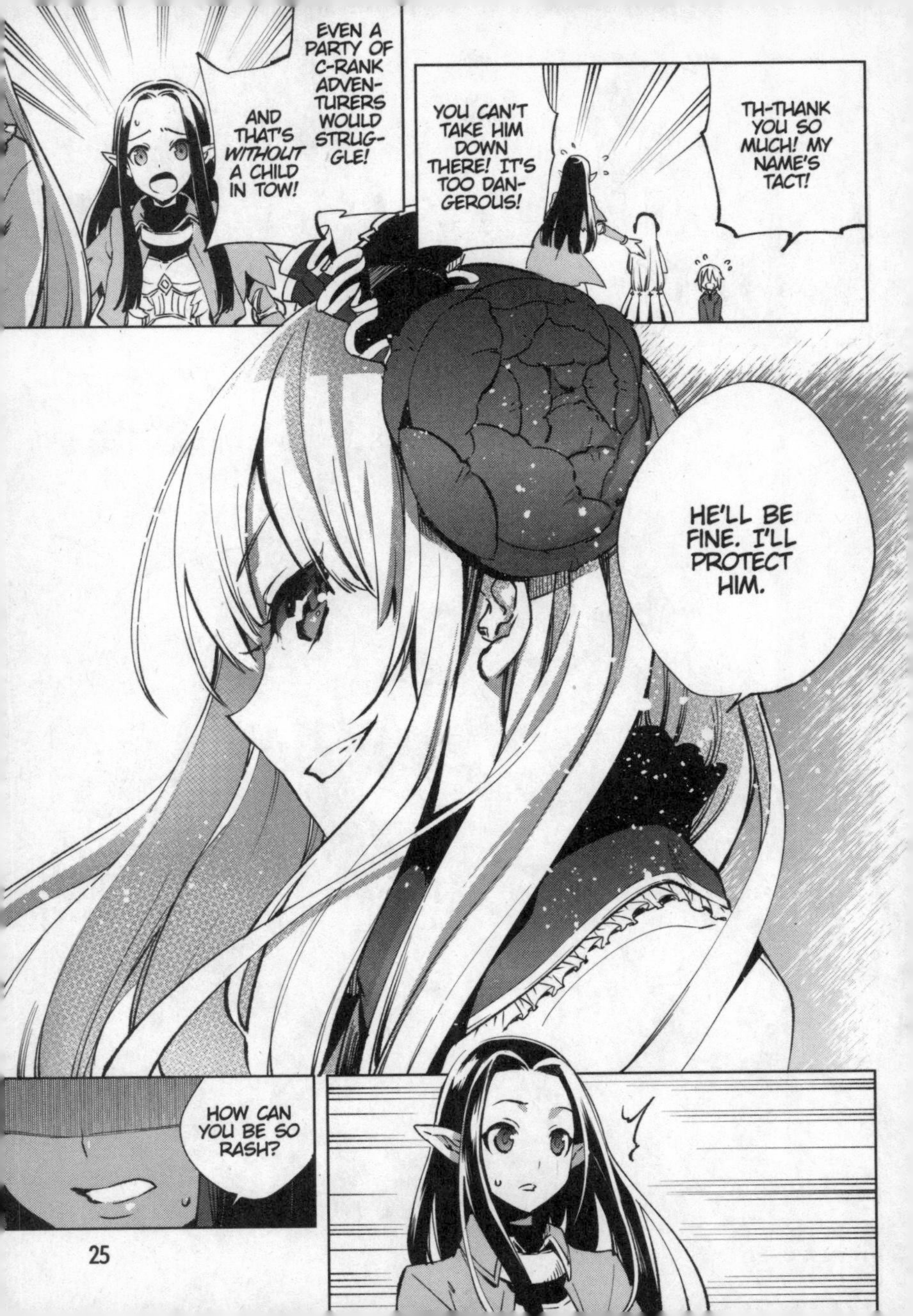
TH-THANK YOU SO MUCH! MY NAME'S TACT!
YOU CAN'T TAKE HIM DOWN THERE! IT'S TOO DANGEROUS!
EVEN A PARTY OF C-RANK ADVENTURERS WOULD STRUGGLE!
AND THAT'S *WITHOUT* A CHILD IN TOW!
HE'LL BE FINE. I'LL PROTECT HIM.
HOW CAN YOU BE SO RASH?

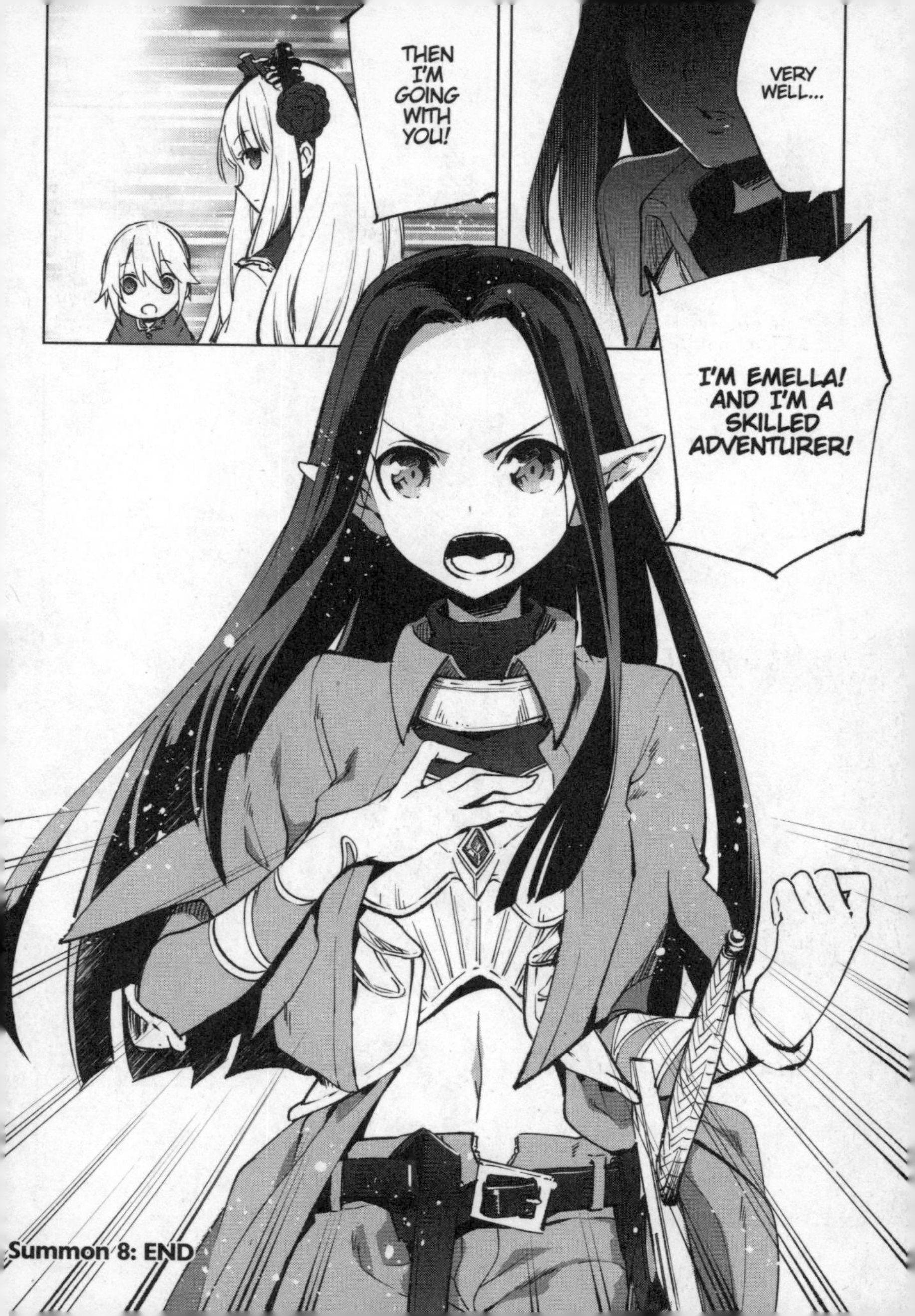
VERY WELL...
THEN I'M GOING WITH YOU!
I'M EMELLA! AND I'M A SKILLED ADVENTURER!

Summon 8: END

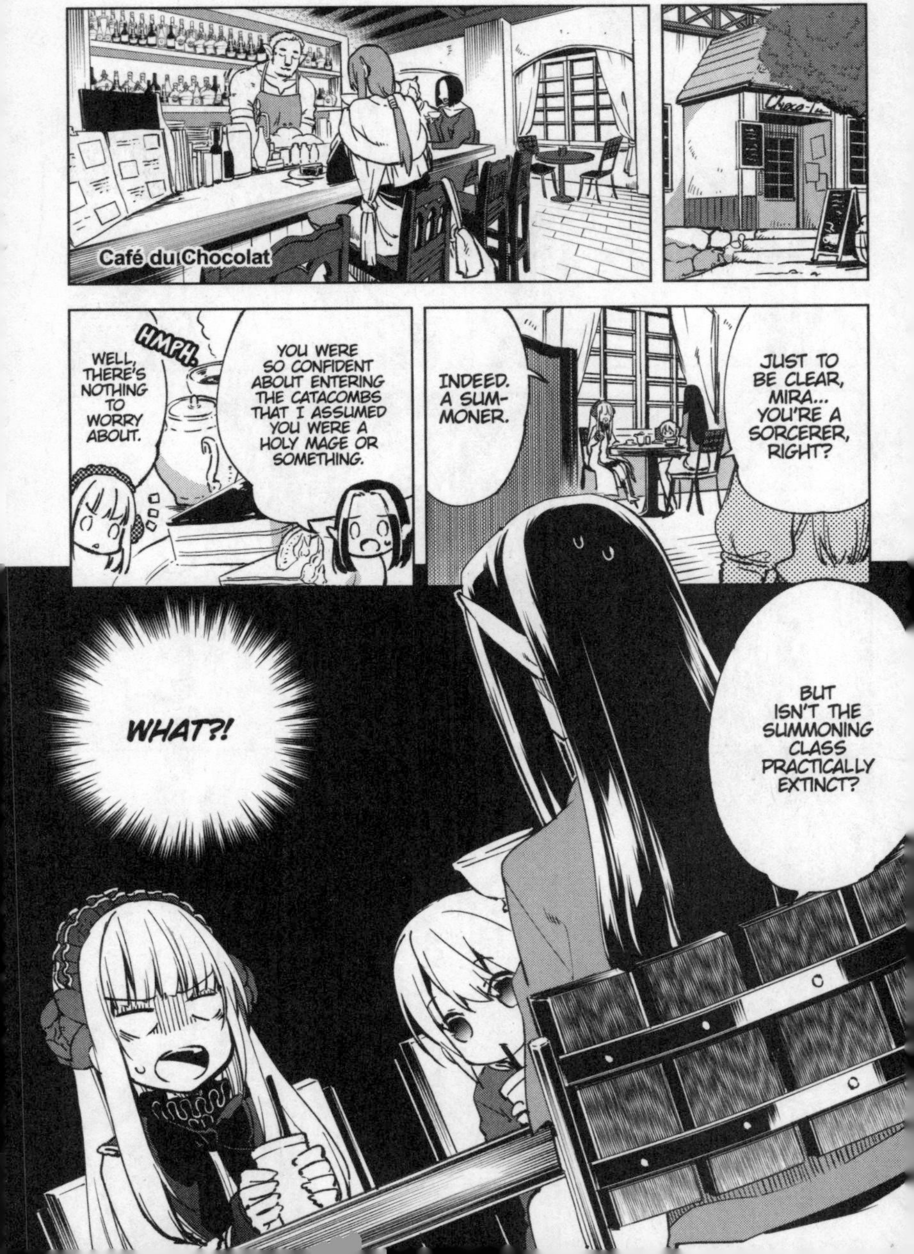
Café du Chocolat
JUST TO BE CLEAR, MIRA... YOU'RE A SORCERER, RIGHT?
INDEED. A SUMMONER.
YOU WERE SO CONFIDENT ABOUT ENTERING THE CATACOMBS THAT I ASSUMED YOU WERE A HOLY MAGE OR SOMETHING.
HMPH.
WELL, THERE'S NOTHING TO WORRY ABOUT.
BUT ISN'T THE SUMMONING CLASS PRACTICALLY EXTINCT?
WHAT?!

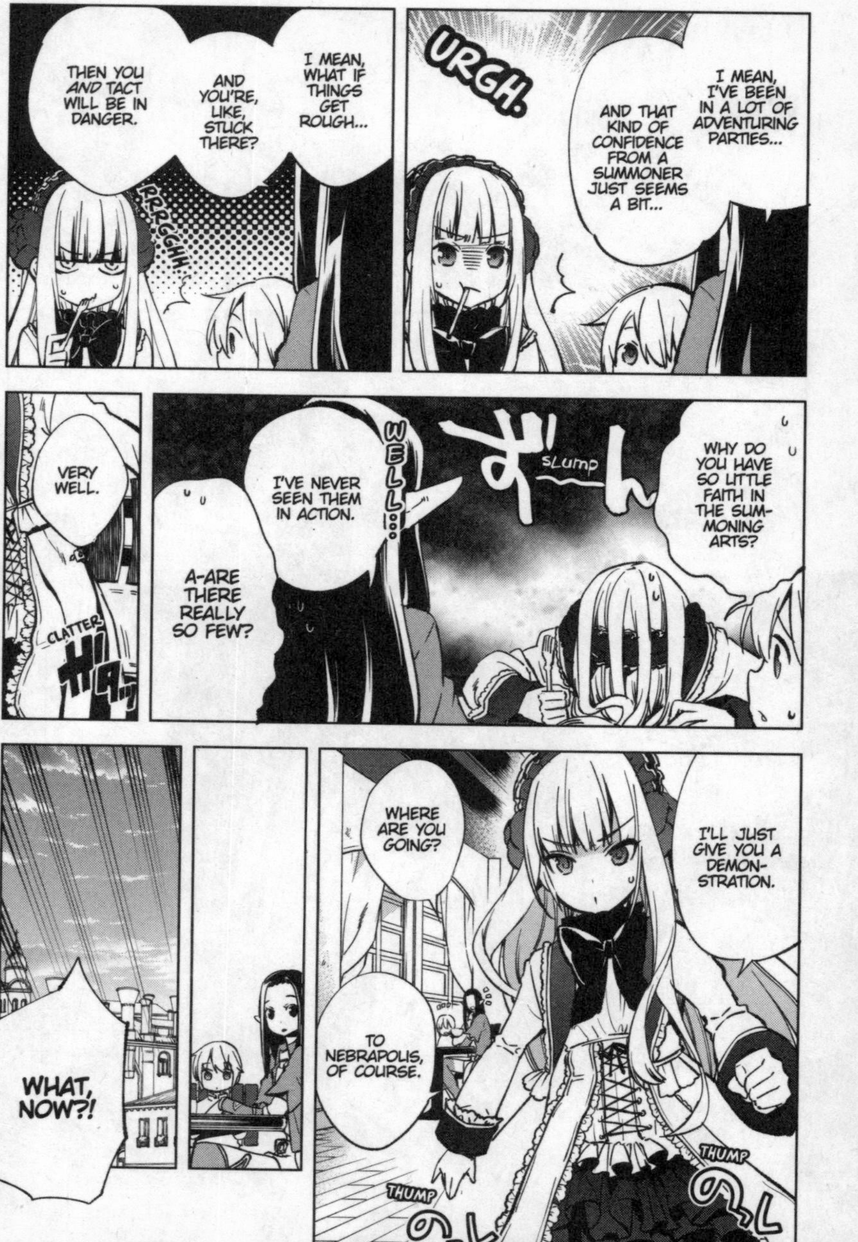
URGH.
I MEAN, I'VE BEEN IN A LOT OF ADVENTURING PARTIES...
AND THAT KIND OF CONFIDENCE FROM A SUMMONER JUST SEEMS A BIT...
I MEAN, WHAT IF THINGS GET ROUGH...
AND YOU'RE, LIKE, STUCK THERE?
THEN YOU *AND* TACT WILL BE IN DANGER.
RRRGGHH
WHY DO YOU HAVE SO LITTLE FAITH IN THE SUMMONING ARTS?
ずん
SLUMP
WELL...
I'VE NEVER SEEN THEM IN ACTION.
A-ARE THERE REALLY SO FEW?
VERY WELL.
CLATTER
I'LL JUST GIVE YOU A DEMONSTRATION.
WHERE ARE YOU GOING?
TO NEBRAPOLIS, OF COURSE.
THUMP
のし
THUMP
のし
WHAT, NOW?!

Summon 9: [Écarlate Carillon]

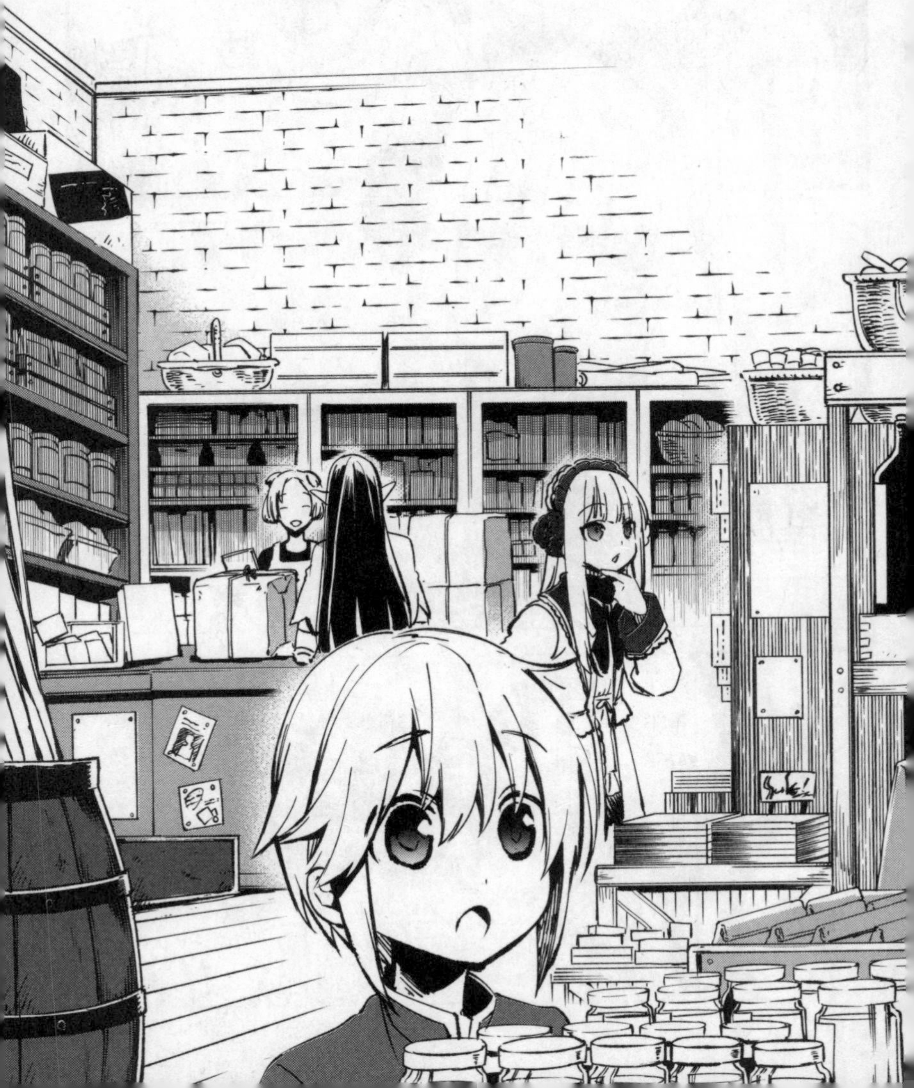

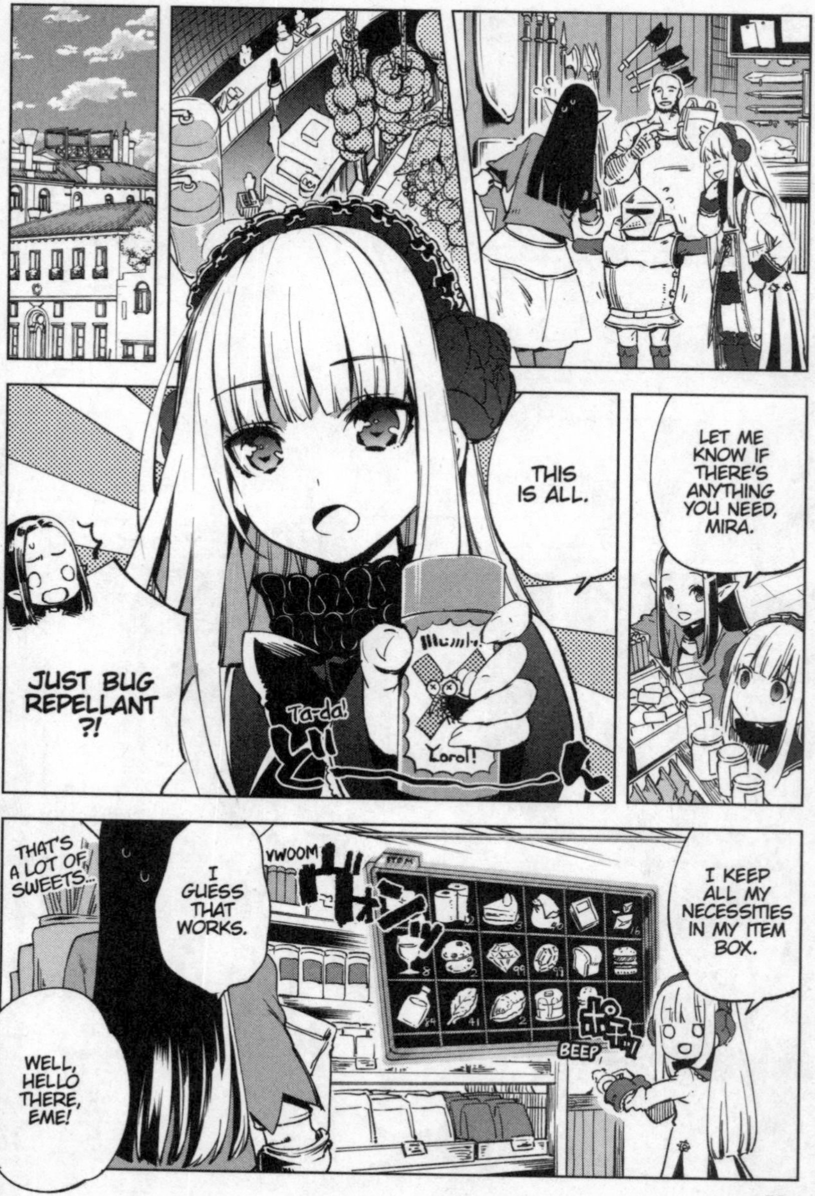
LET ME KNOW IF THERE'S ANYTHING YOU NEED, MIRA.
THIS IS ALL.
Ta-da!
JUST BUG REPELLANT ?!
I KEEP ALL MY NECESSITIES IN MY ITEM BOX.
BEEP
VWOOM
I GUESS THAT WORKS.
THAT'S A LOT OF SWEETS...
WELL, HELLO THERE, EME!

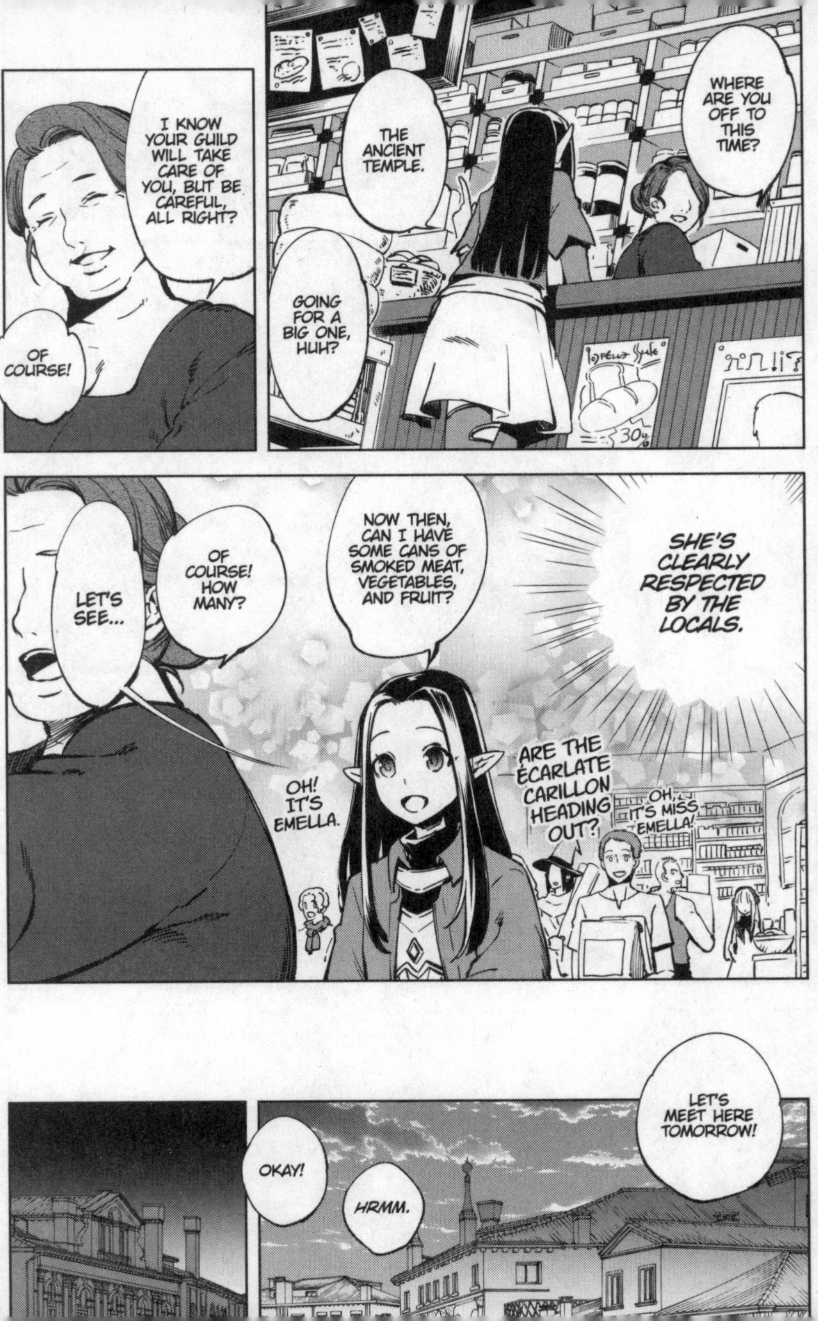
WHERE ARE YOU OFF TO THIS TIME?
THE ANCIENT TEMPLE.
GOING FOR A BIG ONE, HUH?
I KNOW YOUR GUILD WILL TAKE CARE OF YOU, BUT BE CAREFUL, ALL RIGHT?
OF COURSE!
SHE'S CLEARLY RESPECTED BY THE LOCALS.
NOW THEN, CAN I HAVE SOME CANS OF SMOKED MEAT, VEGETABLES, AND FRUIT?
OF COURSE! HOW MANY?
LET'S SEE...
OH, IT'S MISS EMELLA!
ARE THE ÉCARLATE CARILLON HEADING OUT?
OH! IT'S EMELLA.
LET'S MEET HERE TOMORROW!
OKAY!
HRMM.

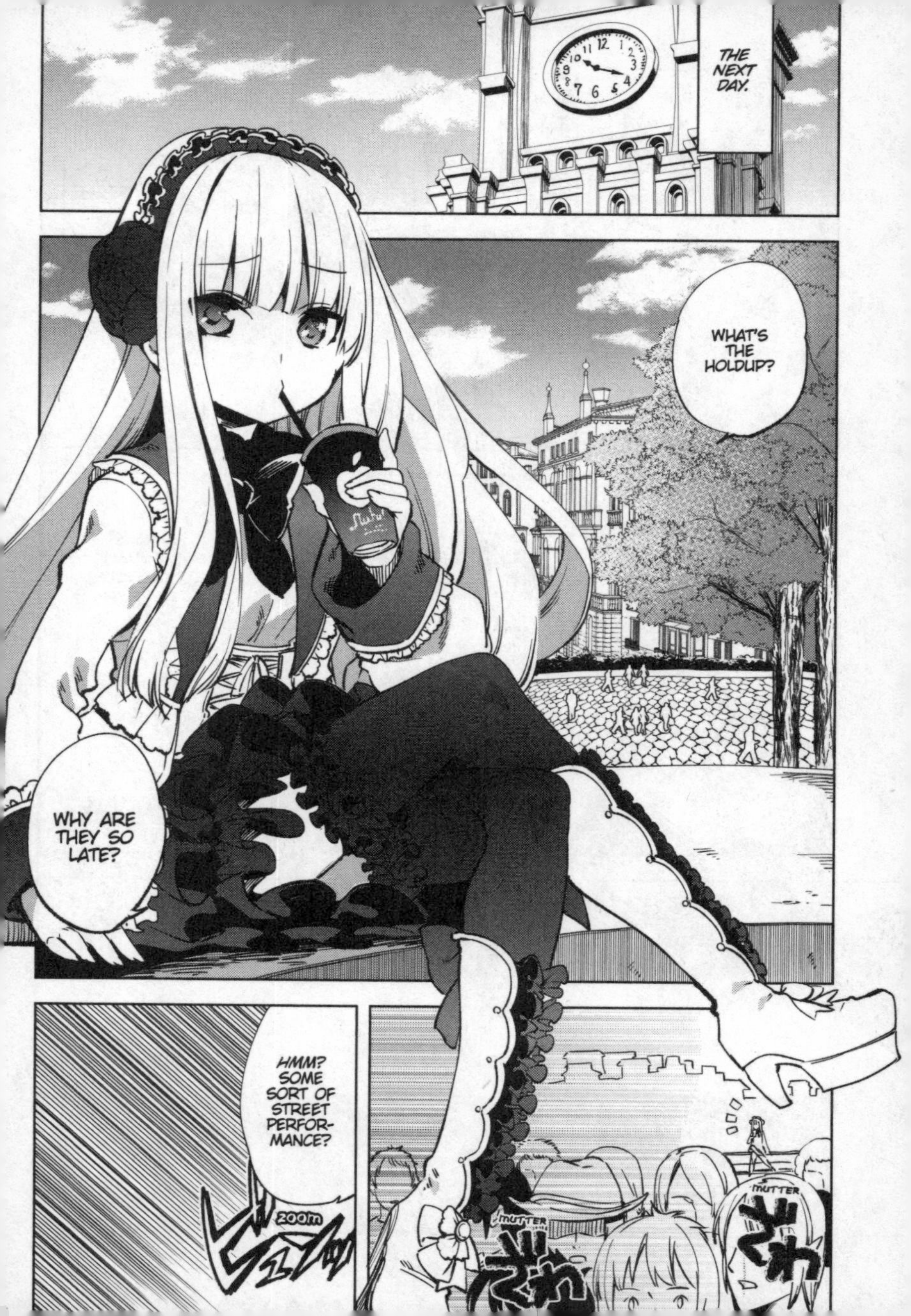
THE NEXT DAY.
WHAT'S THE HOLDUP?
WHY ARE THEY SO LATE?
MUTTER
ざわ
MUTTER
ざわ
HMM? SOME SORT OF STREET PERFORMANCE?
zoom

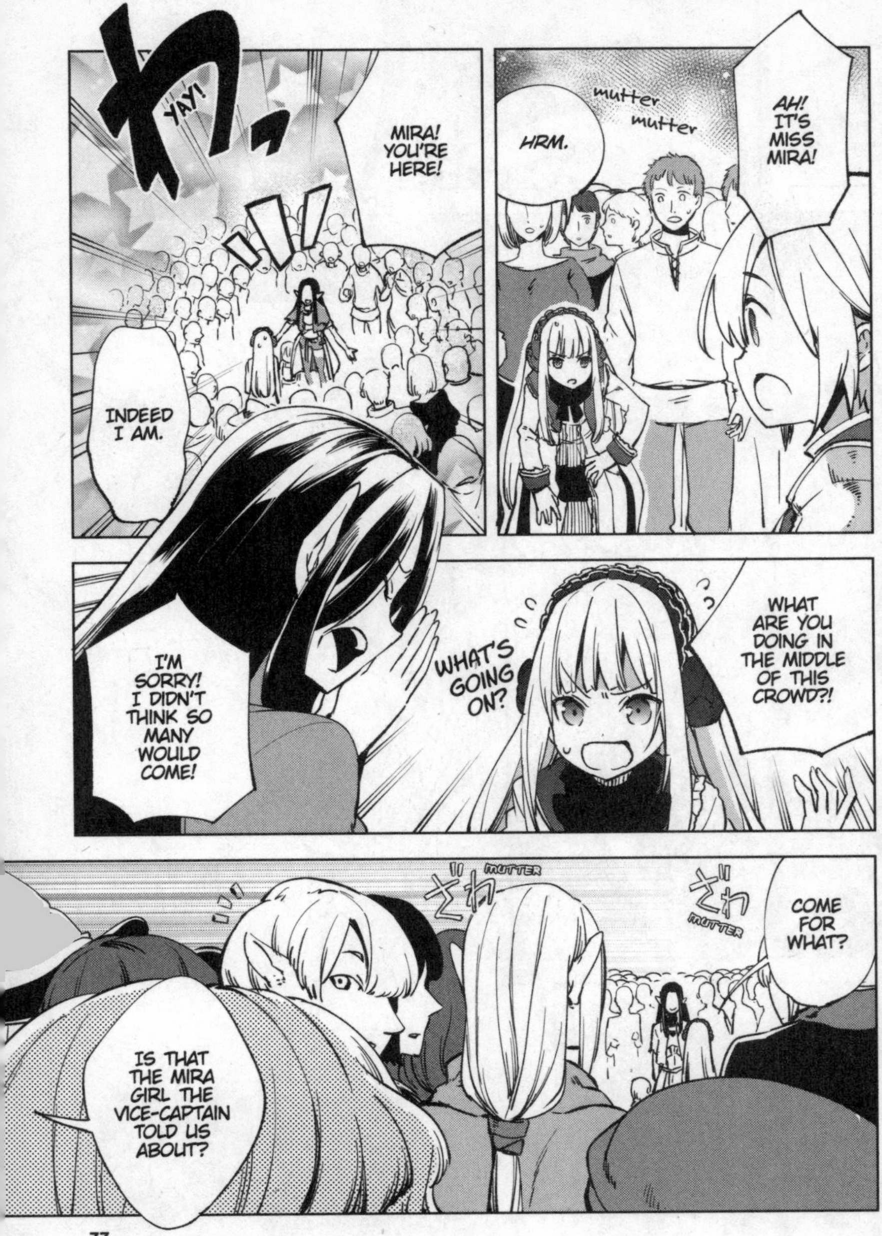
AH! IT'S MISS MIRA!
mutter mutter
HRM.
MIRA! YOU'RE HERE!
ヤッ
YAY!
INDEED I AM.
WHAT ARE YOU DOING IN THE MIDDLE OF THIS CROWD?!
WHAT'S GOING ON?
I'M SORRY! I DIDN'T THINK SO MANY WOULD COME!
COME FOR WHAT?
ざわ
MUTTER
ざわ
MUTTER
IS THAT THE MIRA GIRL THE VICE-CAPTAIN TOLD US ABOUT?

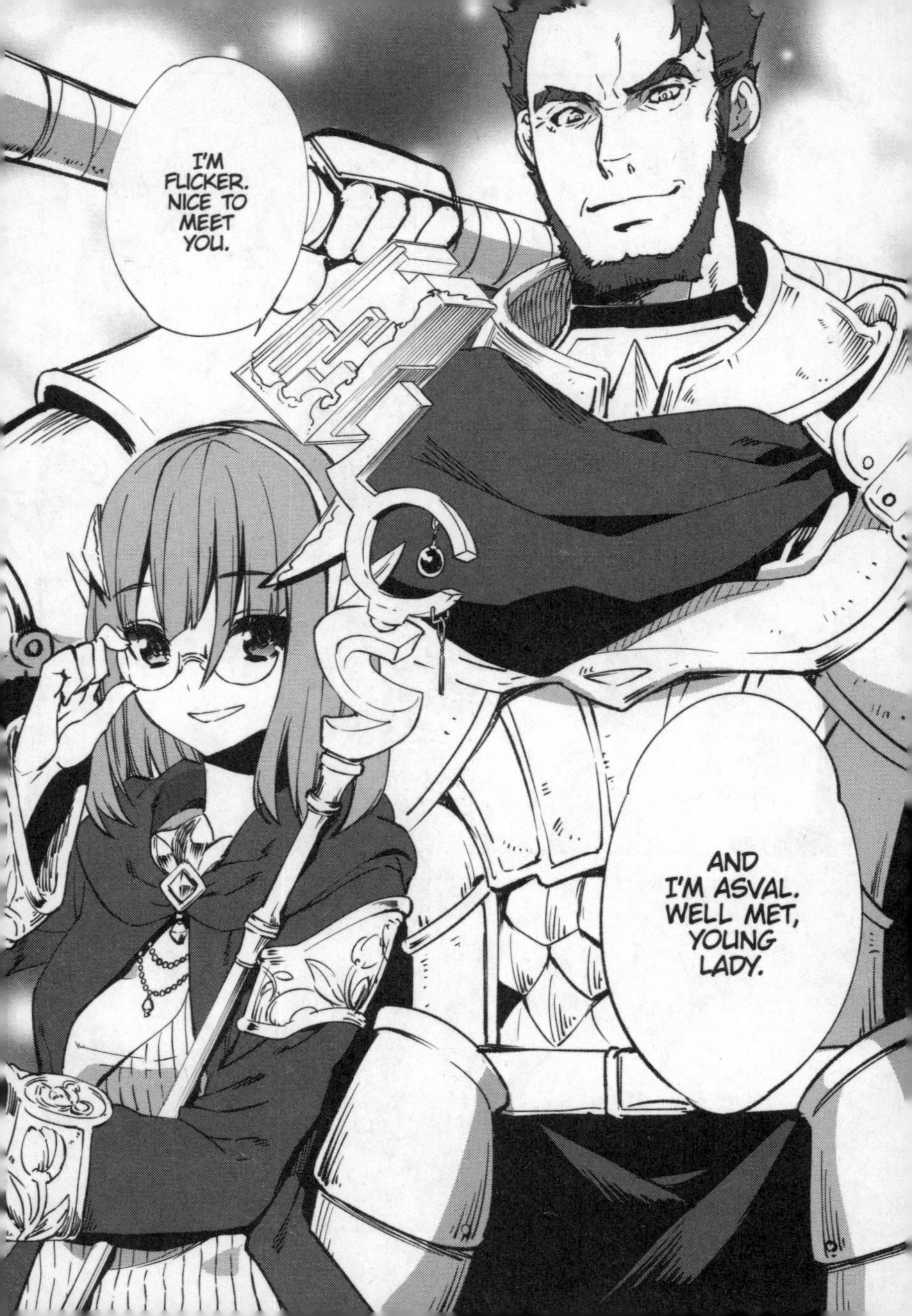
I'M FLICKER. NICE TO MEET YOU.
AND I'M ASVAL. WELL MET, YOUNG LADY.

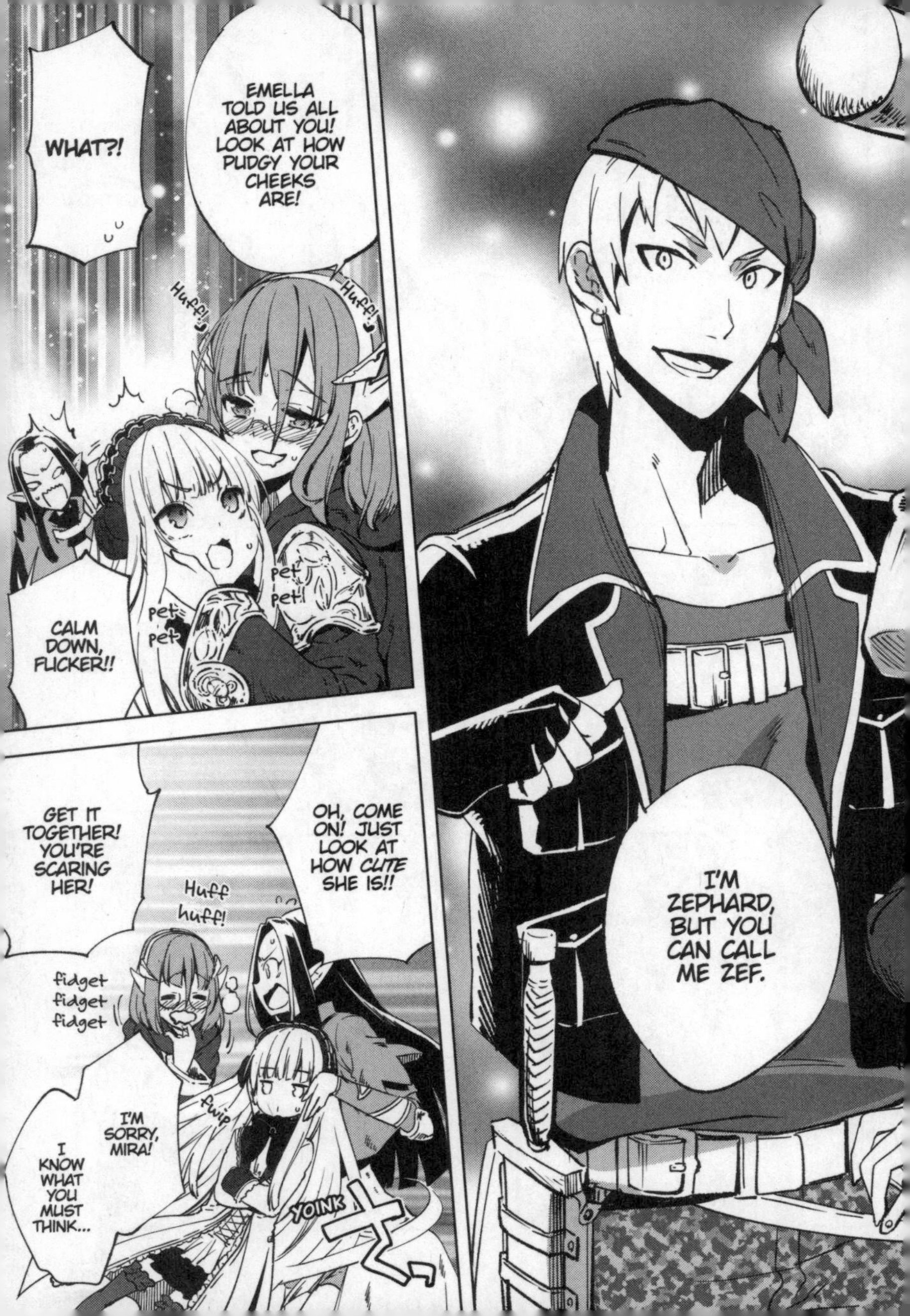
I'M ZEPHARD, BUT YOU CAN CALL ME ZEF.
EMELLA TOLD US ALL ABOUT YOU! LOOK AT HOW PUDGY YOUR CHEEKS ARE!
WHAT?!
Huff!
Huff!
pet pet
pet pet
CALM DOWN, FLICKER!!
OH, COME ON! JUST LOOK AT HOW *CUTE* SHE IS!!
GET IT TOGETHER! YOU'RE SCARING HER!
Huff huff!
fidget fidget fidget
fwip
I'M SORRY, MIRA!
YOINK
I KNOW WHAT YOU MUST THINK...

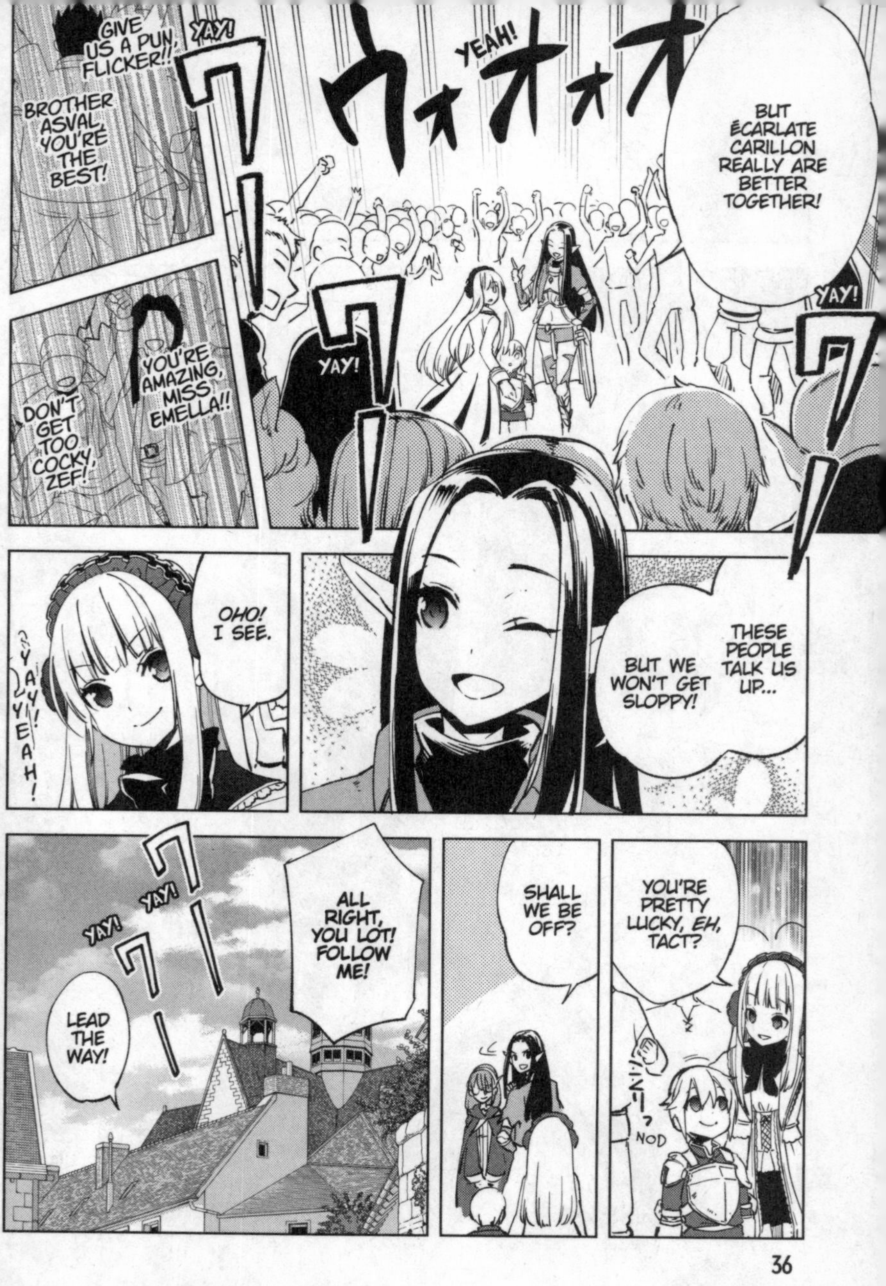
BUT ÉCARLATE CARILLON REALLY ARE BETTER TOGETHER!
YAY!
ウォオォオ
YEAH!
YAY!
GIVE US A PUN FLICKER!!
YAY!
BROTHER ASVAL, YOU'RE THE BEST!
YOU'RE AMAZING, MISS EMELLA!!
DON'T GET TOO COCKY, ZEF!
THESE PEOPLE TALK US UP...
BUT WE WON'T GET SLOPPY!
OHO! I SEE.
YAY! YEAH!
YOU'RE PRETTY LUCKY, EH, TACT?
NOD
SHALL WE BE OFF?
ALL RIGHT, YOU LOT! FOLLOW ME!
YAY!
YAY!
LEAD THE WAY!

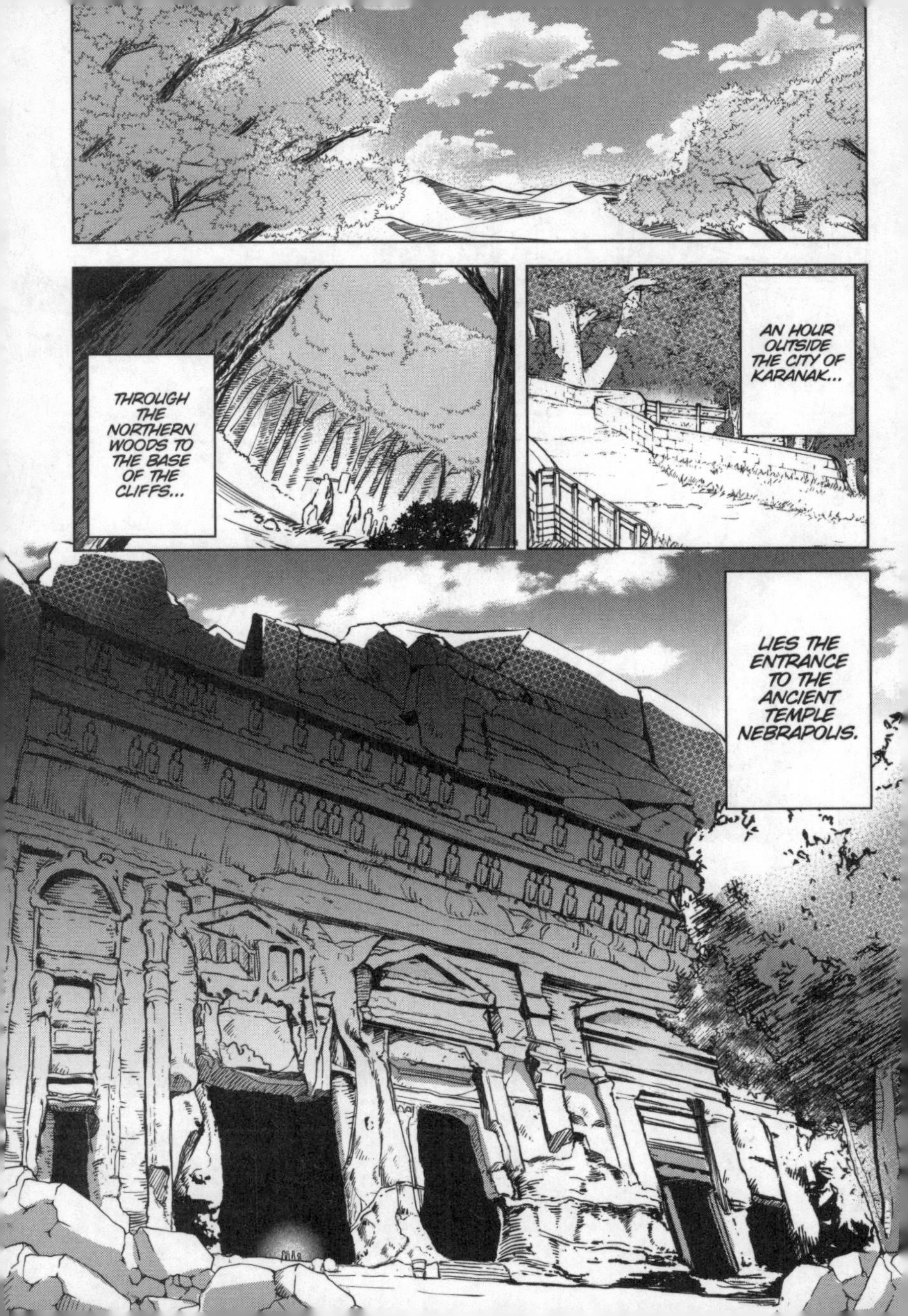
AN HOUR OUTSIDE THE CITY OF KARANAK...
THROUGH THE NORTHERN WOODS TO THE BASE OF THE CLIFFS...
LIES THE ENTRANCE TO THE ANCIENT TEMPLE NEBRAPOLIS.

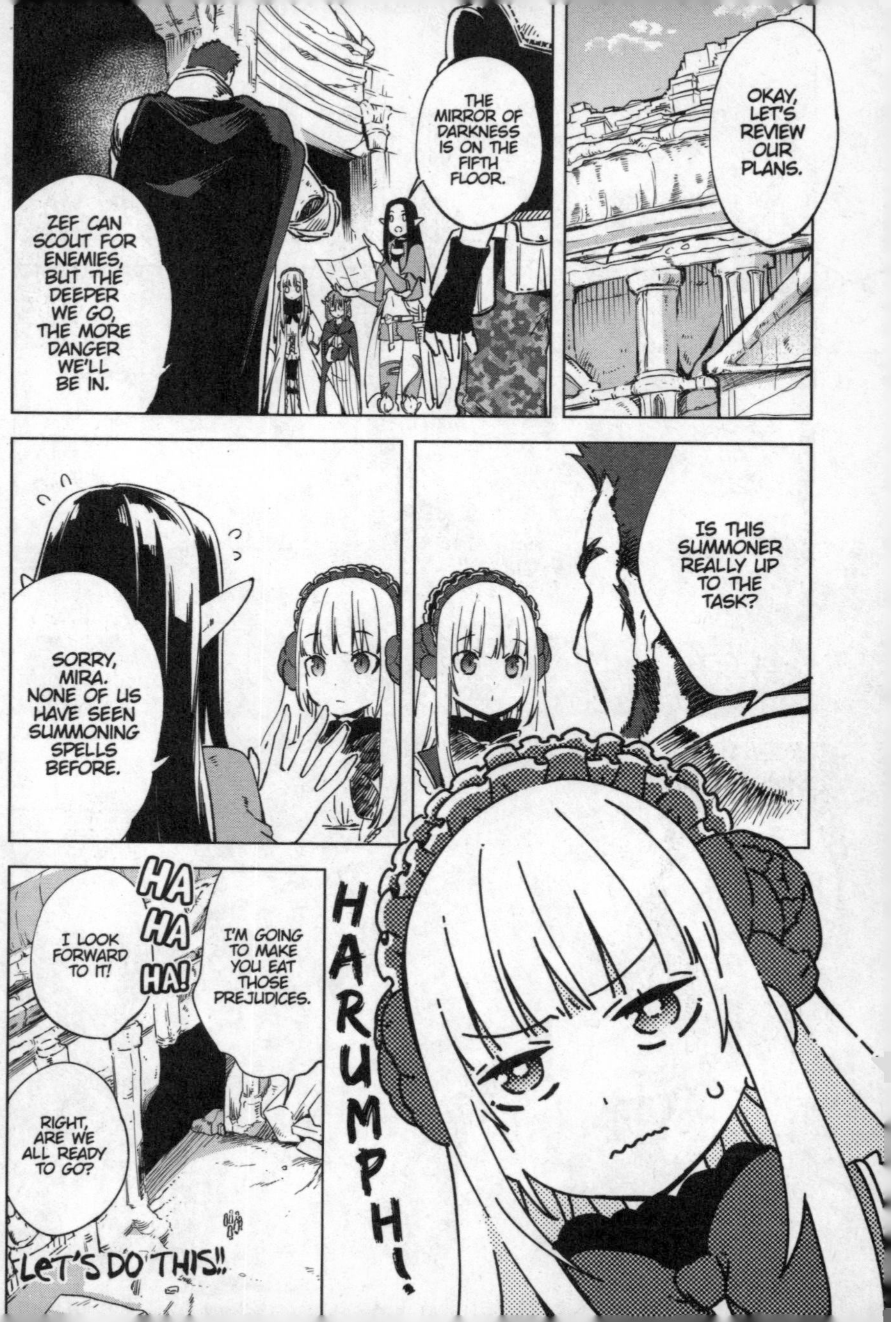
OKAY, LET'S REVIEW OUR PLANS.
THE MIRROR OF DARKNESS IS ON THE FIFTH FLOOR.
ZEF CAN SCOUT FOR ENEMIES, BUT THE DEEPER WE GO, THE MORE DANGER WE'LL BE IN.
IS THIS SUMMONER REALLY UP TO THE TASK?
SORRY, MIRA. NONE OF US HAVE SEEN SUMMONING SPELLS BEFORE.
HARUMPH!
I'M GOING TO MAKE YOU EAT THOSE PREJUDICES.
HA HA HA!
I LOOK FORWARD TO IT!
RIGHT, ARE WE ALL READY TO GO?
LET'S DO THIS!!

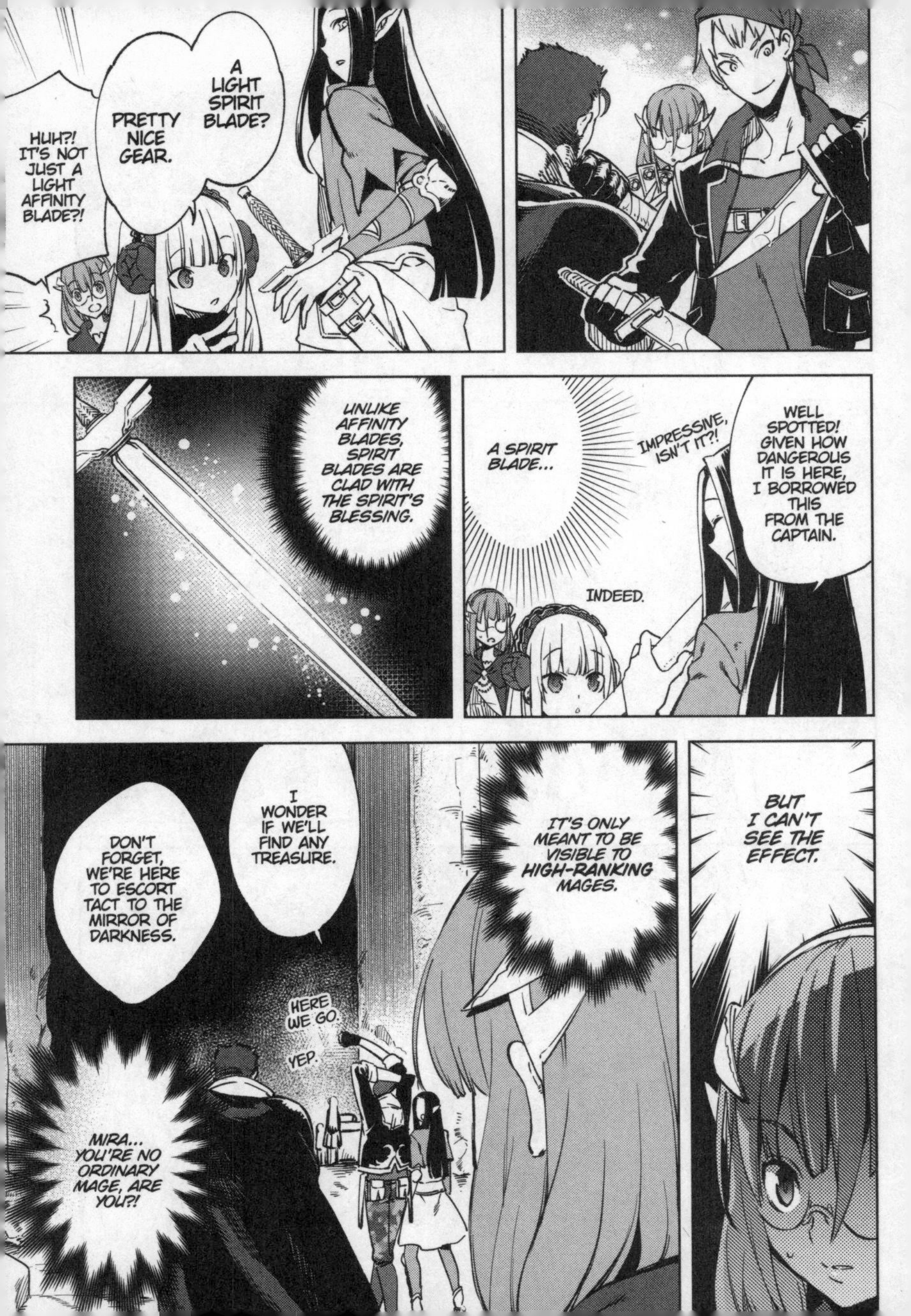
A LIGHT SPIRIT BLADE?
PRETTY NICE GEAR.
HUH?! IT'S NOT JUST A LIGHT AFFINITY BLADE?!
WELL SPOTTED! GIVEN HOW DANGEROUS IT IS HERE, I BORROWED THIS FROM THE CAPTAIN.
IMPRESSIVE, ISN'T IT?!
A SPIRIT BLADE...
INDEED.
UNLIKE AFFINITY BLADES, SPIRIT BLADES ARE CLAD WITH THE SPIRIT'S BLESSING.
BUT I CAN'T SEE THE EFFECT.
IT'S ONLY MEANT TO BE VISIBLE TO HIGH-RANKING MAGES.
I WONDER IF WE'LL FIND ANY TREASURE.
DON'T FORGET, WE'RE HERE TO ESCORT TACT TO THE MIRROR OF DARKNESS.
HERE WE GO.
YEP.
MIRA... YOU'RE NO ORDINARY MAGE, ARE YOU?!

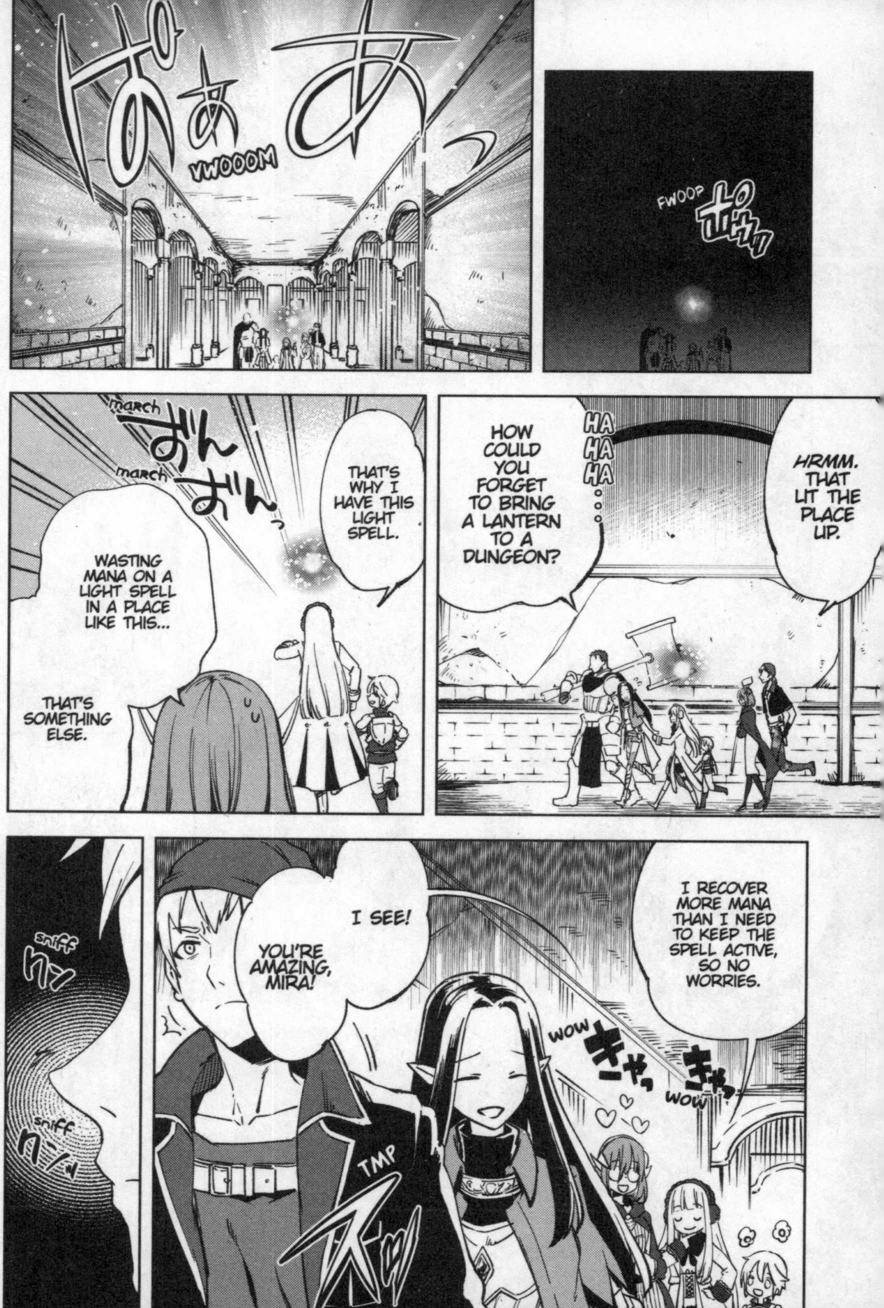
FWOOP
VWOOOM
HRMM. THAT LIT THE PLACE UP.
HA HA HA...
HOW COULD YOU FORGET TO BRING A LANTERN TO A DUNGEON?
THAT'S WHY I HAVE THIS LIGHT SPELL.
march
march
WASTING MANA ON A LIGHT SPELL IN A PLACE LIKE THIS...
THAT'S SOMETHING ELSE.
I RECOVER MORE MANA THAN I NEED TO KEEP THE SPELL ACTIVE, SO NO WORRIES.
WOW
WOW
I SEE!
YOU'RE AMAZING, MIRA!
TMP
sniff
sniff

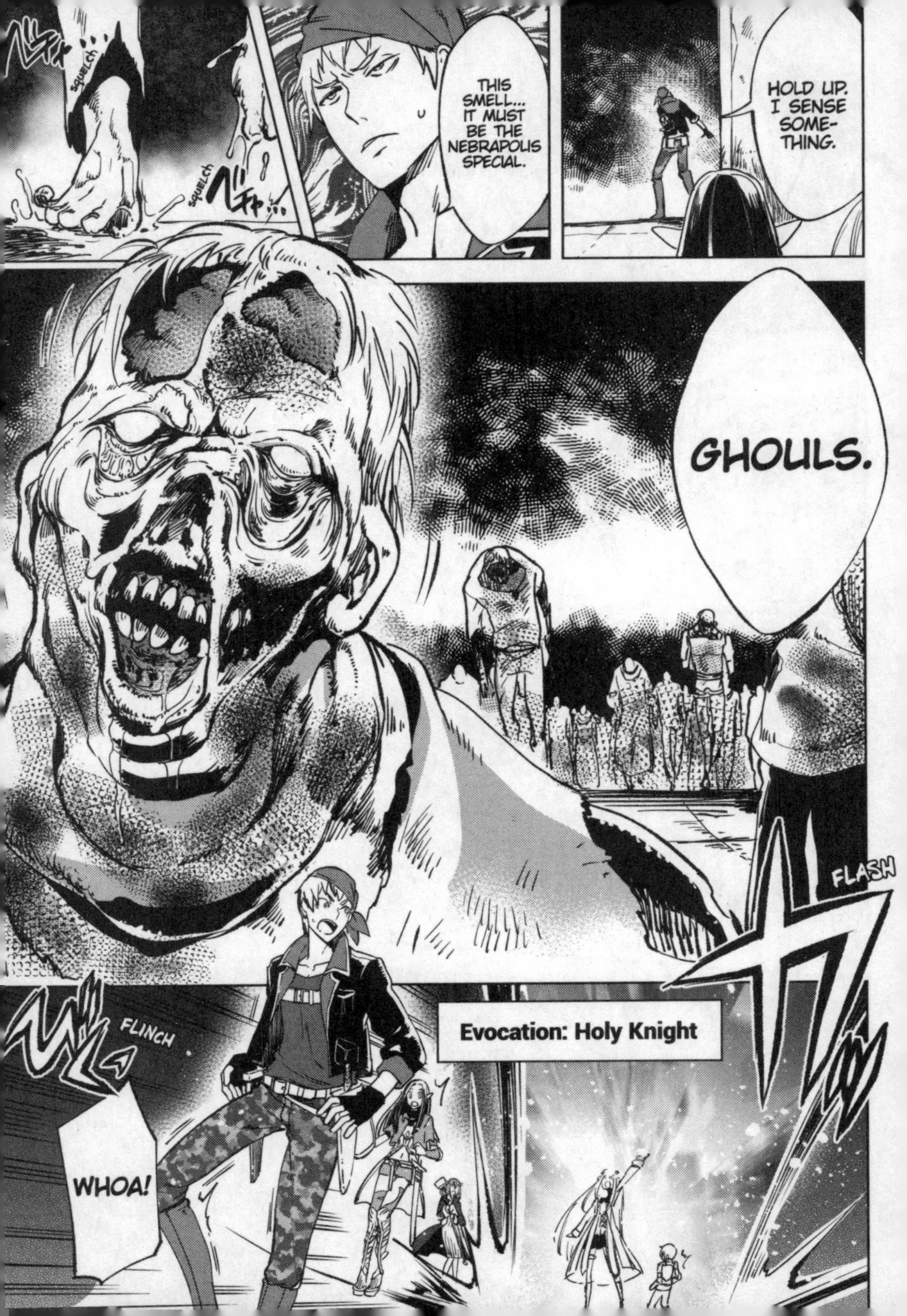
HOLD UP. I SENSE SOME-THING.
THIS SMELL... IT MUST BE THE NEBRAPOLIS SPECIAL.
squelch
squelch
GHOULS.
FLASH
Evocation: Holy Knight
FLINCH
WHOA!

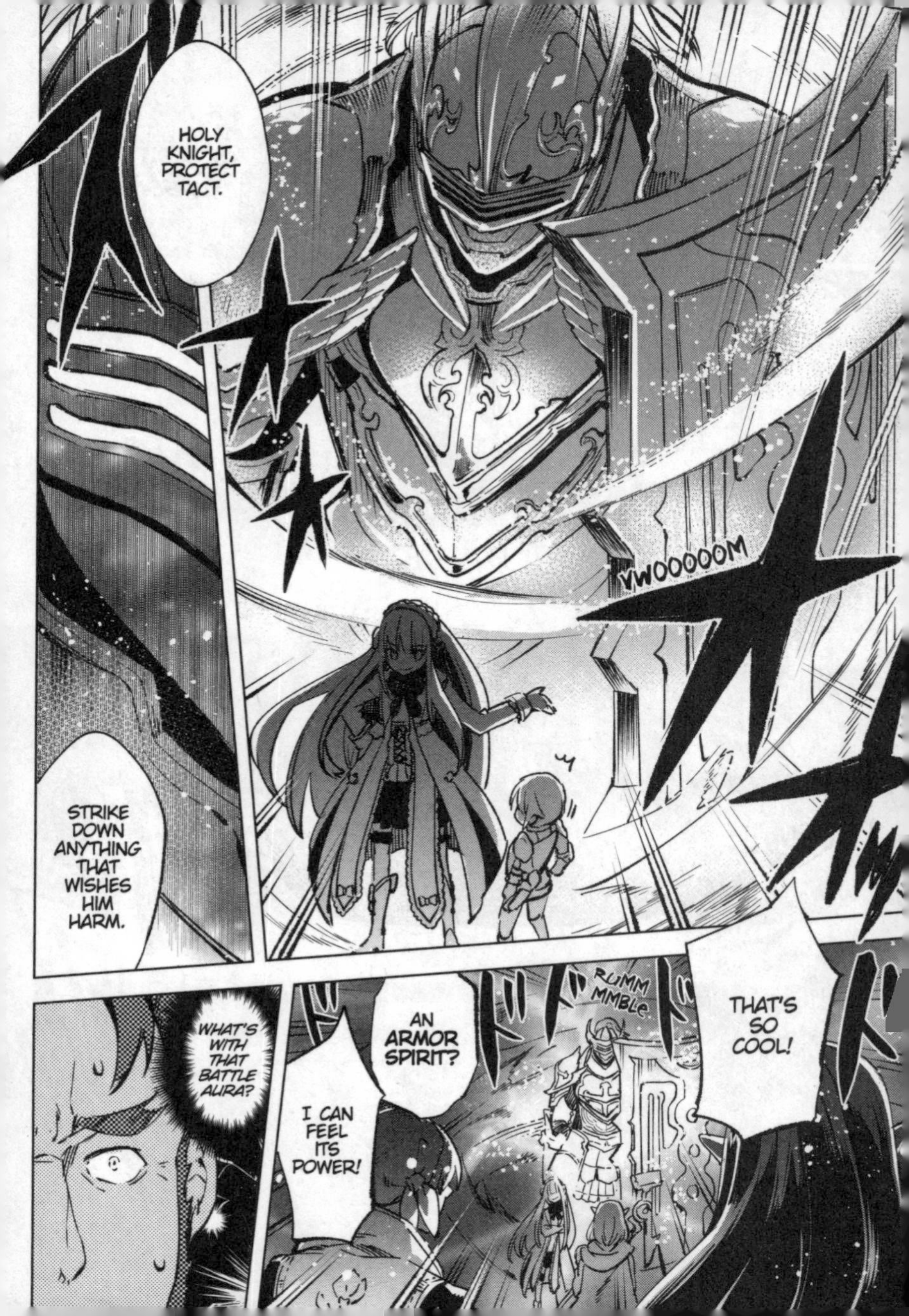
HOLY KNIGHT, PROTECT TACT.
YWOOOOOM
STRIKE DOWN ANYTHING THAT WISHES HIM HARM.
THAT'S SO COOL!
RUMMMMBLe
AN ARMOR SPIRIT?
I CAN FEEL ITS POWER!
WHAT'S WITH THAT BATTLE AURA?

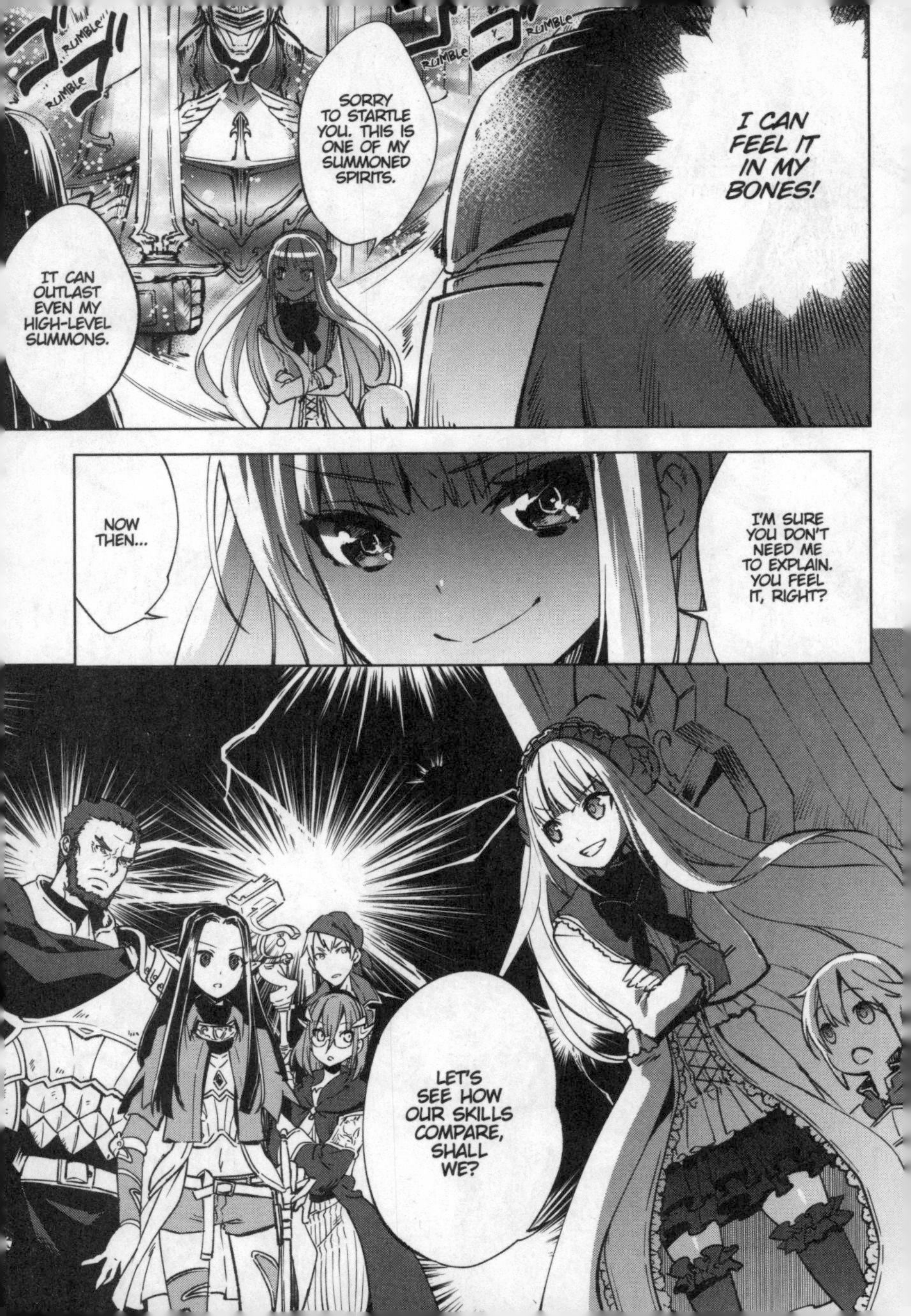
RUMBLE RUMBLE
I CAN FEEL IT IN MY BONES!
RUMBLE RUMBLE
SORRY TO STARTLE YOU. THIS IS ONE OF MY SUMMONED SPIRITS.
IT CAN OUTLAST EVEN MY HIGH-LEVEL SUMMONS.
I'M SURE YOU DON'T NEED ME TO EXPLAIN. YOU FEEL IT, RIGHT?
NOW THEN...
LET'S SEE HOW OUR SKILLS COMPARE, SHALL WE?

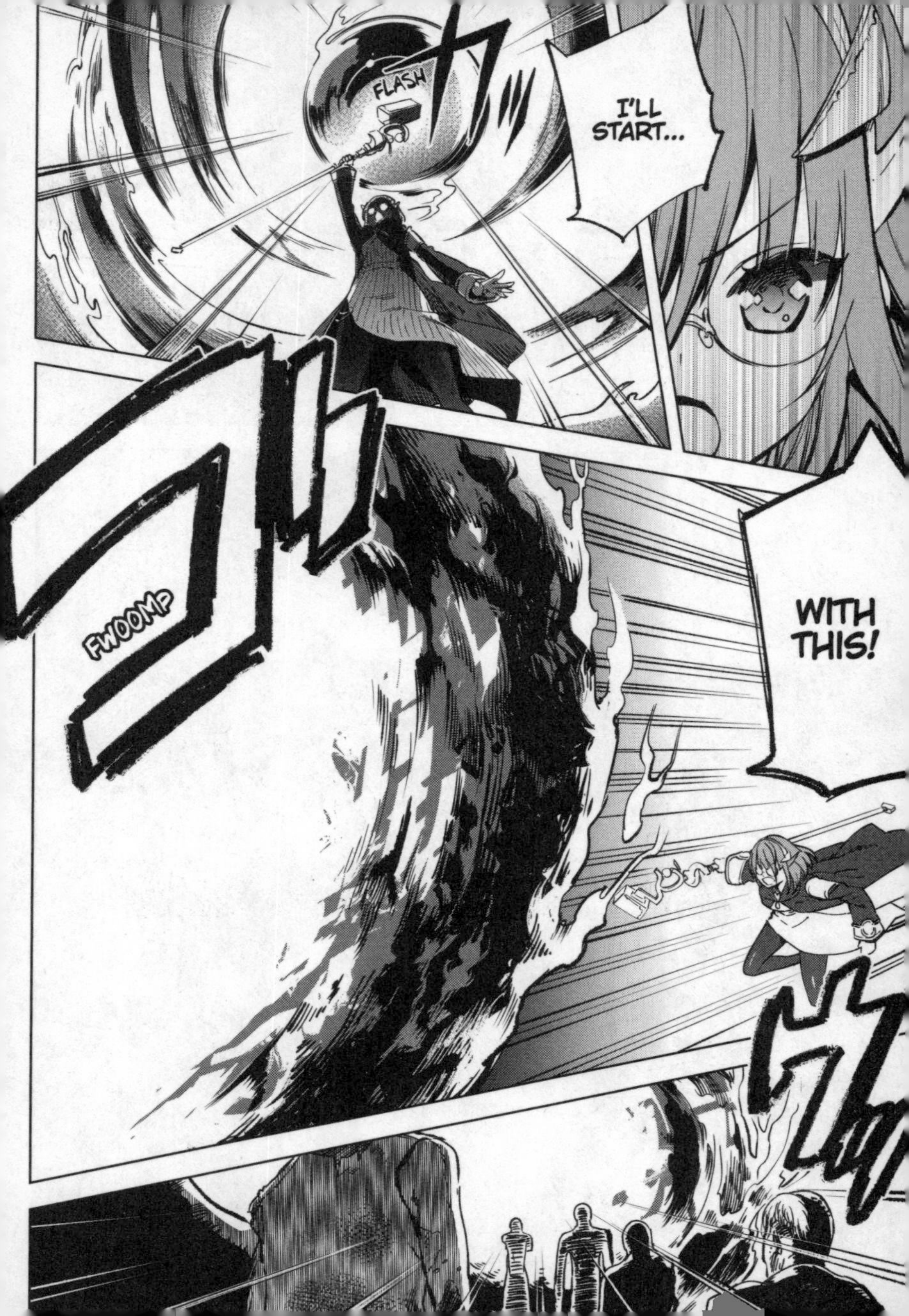
I'LL START...
FLASH
WITH THIS!
FWOOMP

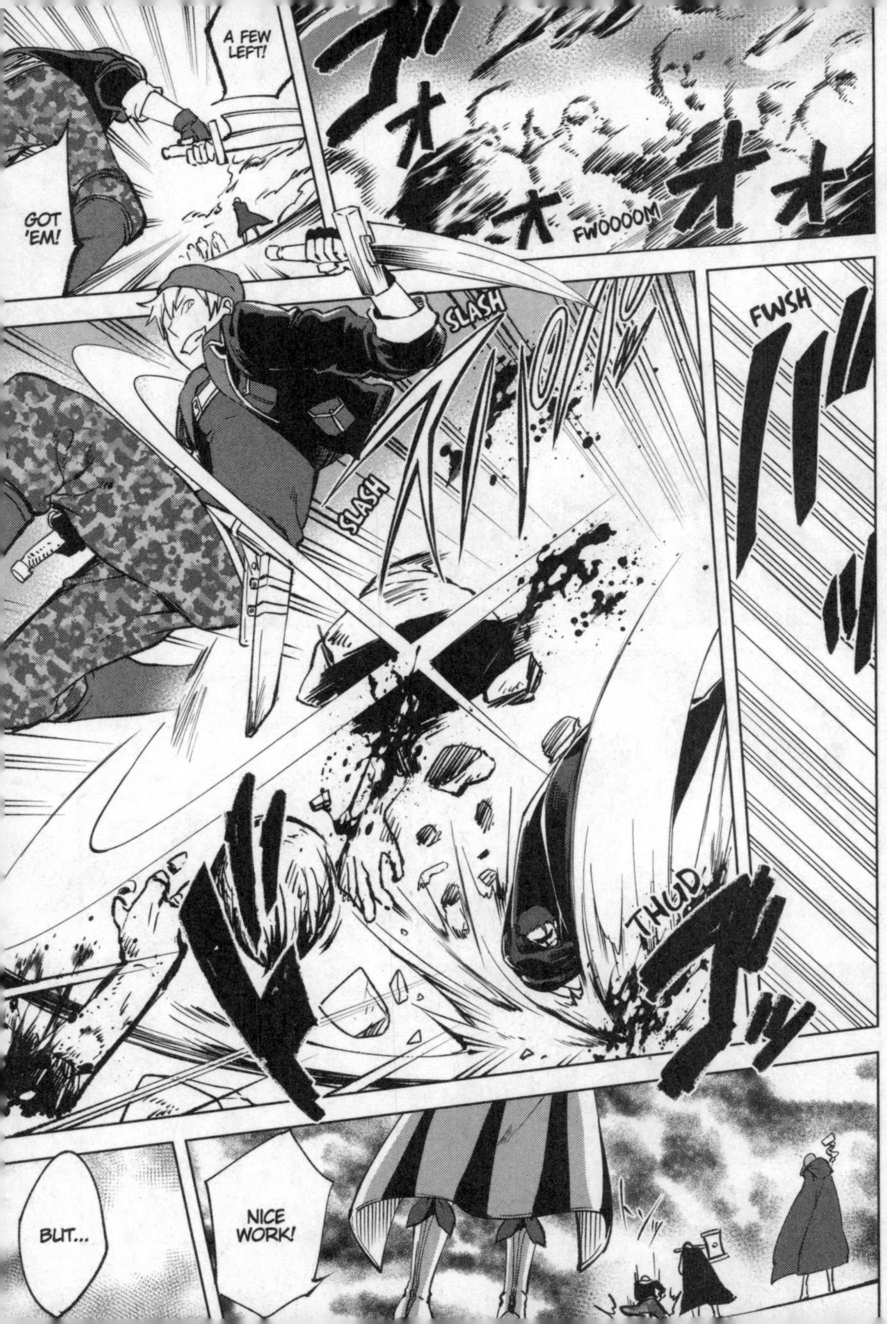
FWOOOOM
A FEW LEFT!
GOT 'EM!
FWSH
SLASH
SLASH
THUD
NICE WORK!
BUT...

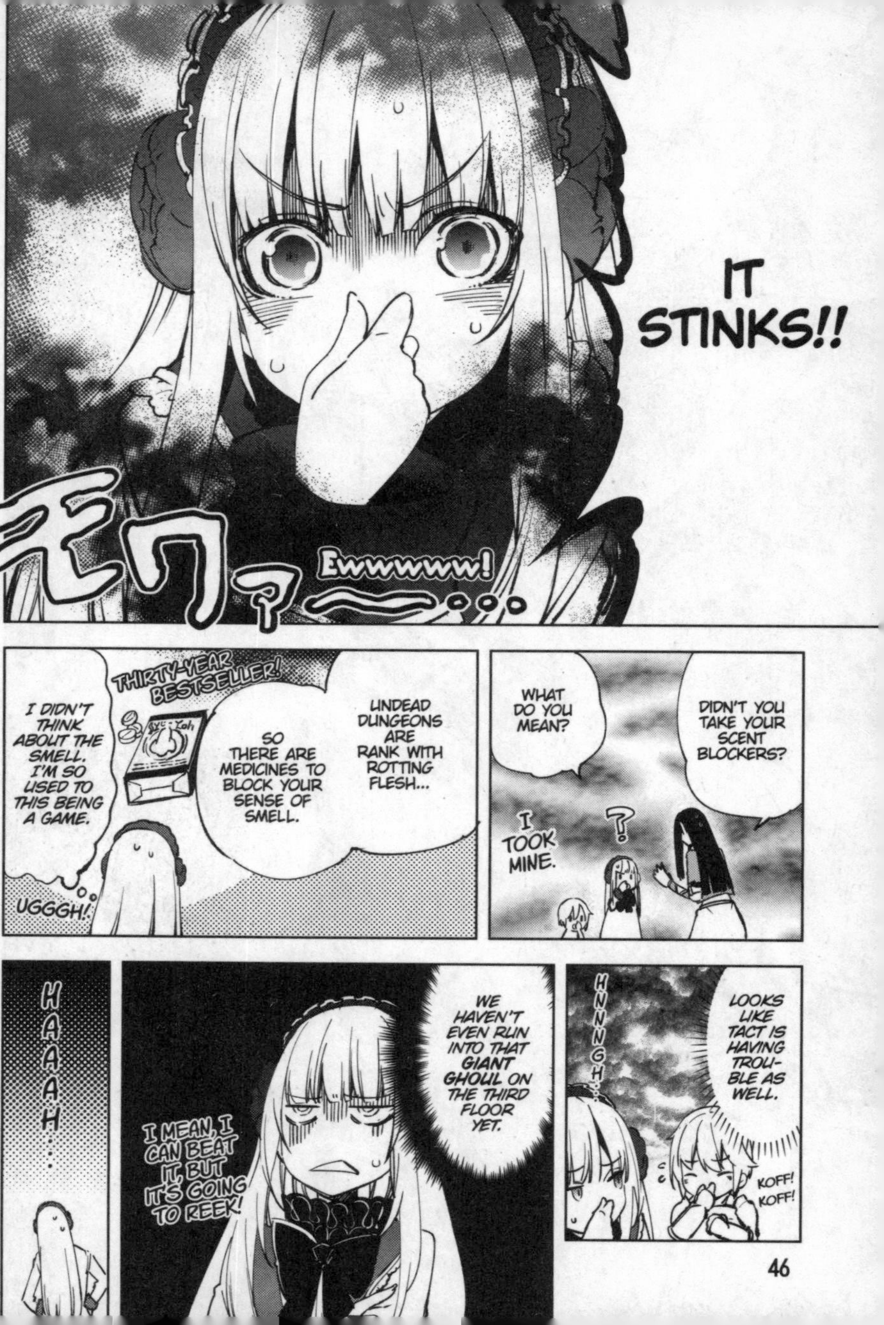
IT STINKS!!
モワァー…
Ewwwww!
DIDN'T YOU TAKE YOUR SCENT BLOCKERS?
WHAT DO YOU MEAN?
?
I TOOK MINE.
UNDEAD DUNGEONS ARE RANK WITH ROTTING FLESH...
SO THERE ARE MEDICINES TO BLOCK YOUR SENSE OF SMELL.
THIRTY-YEAR BESTSELLER!
I DIDN'T THINK ABOUT THE SMELL. I'M SO USED TO THIS BEING A GAME.
UGGGH!
LOOKS LIKE TACT IS HAVING TROUBLE AS WELL.
HNNNGH...
KOFF! KOFF!
WE HAVEN'T EVEN RUN INTO THAT GIANT GHOUL ON THE THIRD FLOOR YET.
I MEAN, I CAN BEAT IT, BUT IT'S GOING TO REEK!
HAAAAH...

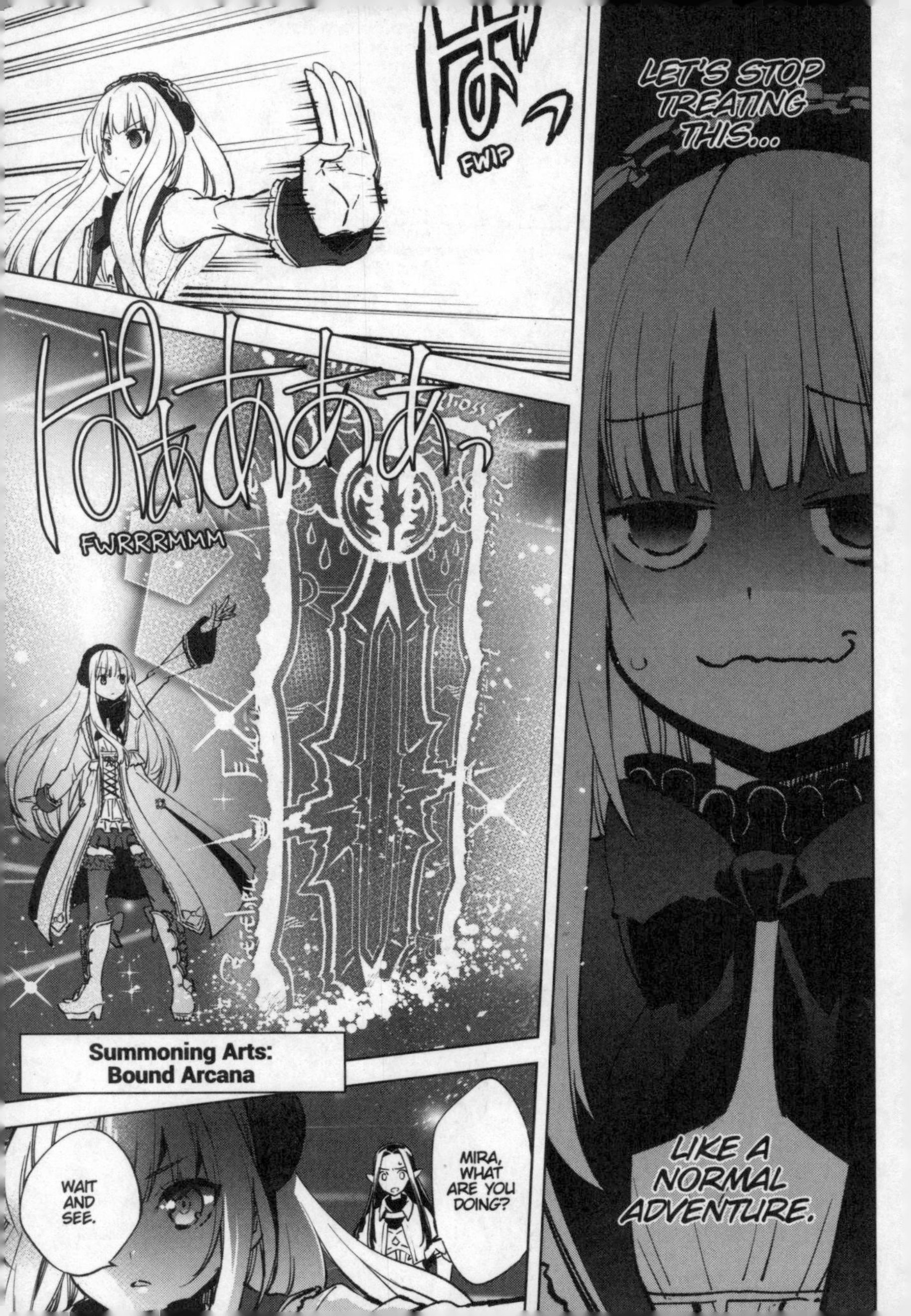

LET'S STOP TREATING THIS...
LIKE A NORMAL ADVENTURE.
FWIP
FWRRRMMM
Summoning Arts: Bound Arcana
MIRA, WHAT ARE YOU DOING?
WAIT AND SEE.

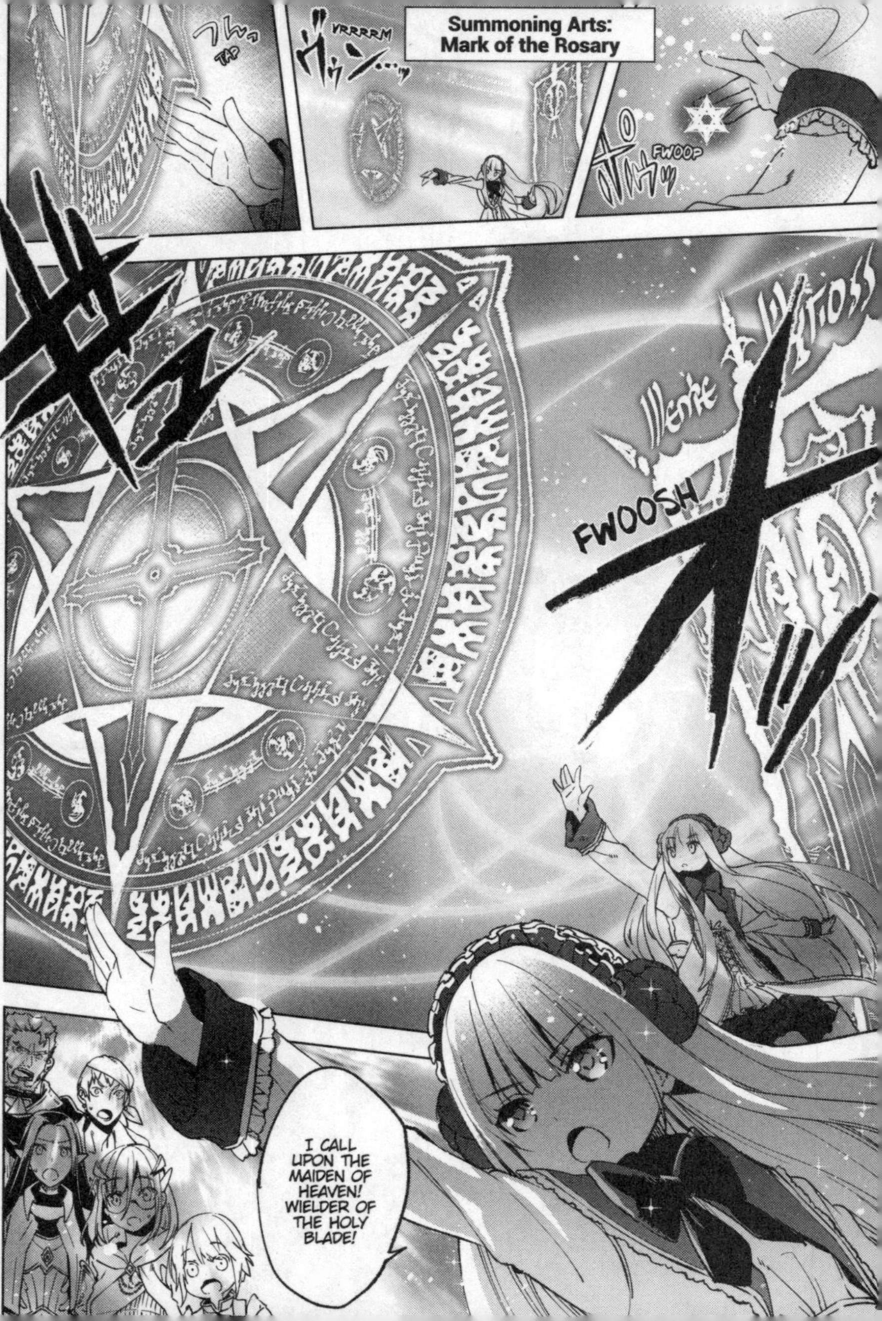
Summoning Arts: Mark of the Rosary
FWOOP
VRRRRM
TAP
FWOOSH
I CALL UPON THE MAIDEN OF HEAVEN! WIELDER OF THE HOLY BLADE!

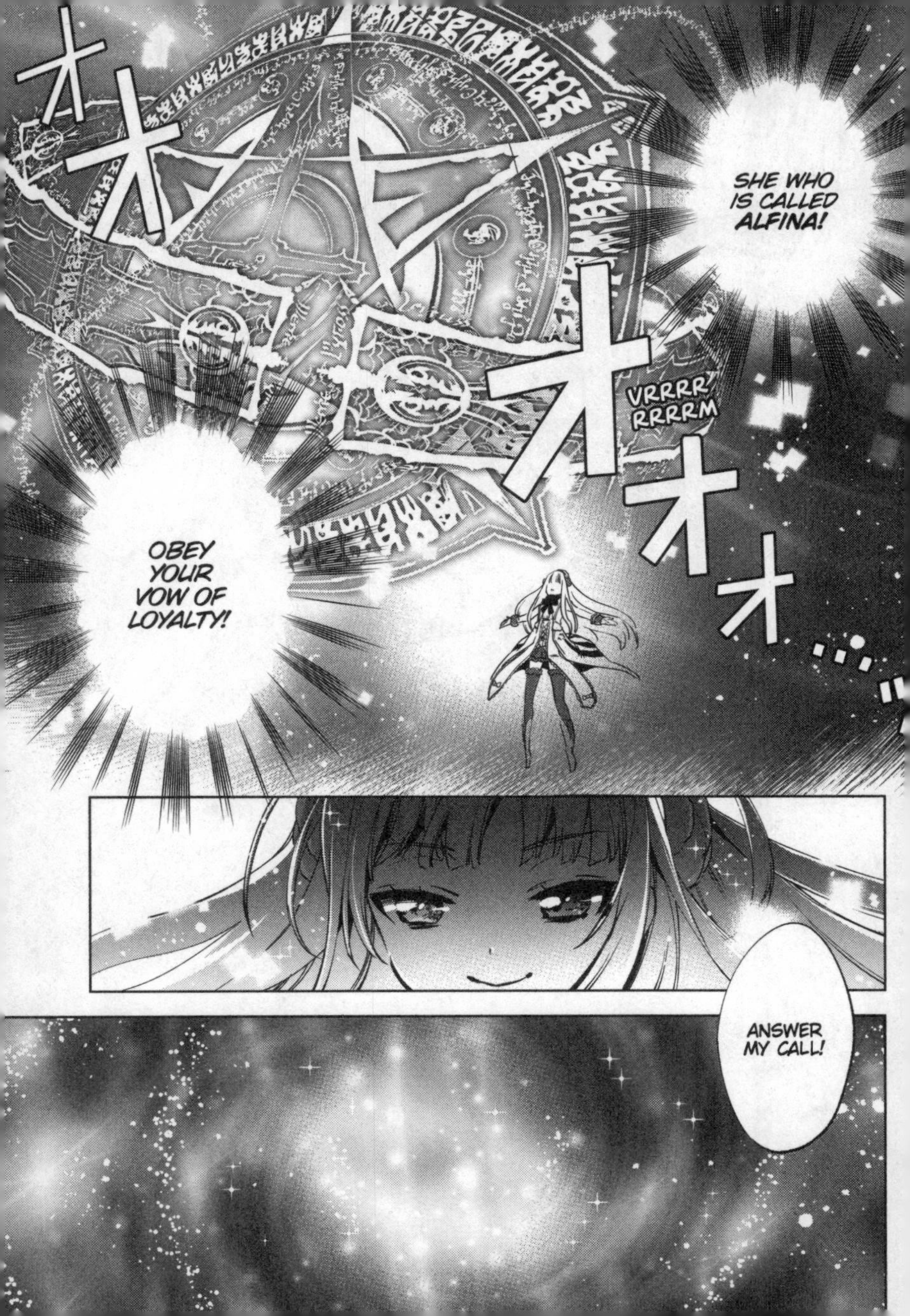
SHE WHO IS CALLED ALFINA!
VRRRR RRRRM
OBEY YOUR VOW OF LOYALTY!
ANSWER MY CALL!

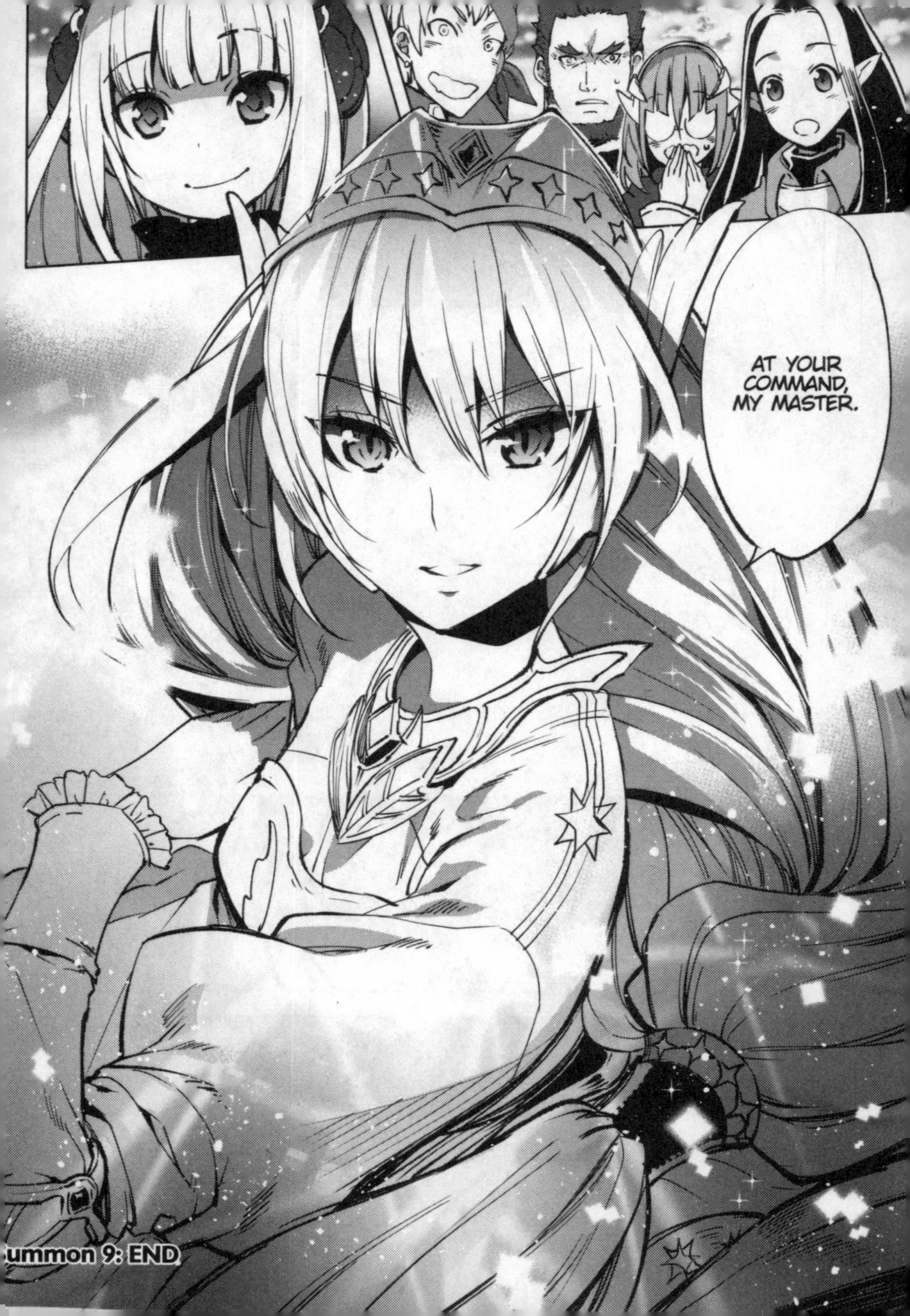
AT YOUR COMMAND, MY MASTER.
ummon 9: END

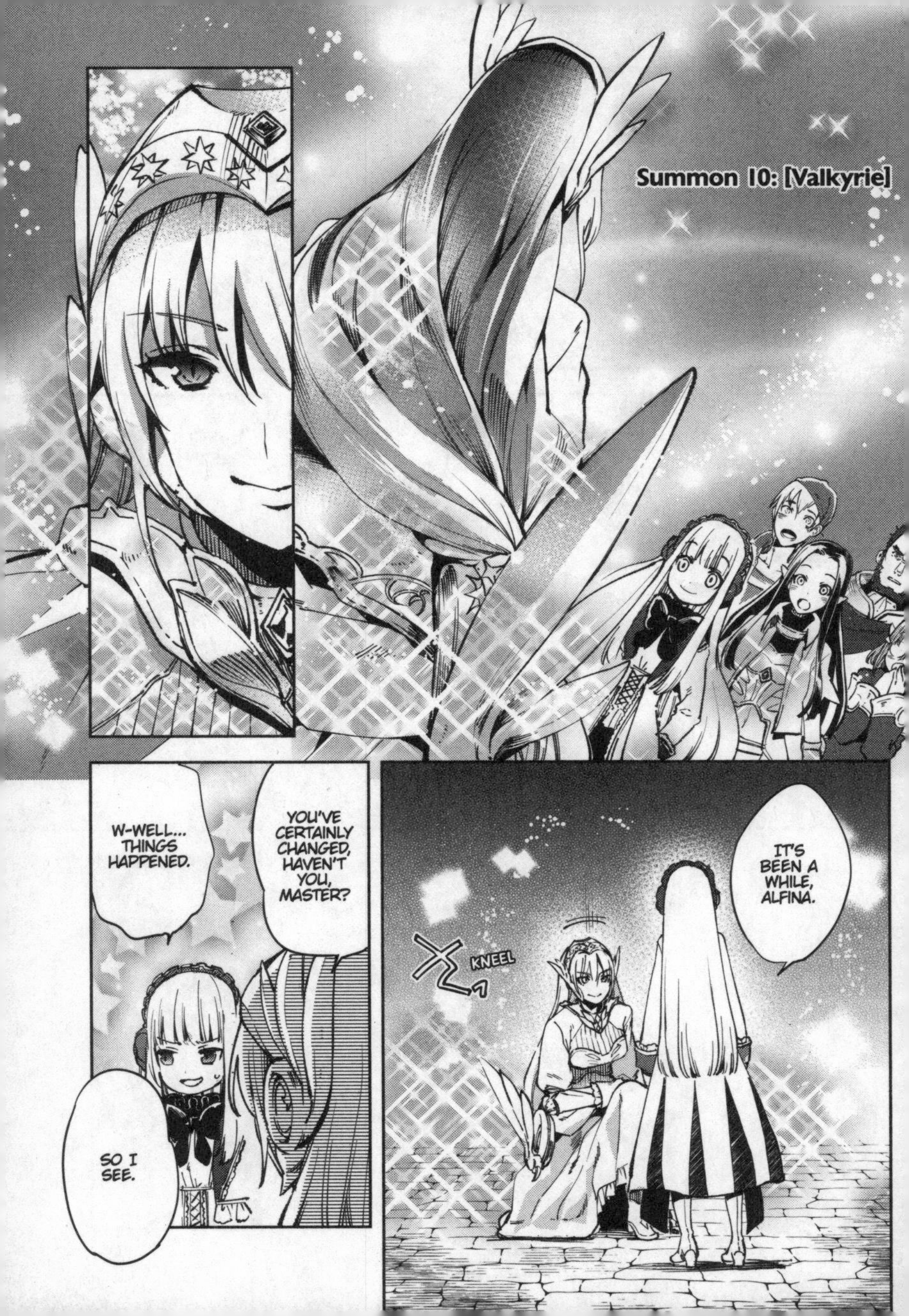
Summon 10: [Valkyrie]
IT'S BEEN A WHILE, ALFINA.
KNEEL
YOU'VE CERTAINLY CHANGED, HAVEN'T YOU, MASTER?
W-WELL... THINGS HAPPENED.
SO I SEE.

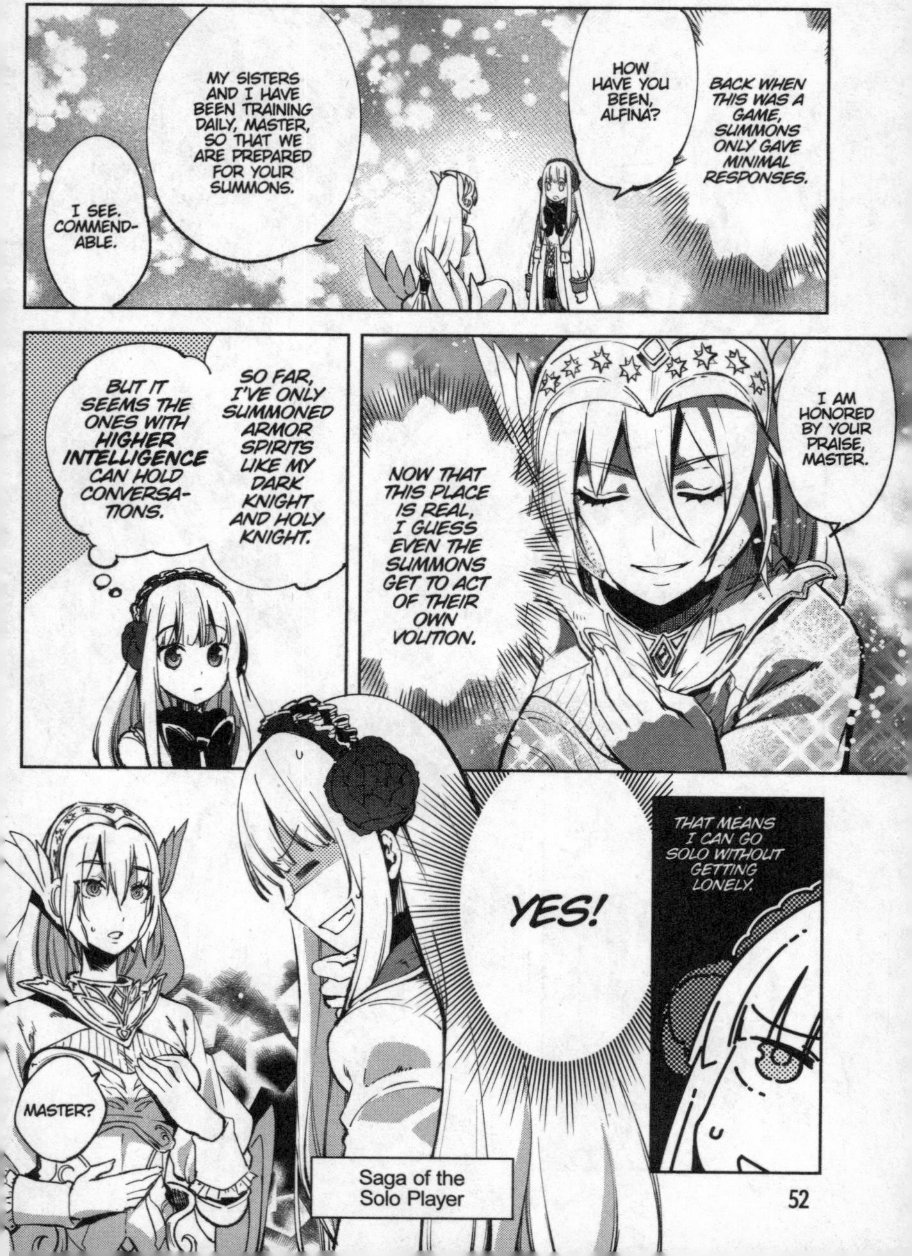
BACK WHEN THIS WAS A GAME, SUMMONS ONLY GAVE MINIMAL RESPONSES.
HOW HAVE YOU BEEN, ALFINA?
MY SISTERS AND I HAVE BEEN TRAINING DAILY, MASTER, SO THAT WE ARE PREPARED FOR YOUR SUMMONS.
I SEE. COMMENDABLE.
I AM HONORED BY YOUR PRAISE, MASTER.
NOW THAT THIS PLACE IS REAL, I GUESS EVEN THE SUMMONS GET TO ACT OF THEIR OWN VOLITION.
SO FAR, I'VE ONLY SUMMONED ARMOR SPIRITS LIKE MY DARK KNIGHT AND HOLY KNIGHT.
BUT IT SEEMS THE ONES WITH HIGHER INTELLIGENCE CAN HOLD CONVERSATIONS.
THAT MEANS I CAN GO SOLO WITHOUT GETTING LONELY.
YES!
MASTER?

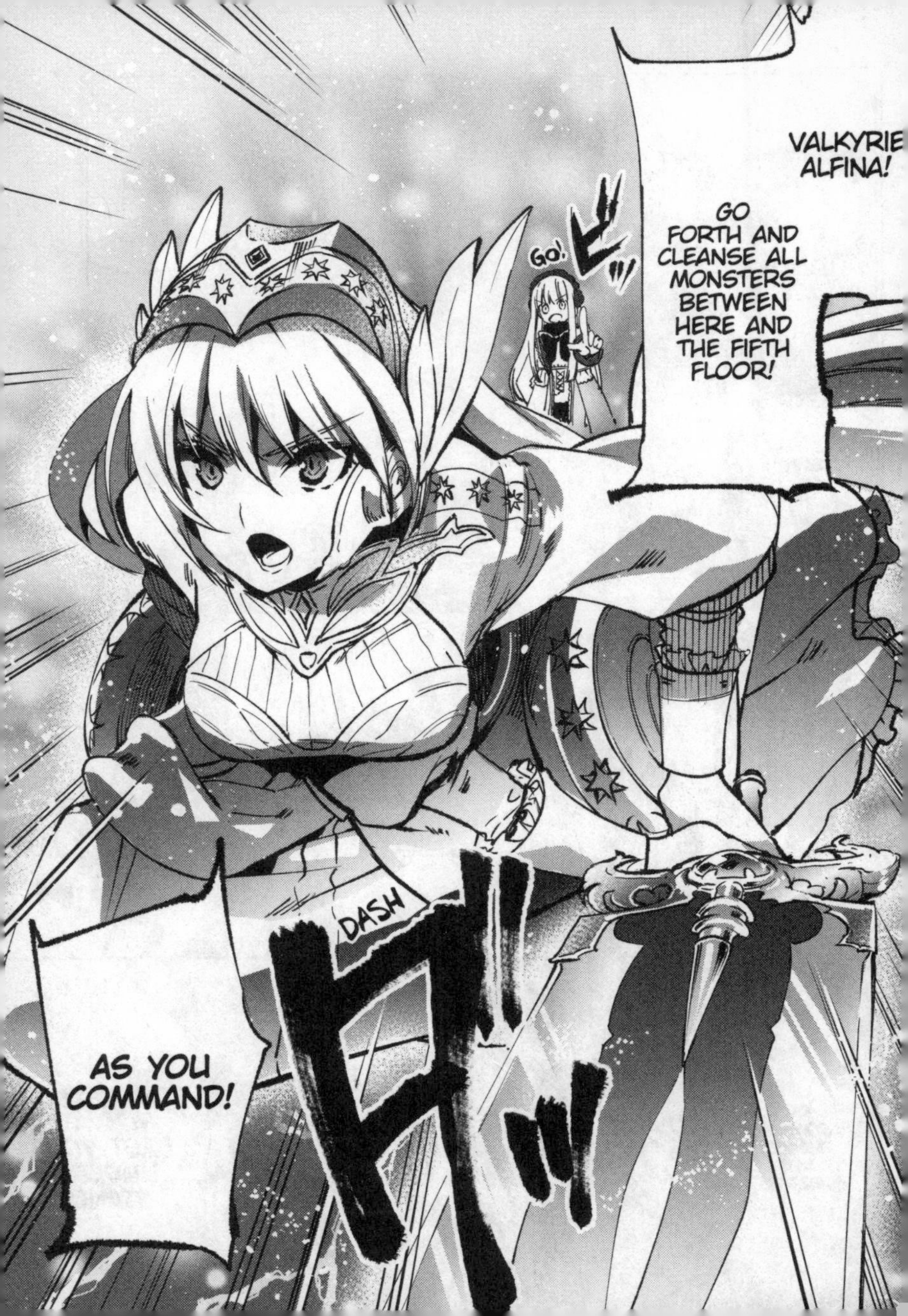
VALKYRIE ALFINA!
GO FORTH AND CLEANSE ALL MONSTERS BETWEEN HERE AND THE FIFTH FLOOR!
GO!
DASH
AS YOU COMMAND!

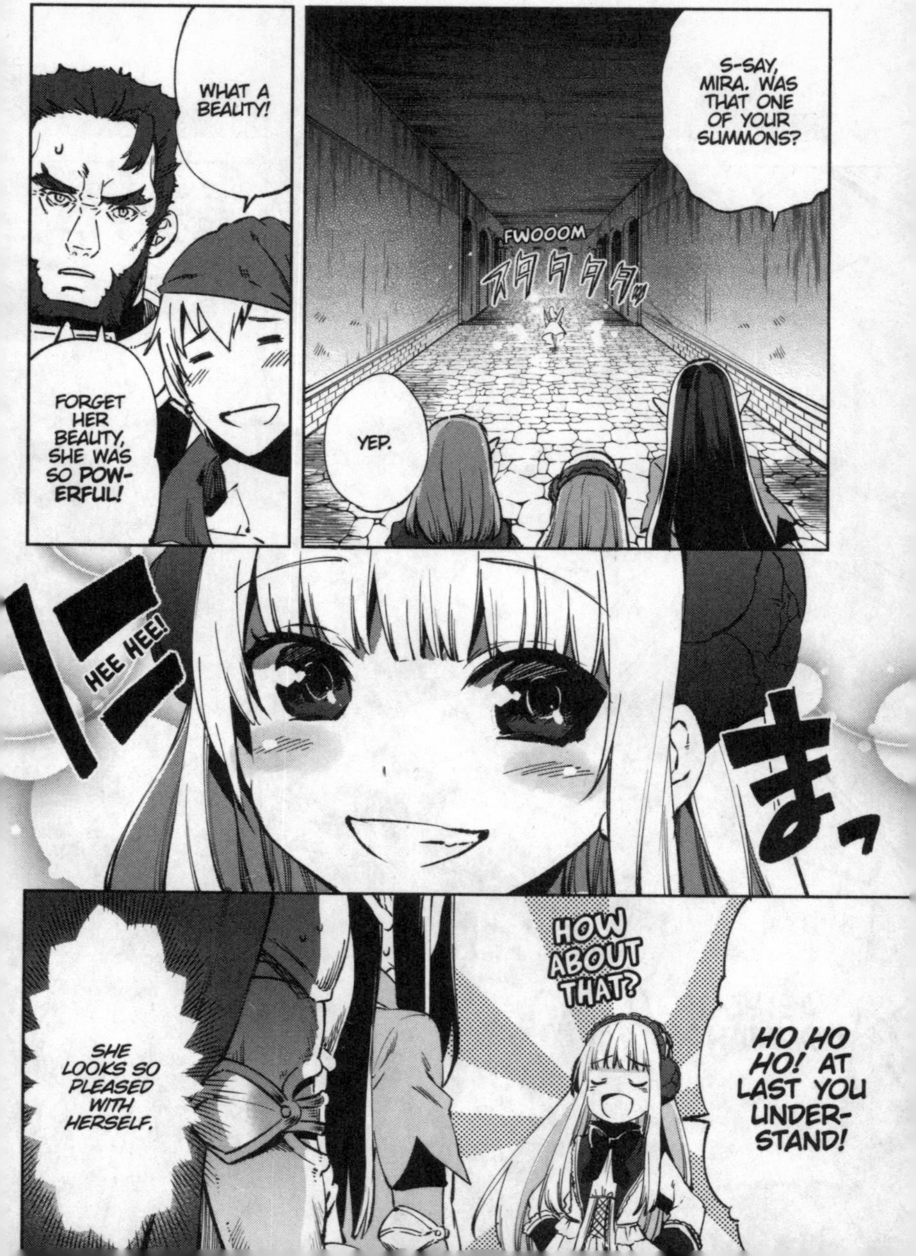
S-SAY, MIRA. WAS THAT ONE OF YOUR SUMMONS?
FWOOOM
スタタタタッ
YEP.
WHAT A BEAUTY!
FORGET HER BEAUTY, SHE WAS SO POW-ERFUL!
HEE HEE!
まっ
HO HO HO! AT LAST YOU UNDER-STAND!
HOW ABOUT THAT?
SHE LOOKS SO PLEASED WITH HERSELF.

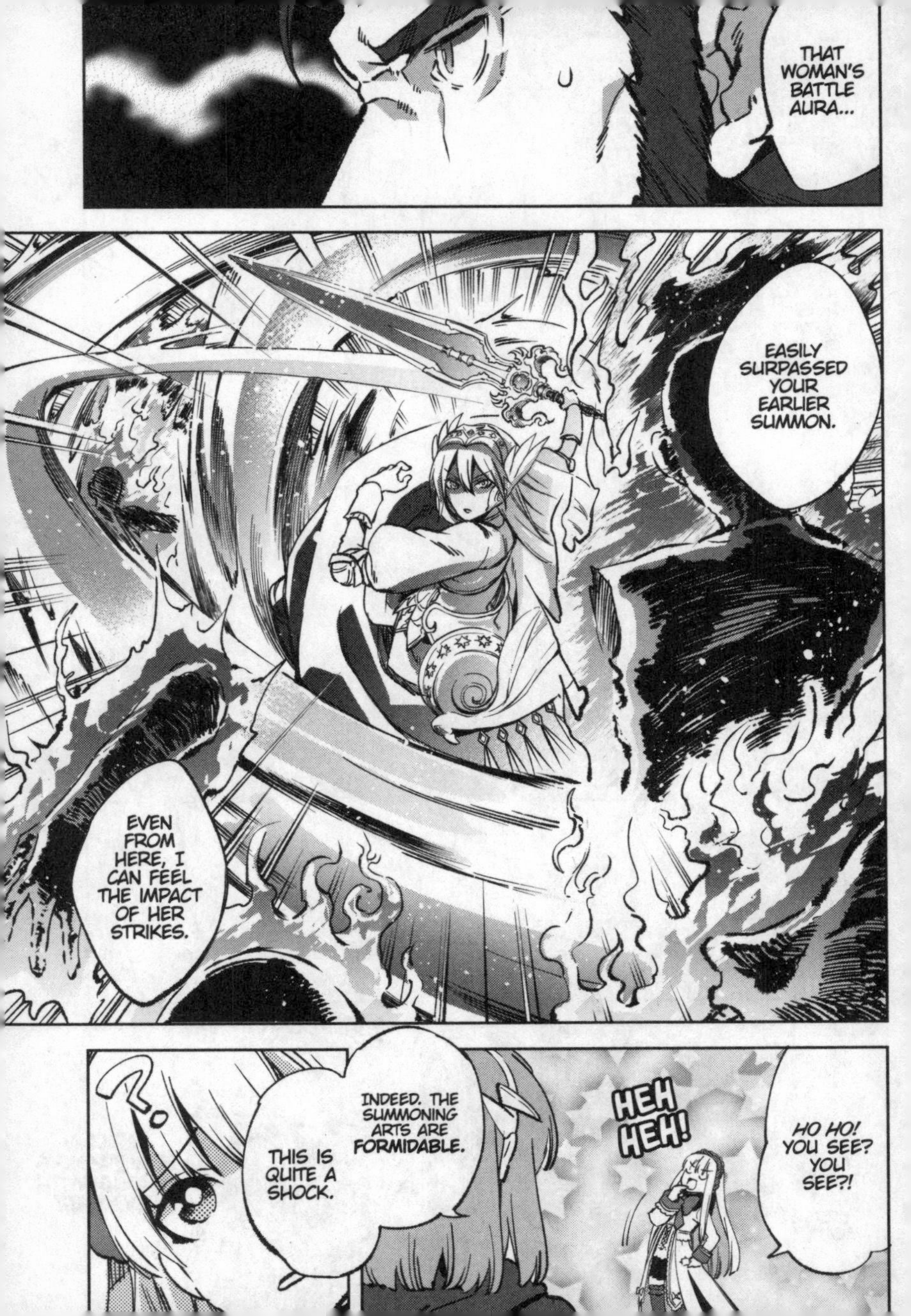
THAT WOMAN'S BATTLE AURA...
EASILY SURPASSED YOUR EARLIER SUMMON.
EVEN FROM HERE, I CAN FEEL THE IMPACT OF HER STRIKES.
HO HO! YOU SEE? YOU SEE?!
HEH HEH!
INDEED. THE SUMMONING ARTS ARE FORMIDABLE.
THIS IS QUITE A SHOCK.
?!

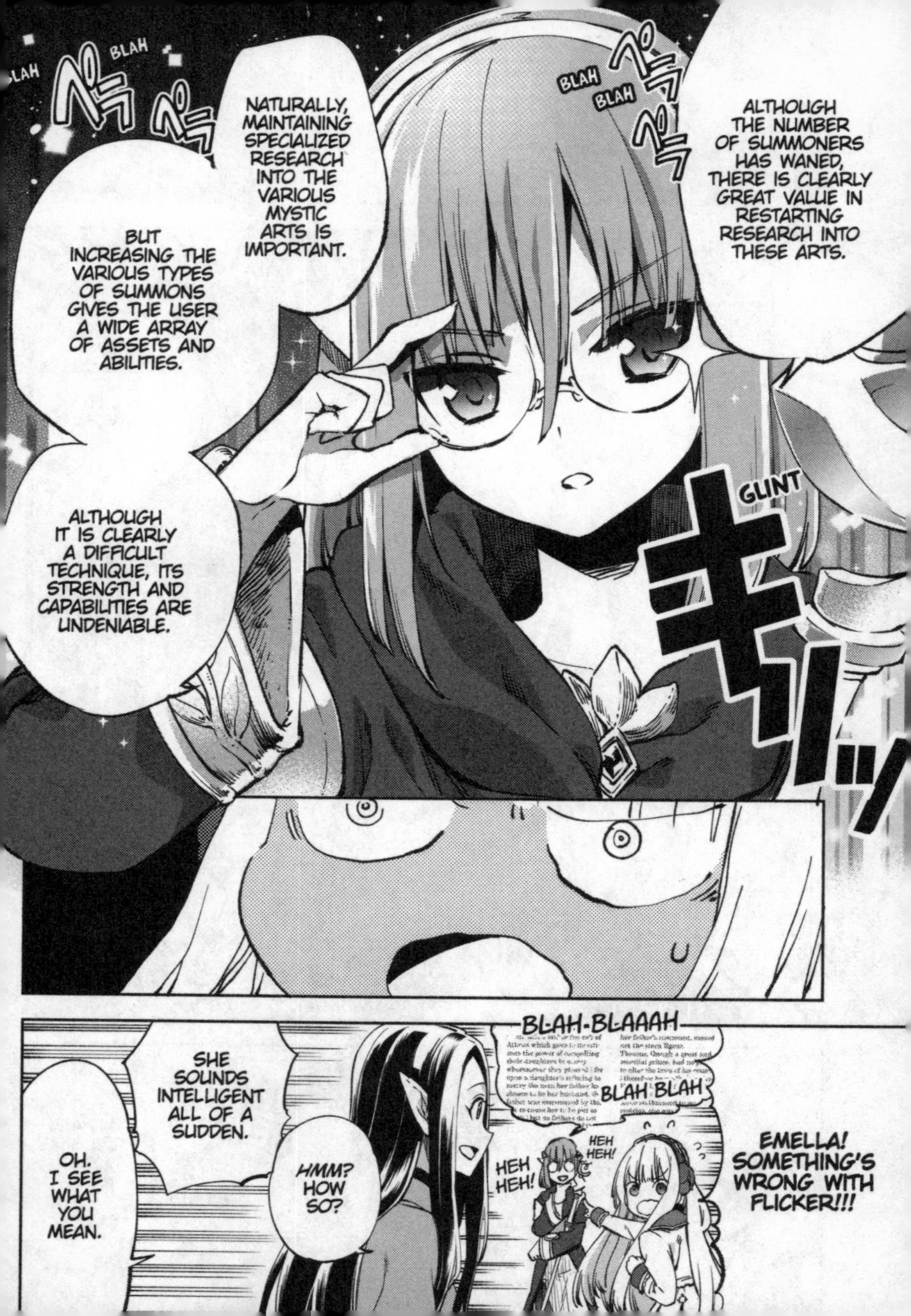
BLAH BLAH
ALTHOUGH THE NUMBER OF SUMMONERS HAS WANED, THERE IS CLEARLY GREAT VALUE IN RESTARTING RESEARCH INTO THESE ARTS.
BLAH BLAH
NATURALLY, MAINTAINING SPECIALIZED RESEARCH INTO THE VARIOUS MYSTIC ARTS IS IMPORTANT.
BUT INCREASING THE VARIOUS TYPES OF SUMMONS GIVES THE USER A WIDE ARRAY OF ASSETS AND ABILITIES.
GLINT
ALTHOUGH IT IS CLEARLY A DIFFICULT TECHNIQUE, ITS STRENGTH AND CAPABILITIES ARE UNDENIABLE.
EMELLA! SOMETHING'S WRONG WITH FLICKER!!!
BLAH-BLAAAH
BLAH BLAH
HEH HEH!
HEH HEH!
SHE SOUNDS INTELLIGENT ALL OF A SUDDEN.
HMM? HOW SO?
OH. I SEE WHAT YOU MEAN.

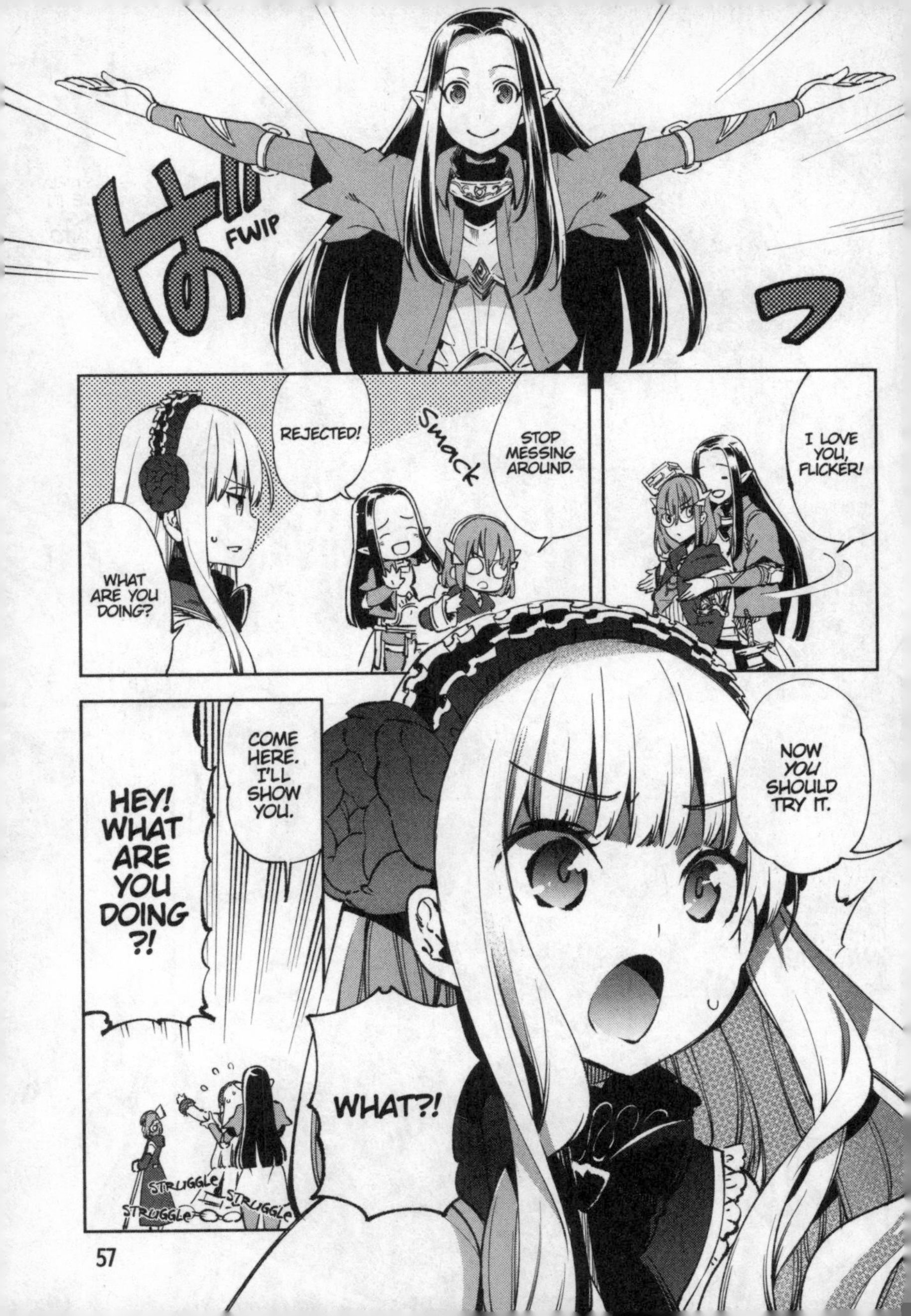
FWIP
I LOVE YOU, FLICKER!
STOP MESSING AROUND.
Smack
REJECTED!
WHAT ARE YOU DOING?
NOW YOU SHOULD TRY IT.
WHAT?!
COME HERE. I'LL SHOW YOU.
HEY! WHAT ARE YOU DOING?!
STRUGGLE
STRUGGLE
STRUGGLE

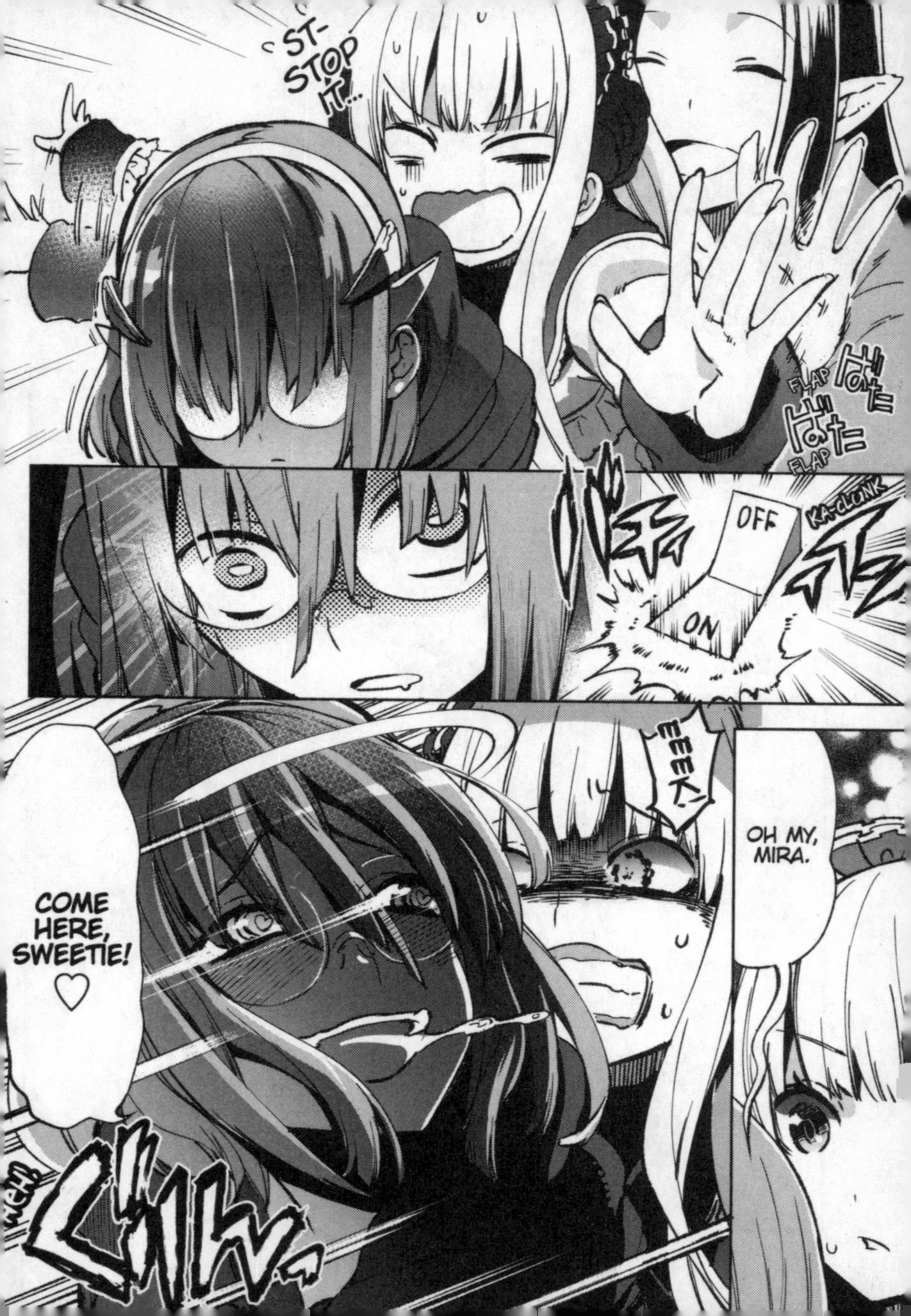
ST-STOP IT...
FLAP
FLAP
KA-CLUNK
OFF
ON
OH MY, MIRA.
EEEK!
COME HERE, SWEETIE! ♡

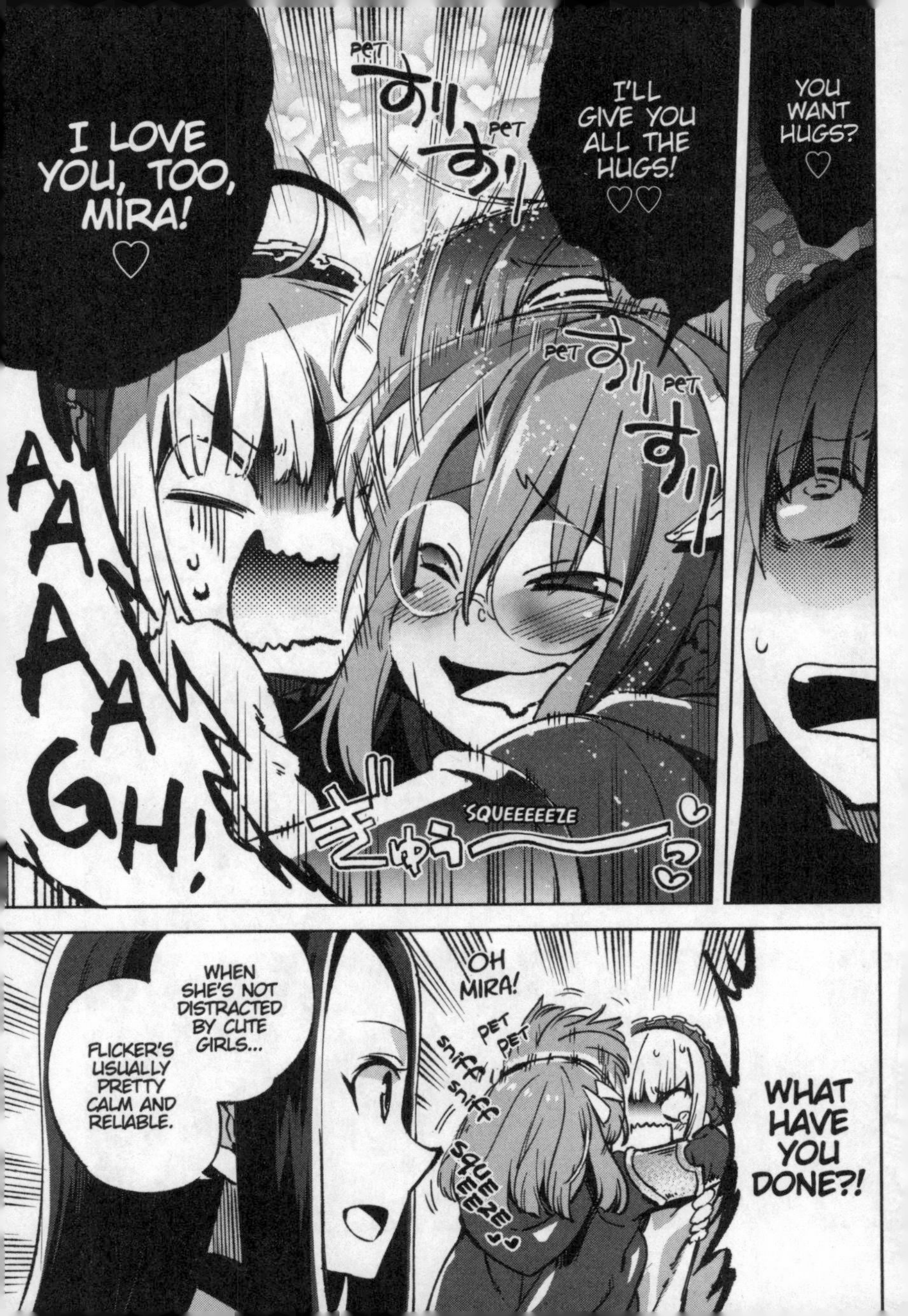
YOU WANT HUGS? ♡
I'LL GIVE YOU ALL THE HUGS! ♡♡
PET PET
I LOVE YOU, TOO, MIRA! ♡
PET PET
AAAAGH!
SQUEEEEEZE
WHAT HAVE YOU DONE?!
OH MIRA!
PET PET
sniff sniff
SQUEEEEZE
WHEN SHE'S NOT DISTRACTED BY CUTE GIRLS...
FLICKER'S USUALLY PRETTY CALM AND RELIABLE.

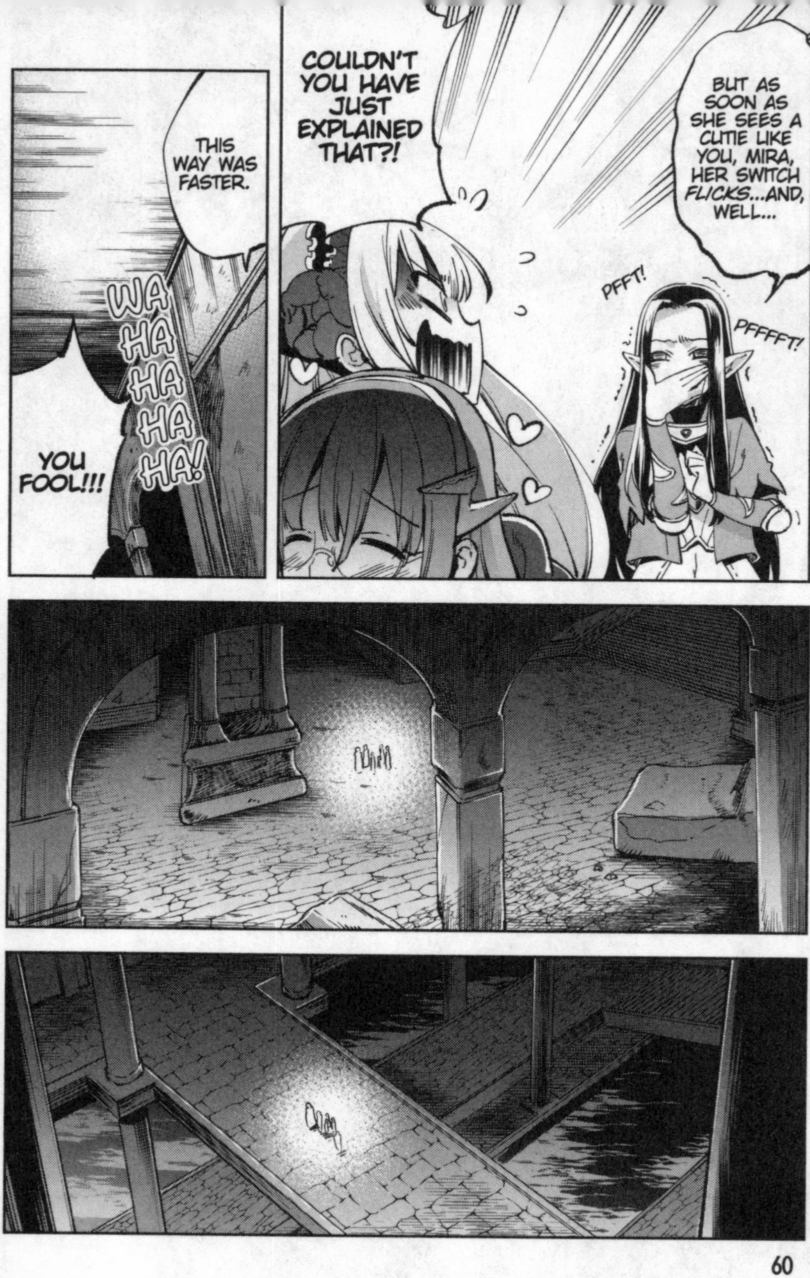
BUT AS SOON AS SHE SEES A CUTIE LIKE YOU, MIRA, HER SWITCH FLICKS...AND, WELL...
COULDN'T YOU HAVE JUST EXPLAINED THAT?!
PFFT!
PFFFFT!
THIS WAY WAS FASTER.
WA HA HA HA HA HA!
YOU FOOL!!!

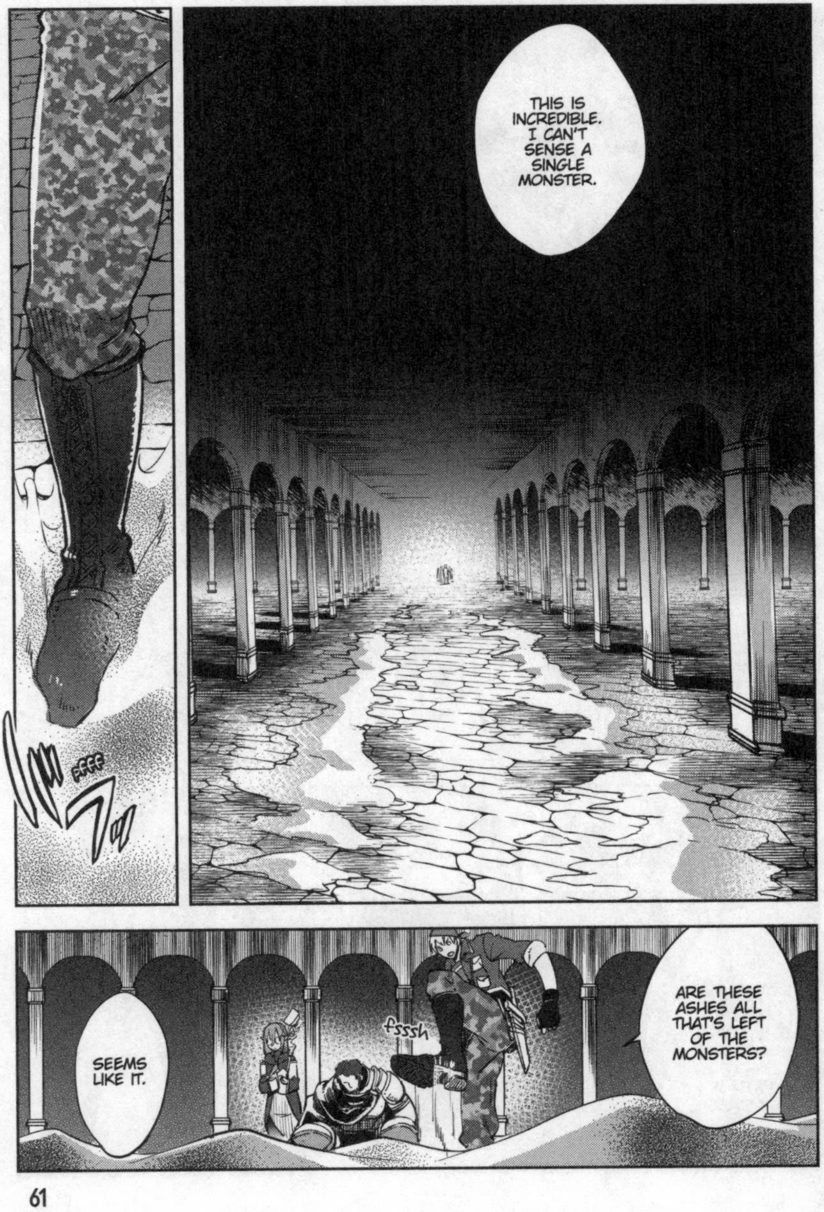
THIS IS INCREDIBLE. I CAN'T SENSE A SINGLE MONSTER.
pfff
ARE THESE ASHES ALL THAT'S LEFT OF THE MONSTERS?
fsssh
SEEMS LIKE IT.

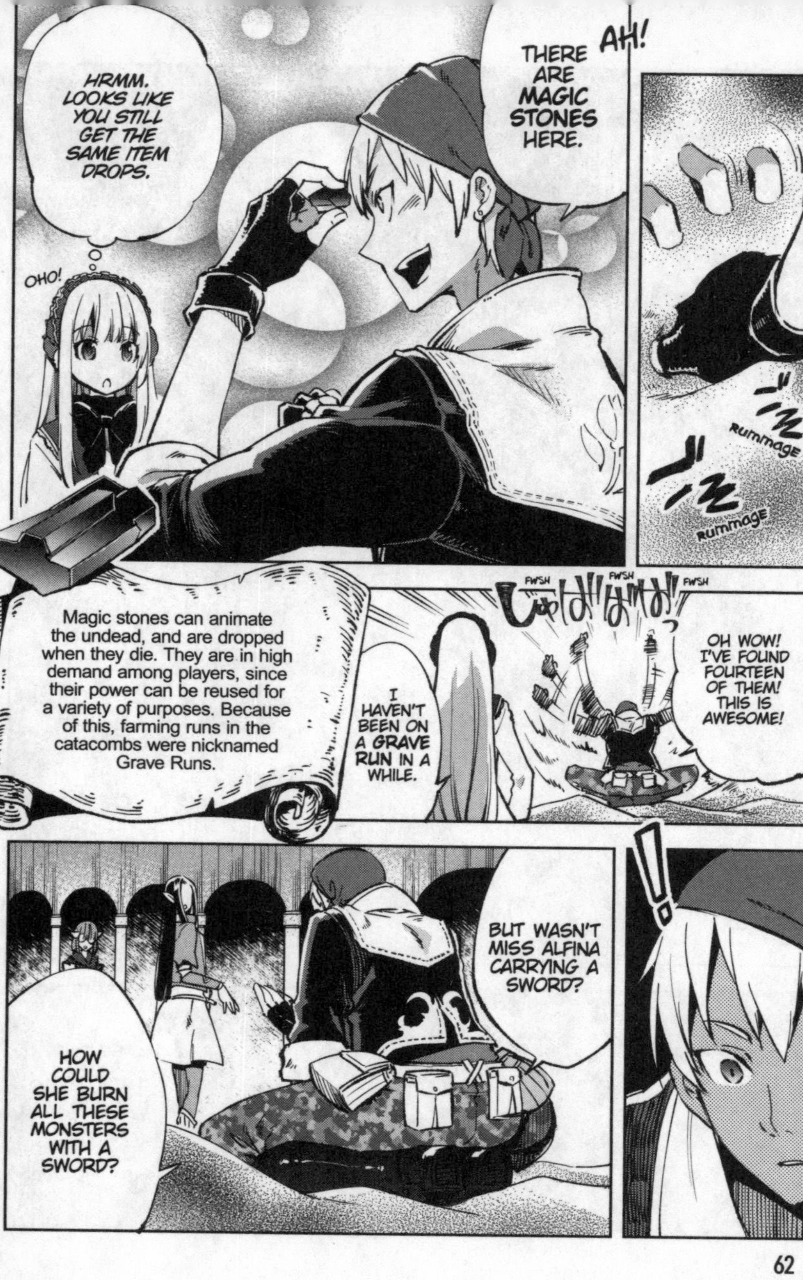
Rummage
Rummage
AH!
THERE ARE MAGIC STONES HERE.
HRMM. LOOKS LIKE YOU STILL GET THE SAME ITEM DROPS.
OHO!
FWSH
FWSH
FWSH
OH WOW! I'VE FOUND FOURTEEN OF THEM! THIS IS AWESOME!
I HAVEN'T BEEN ON A GRAVE RUN IN A WHILE.
Magic stones can animate the undead, and are dropped when they die. They are in high demand among players, since their power can be reused for a variety of purposes. Because of this, farming runs in the catacombs were nicknamed Grave Runs.
!
BUT WASN'T MISS ALFINA CARRYING A SWORD?
HOW COULD SHE BURN ALL THESE MONSTERS WITH A SWORD?

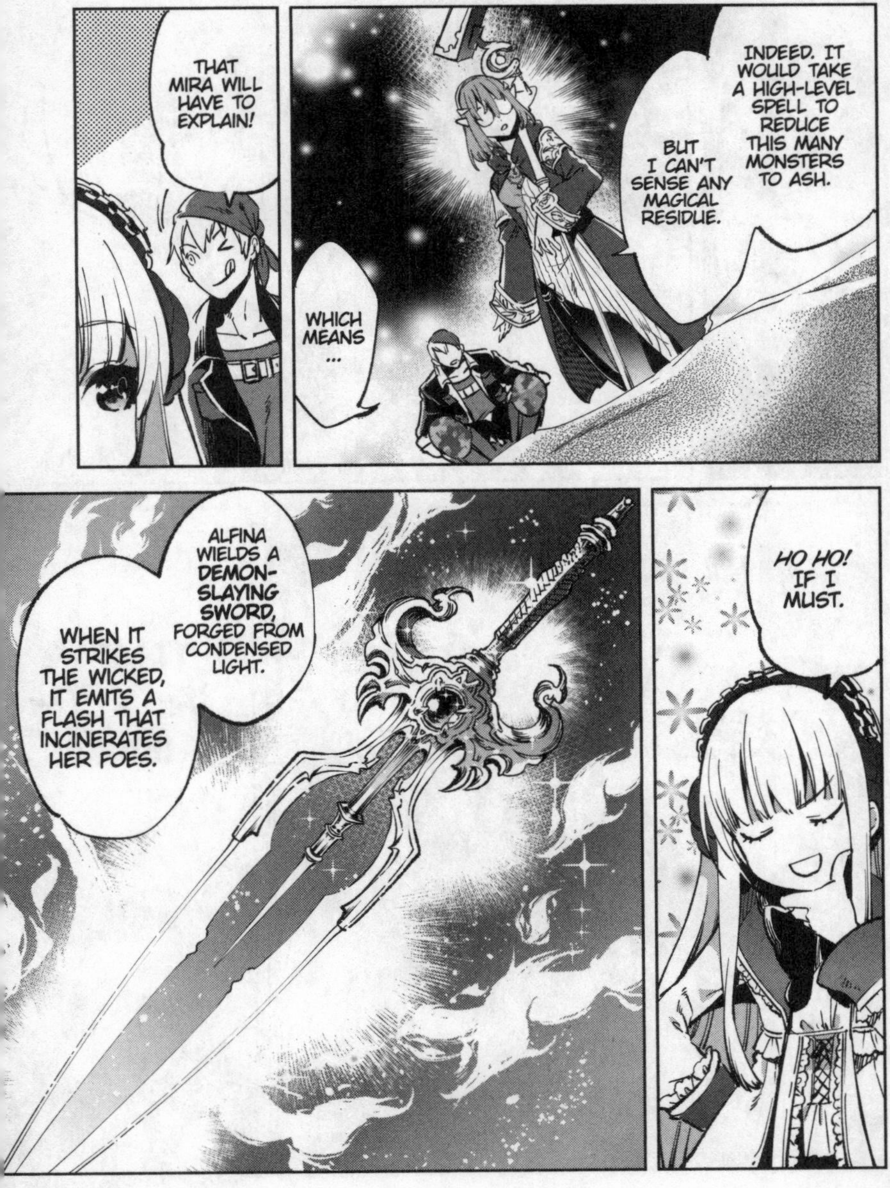
INDEED. IT WOULD TAKE A HIGH-LEVEL SPELL TO REDUCE THIS MANY MONSTERS TO ASH.
BUT I CAN'T SENSE ANY MAGICAL RESIDUE.
WHICH MEANS ...
THAT MIRA WILL HAVE TO EXPLAIN!
HO HO! IF I MUST.
ALFINA WIELDS A DEMON-SLAYING SWORD, FORGED FROM CONDENSED LIGHT.
WHEN IT STRIKES THE WICKED, IT EMITS A FLASH THAT INCINERATES HER FOES.

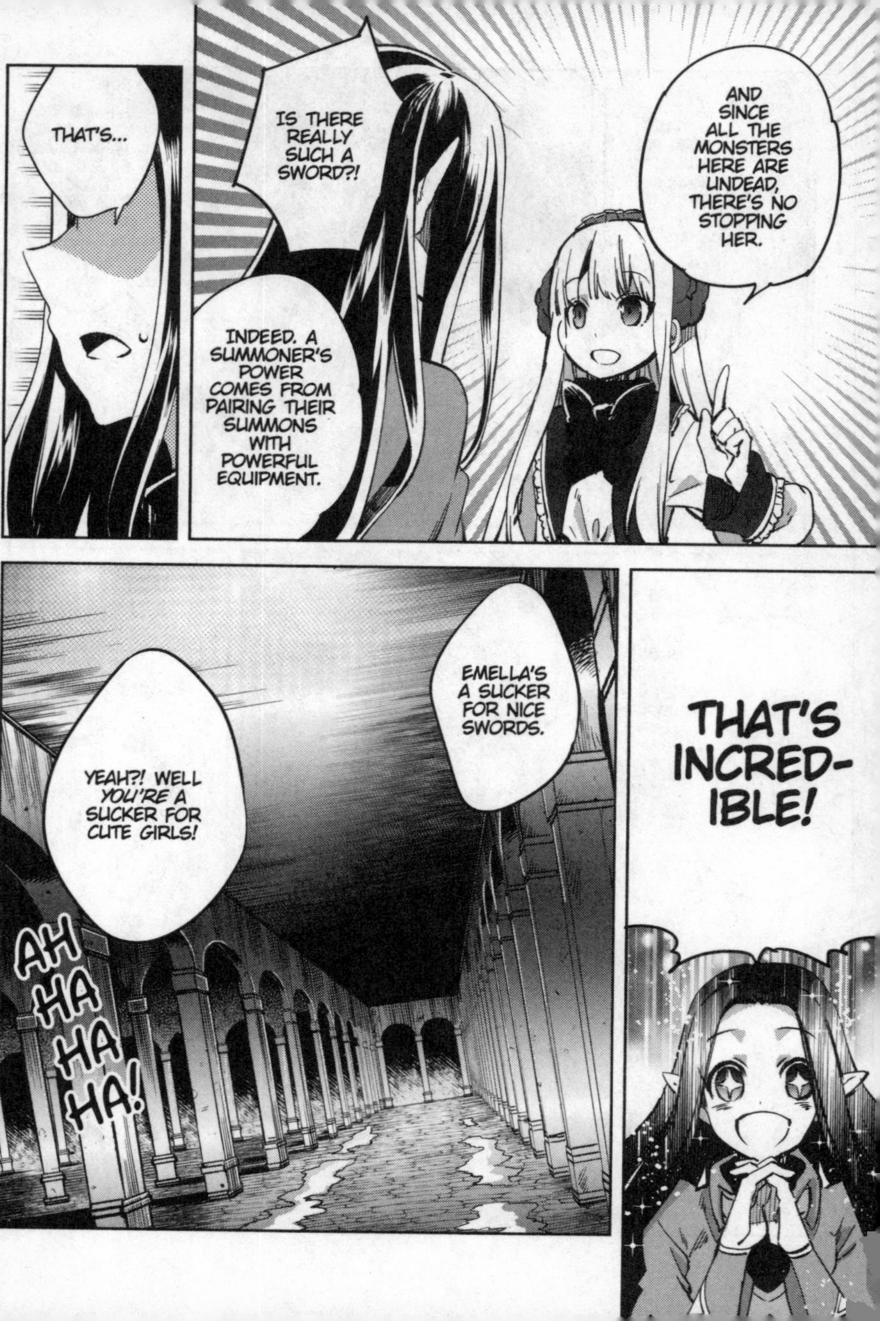
AND SINCE ALL THE MONSTERS HERE ARE UNDEAD, THERE'S NO STOPPING HER.
IS THERE REALLY SUCH A SWORD?!
INDEED. A SUMMONER'S POWER COMES FROM PAIRING THEIR SUMMONS WITH POWERFUL EQUIPMENT.
THAT'S...
THAT'S INCRED-IBLE!
EMELLA'S A SUCKER FOR NICE SWORDS.
YEAH?! WELL YOU'RE A SUCKER FOR CUTE GIRLS!
AH HA HA HA HA!

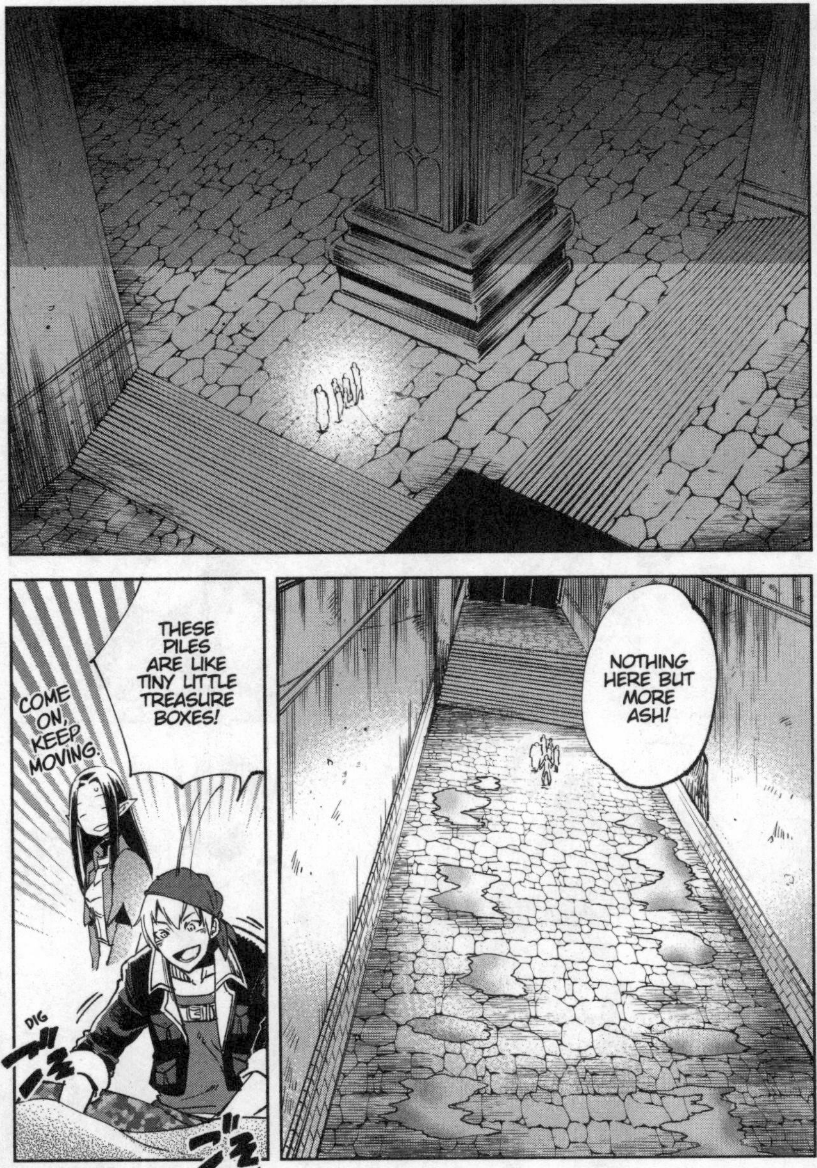
NOTHING HERE BUT MORE ASH!
THESE PILES ARE LIKE TINY LITTLE TREASURE BOXES!
COME ON, KEEP MOVING.
DIG
DIG

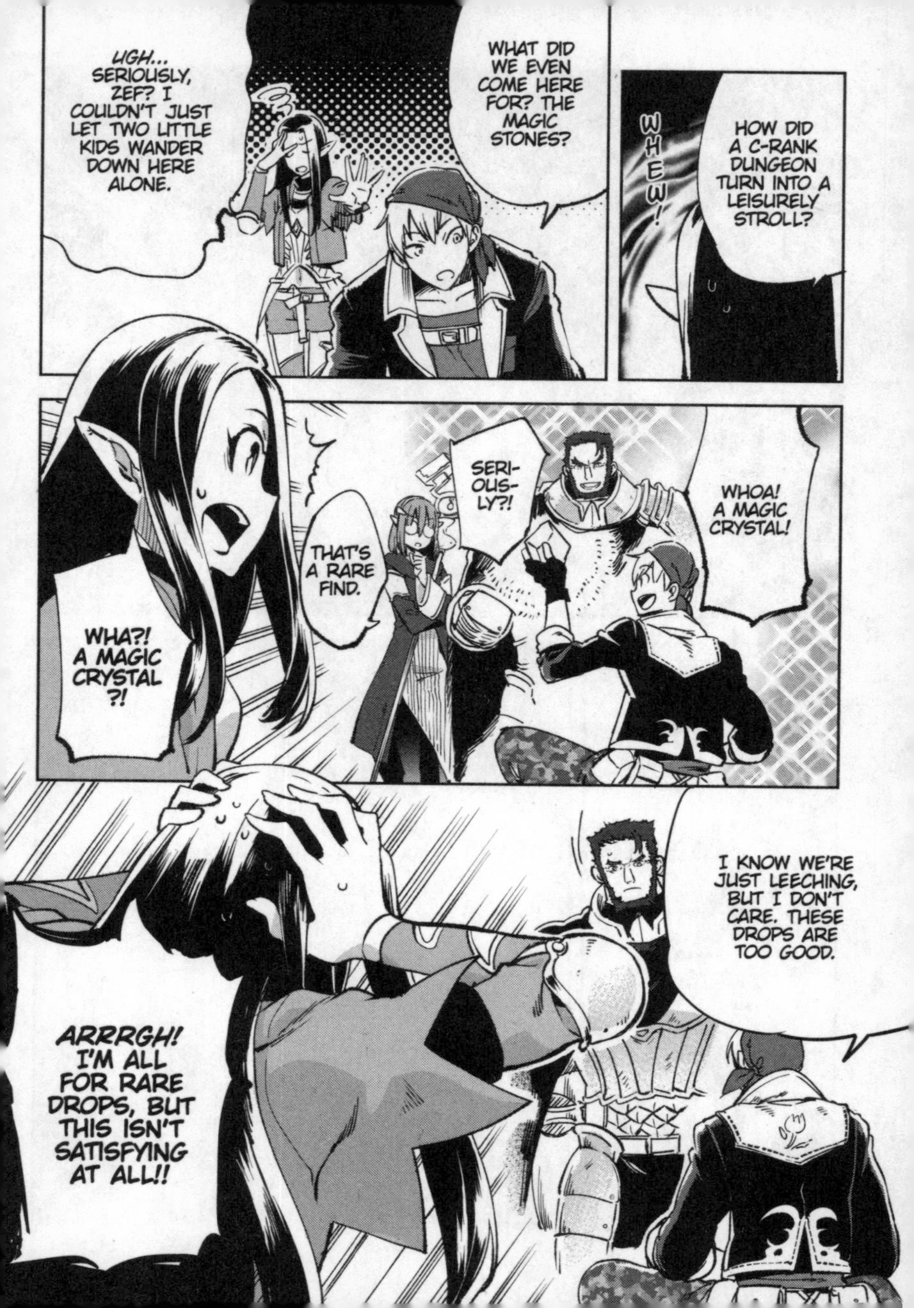
WHEW!
HOW DID A C-RANK DUNGEON TURN INTO A LEISURELY STROLL?
WHAT DID WE EVEN COME HERE FOR? THE MAGIC STONES?
UGH... SERIOUSLY, ZEF? I COULDN'T JUST LET TWO LITTLE KIDS WANDER DOWN HERE ALONE.
WHOA! A MAGIC CRYSTAL!
SERI-OUS-LY?!
THAT'S A RARE FIND.
WHA?! A MAGIC CRYSTAL?!
I KNOW WE'RE JUST LEECHING, BUT I DON'T CARE. THESE DROPS ARE TOO GOOD.
ARRRGH! I'M ALL FOR RARE DROPS, BUT THIS ISN'T SATISFYING AT ALL!!

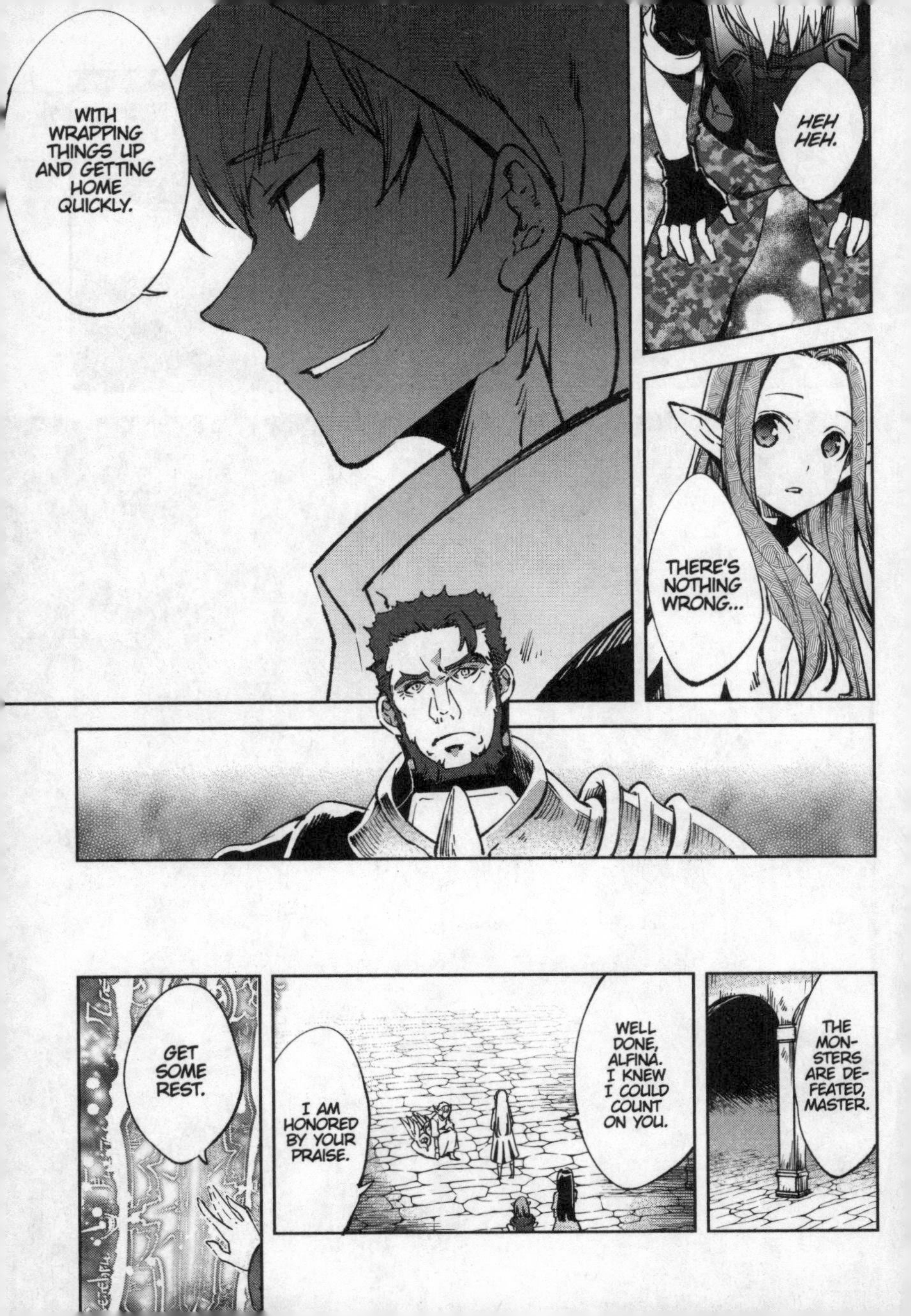
HEH HEH.
THERE'S NOTHING WRONG...
WITH WRAPPING THINGS UP AND GETTING HOME QUICKLY.
THE MONSTERS ARE DEFEATED, MASTER.
WELL DONE, ALFINA. I KNEW I COULD COUNT ON YOU.
I AM HONORED BY YOUR PRAISE.
GET SOME REST.

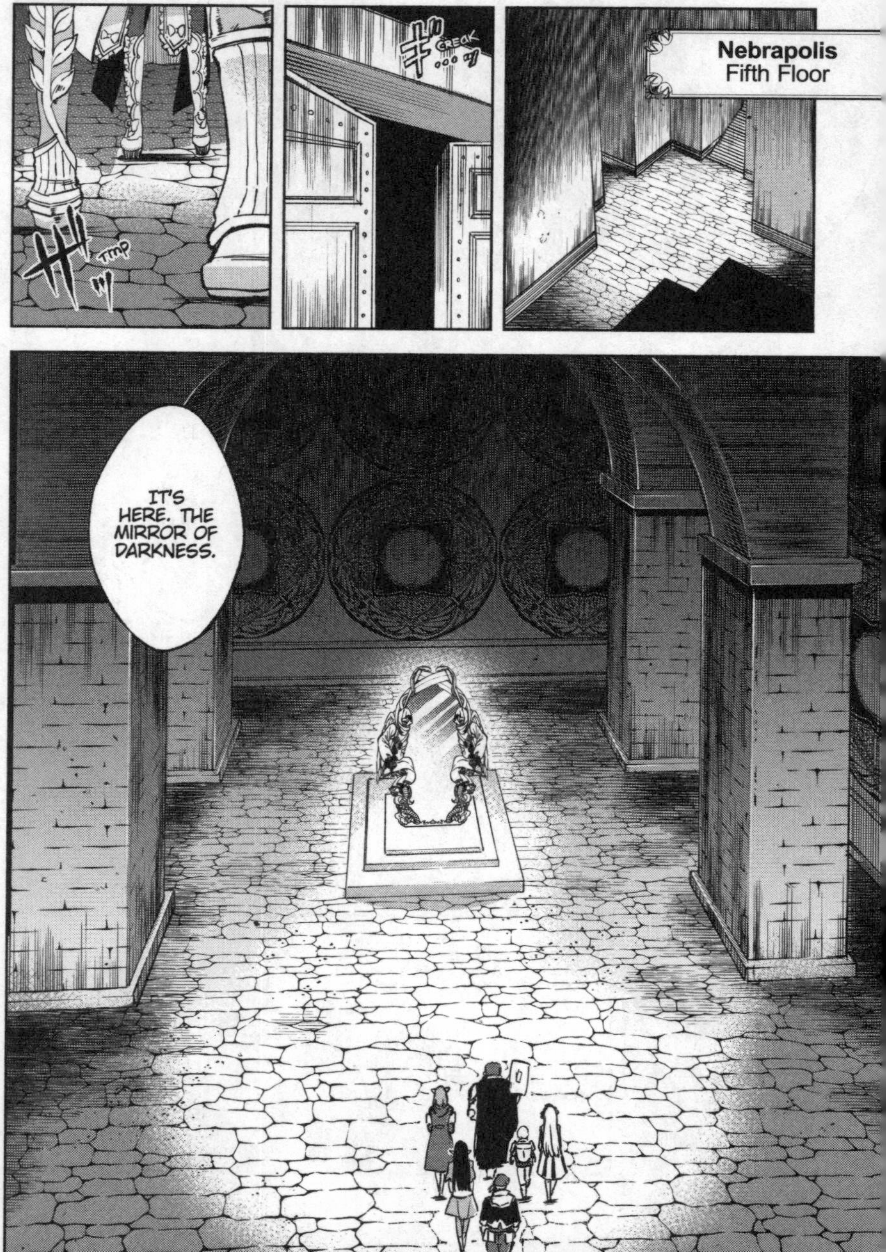
Nebrapolis
Fifth Floor
CREAK
TMP
IT'S HERE. THE MIRROR OF DARKNESS.

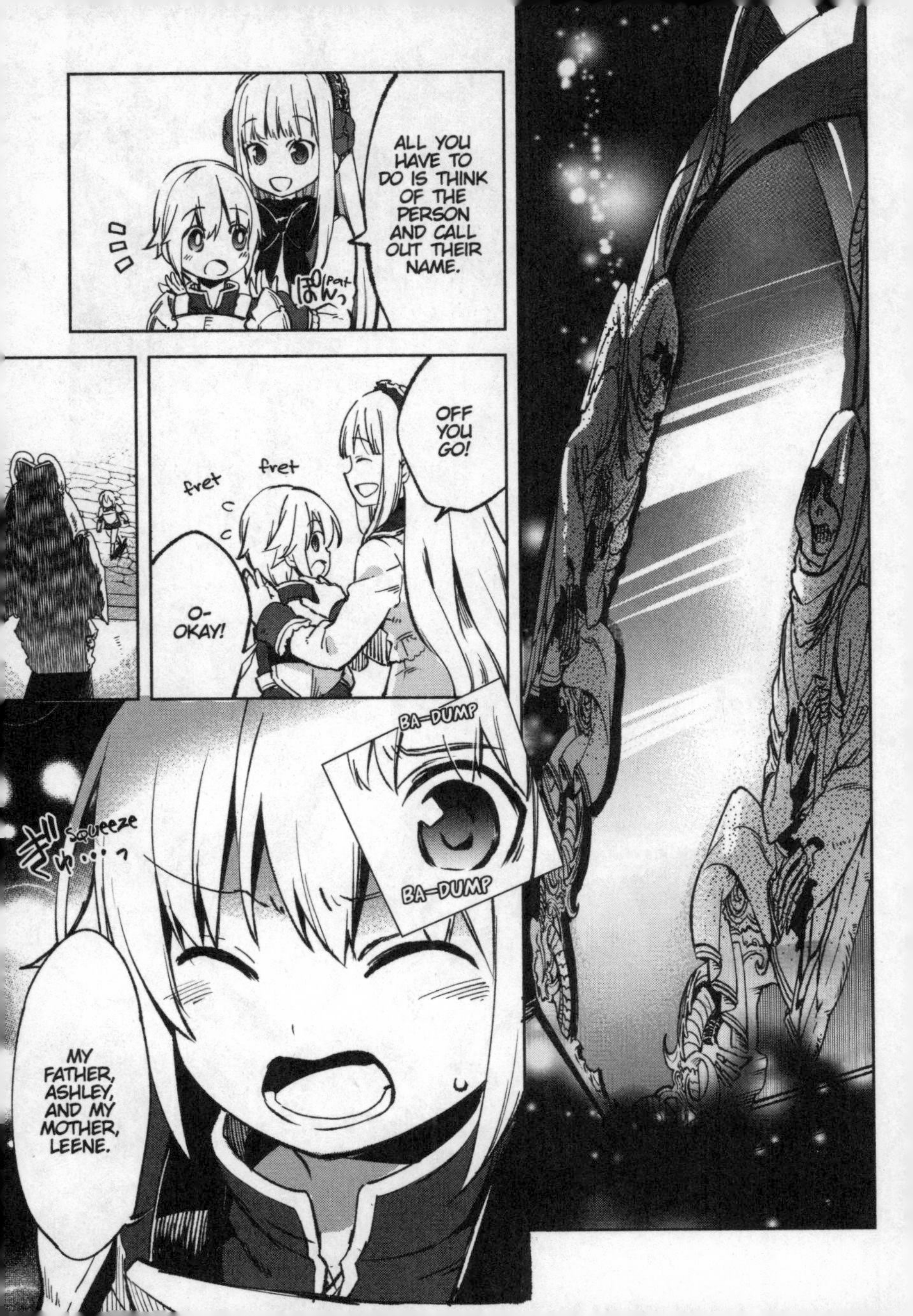
ALL YOU HAVE TO DO IS THINK OF THE PERSON AND CALL OUT THEIR NAME.
pat
OFF YOU GO!
fret fret
O-OKAY!
BA-DUMP
BA-DUMP
squeeze
MY FATHER, ASHLEY, AND MY MOTHER, LEENE.

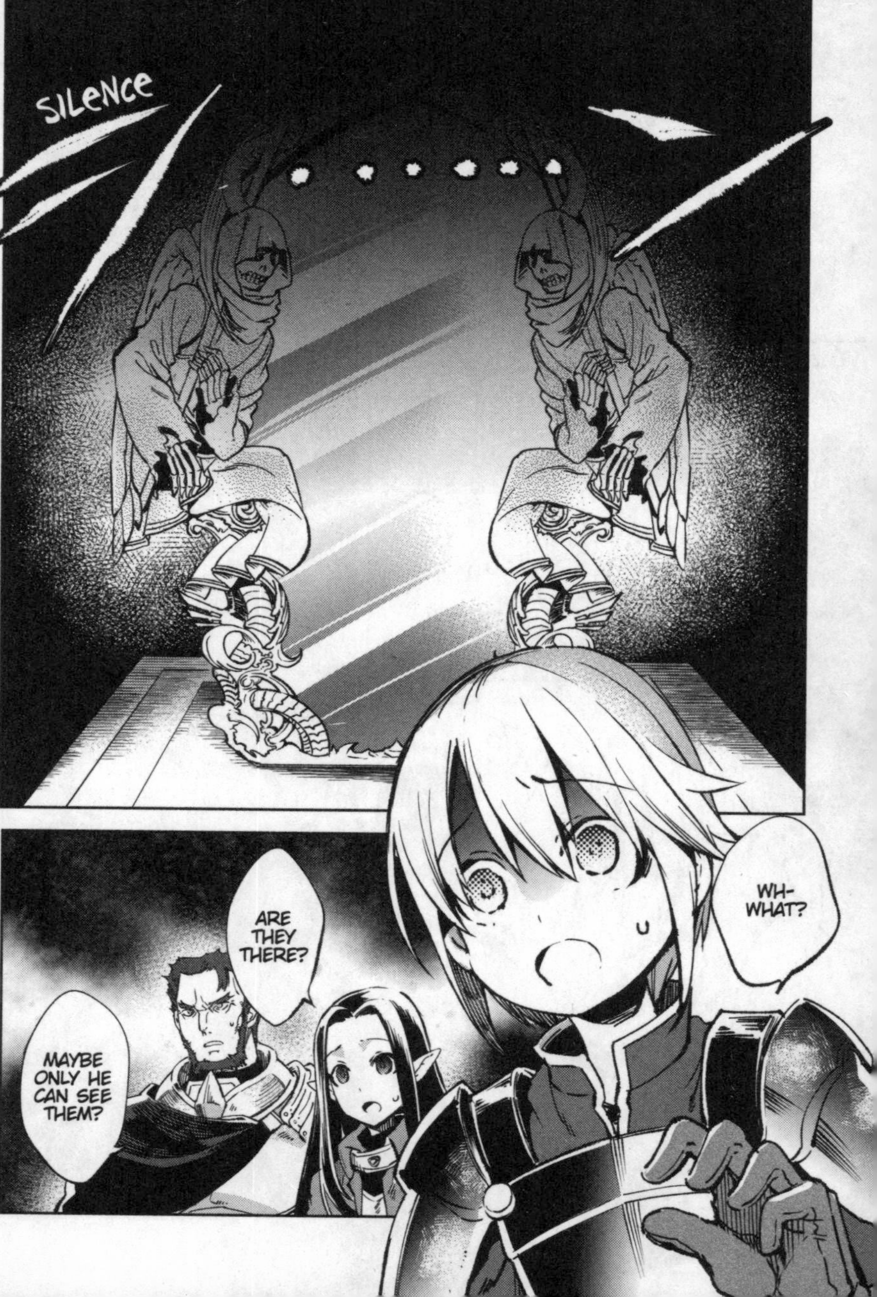
SILENCE
WH-WHAT?
ARE THEY THERE?
MAYBE ONLY HE CAN SEE THEM?

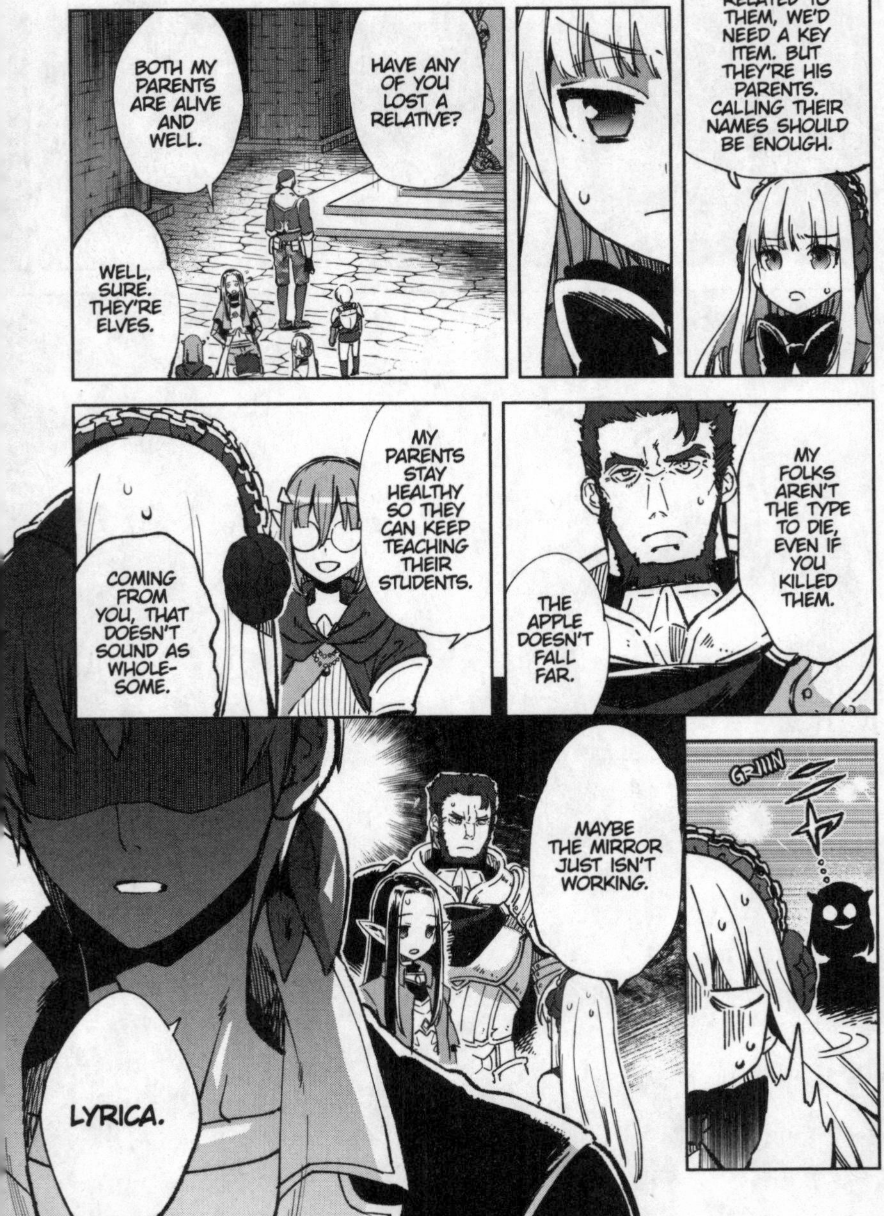
HRMM. IF HE WASN'T RELATED TO THEM, WE'D NEED A KEY ITEM. BUT THEY'RE HIS PARENTS. CALLING THEIR NAMES SHOULD BE ENOUGH.
HAVE ANY OF YOU LOST A RELATIVE?
BOTH MY PARENTS ARE ALIVE AND WELL.
WELL, SURE. THEY'RE ELVES.
MY FOLKS AREN'T THE TYPE TO DIE, EVEN IF YOU KILLED THEM.
THE APPLE DOESN'T FALL FAR.
MY PARENTS STAY HEALTHY SO THEY CAN KEEP TEACHING THEIR STUDENTS.
COMING FROM YOU, THAT DOESN'T SOUND AS WHOLE-SOME.
GRIIIN
MAYBE THE MIRROR JUST ISN'T WORKING.
LYRICA.

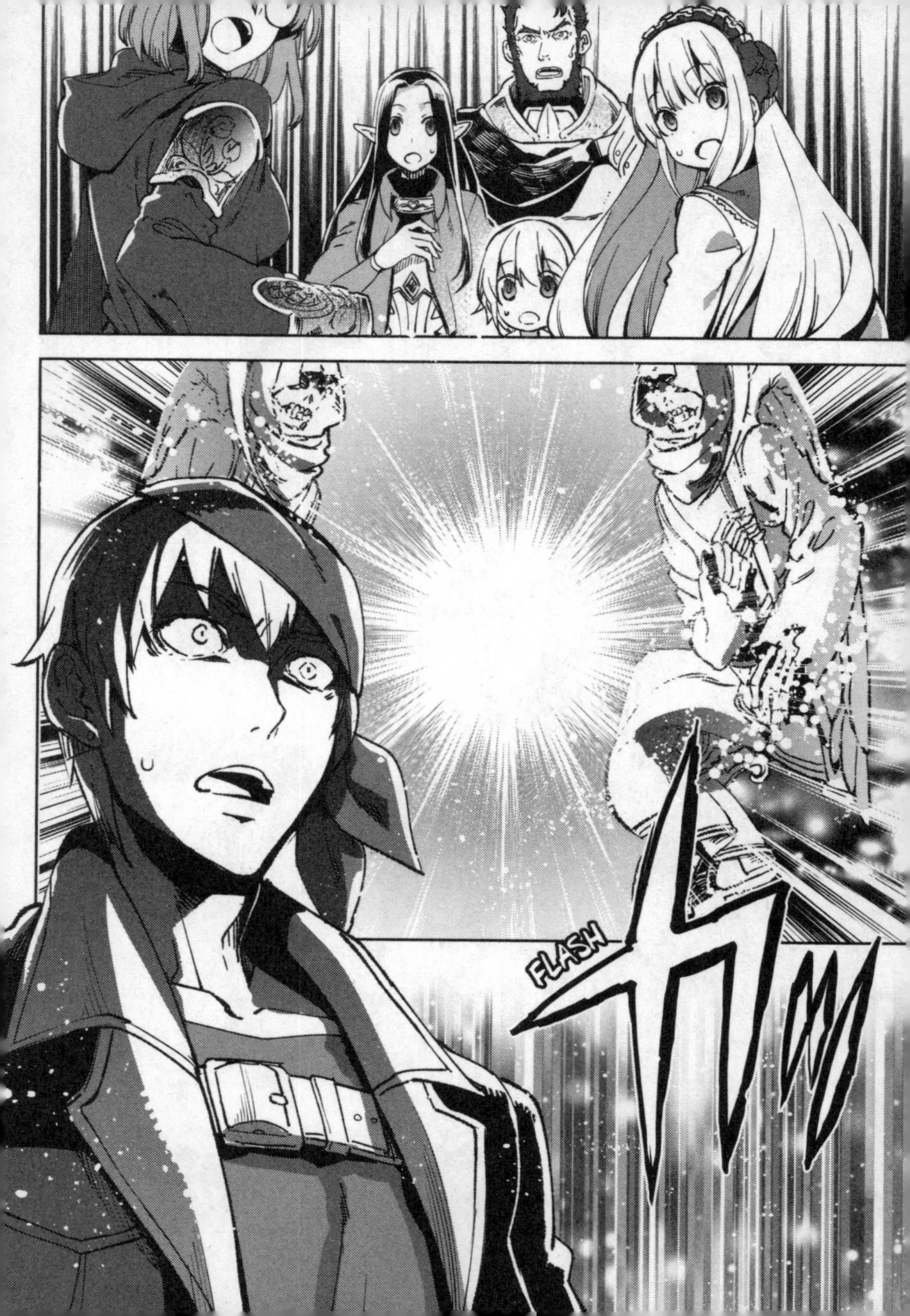
FLASH

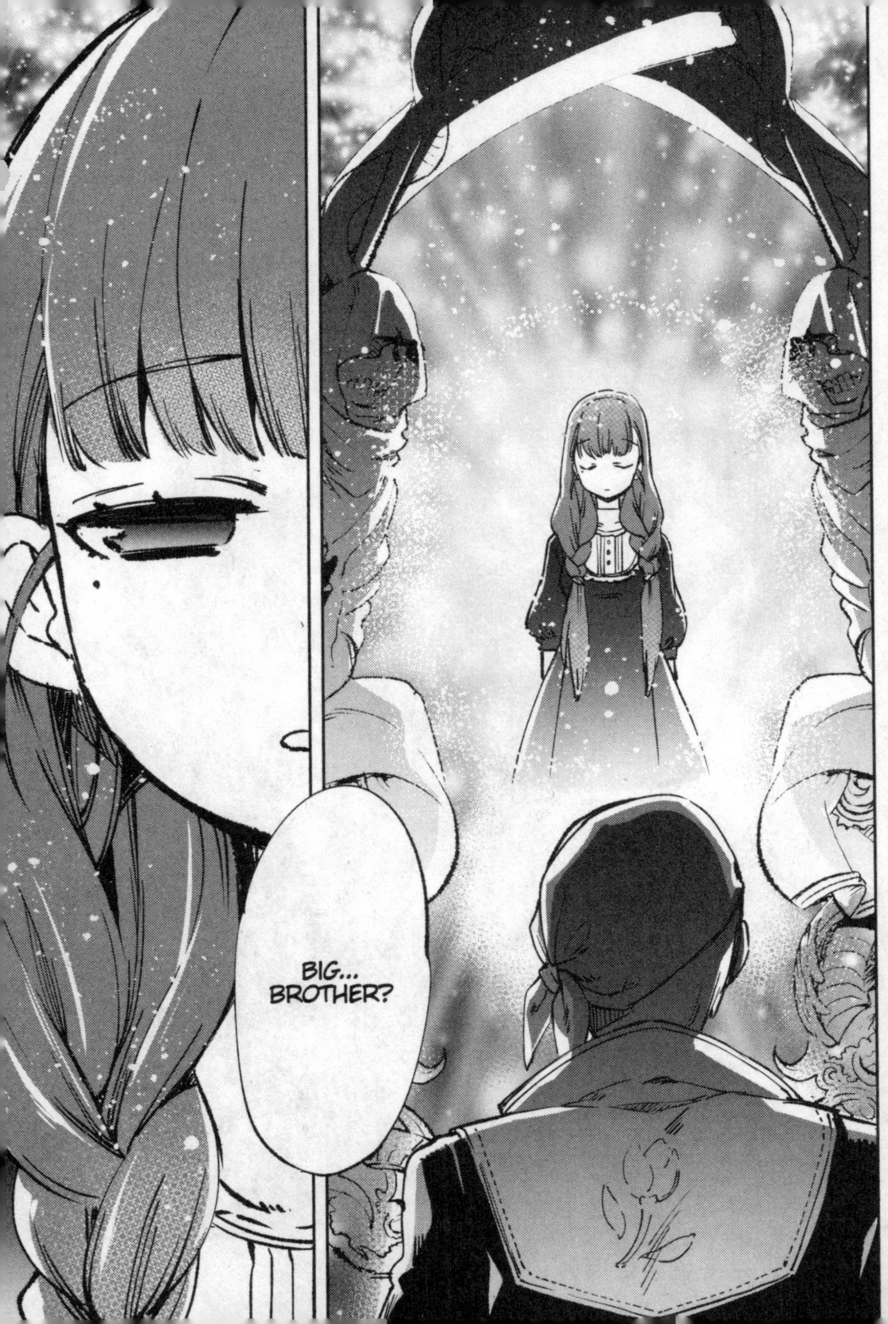
BIG... BROTHER?

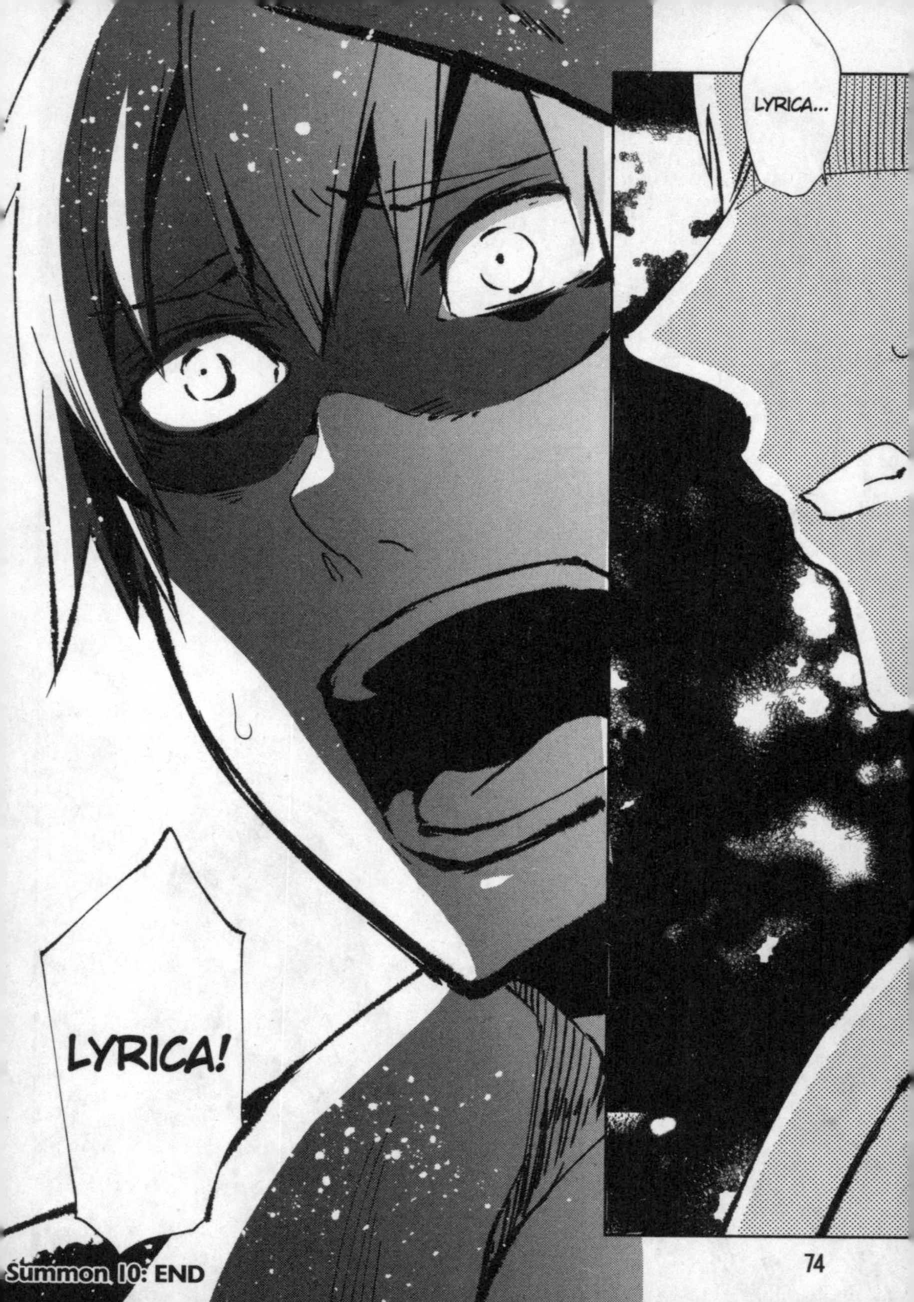
LYRICA...
LYRICA!
Summon 10: END

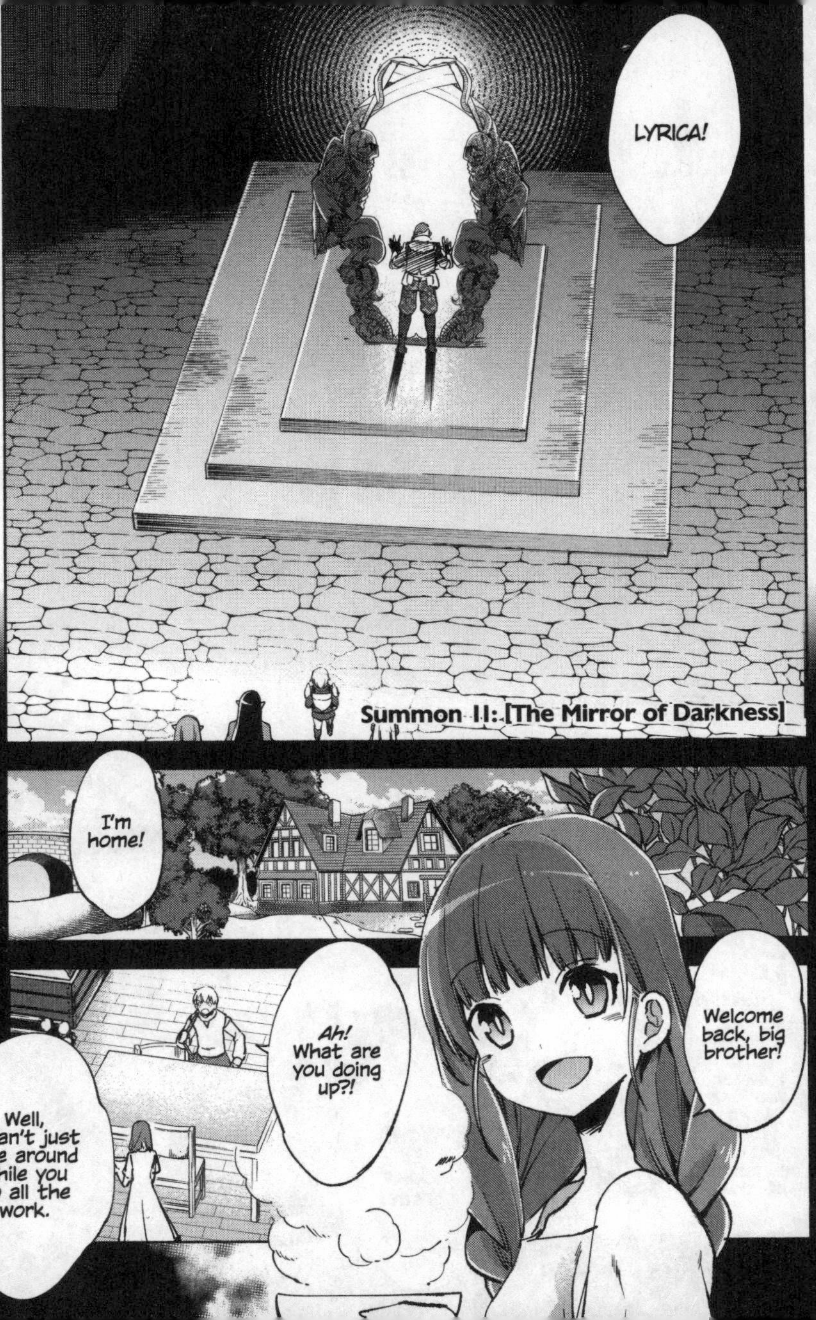
LYRICA!
Summon 11: [The Mirror of Darkness]
I'm home!
Welcome back, big brother!
Ah! What are you doing up?!
Well, I can't just laze around while you do all the work.

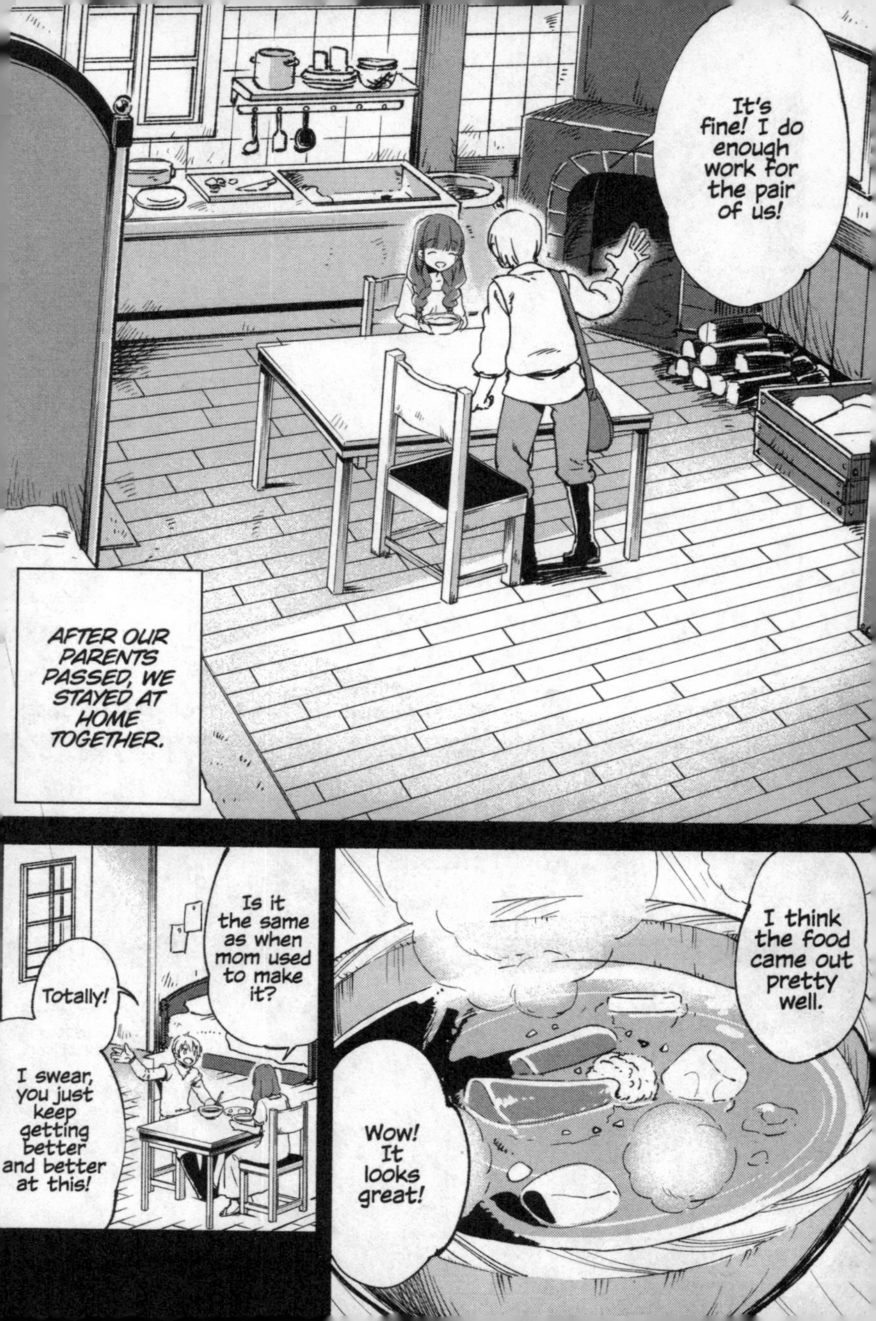
It's fine! I do enough work for the pair of us!
AFTER OUR PARENTS PASSED, WE STAYED AT HOME TOGETHER.
I think the food came out pretty well.
Wow! It looks great!
Is it the same as when mom used to make it?
Totally!
I swear, you just keep getting better and better at this!

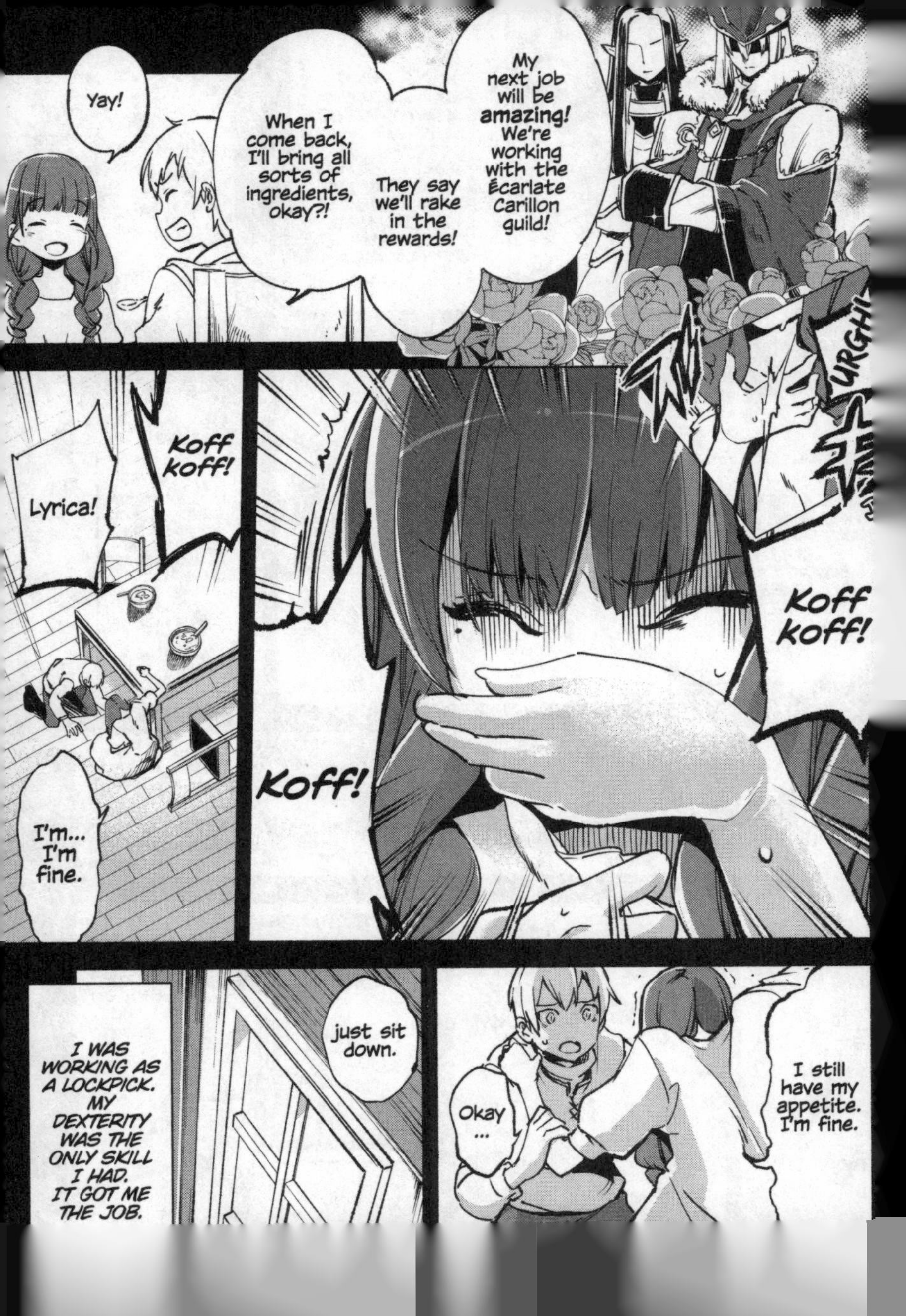
My next job will be amazing! We're working with the Écarlate Carillon guild!
They say we'll rake in the rewards!
When I come back, I'll bring all sorts of ingredients, okay?!
Yay!
URGH!
Koff koff!
Koff!
Koff koff!
Lyrica!
I'm... I'm fine.
I still have my appetite. I'm fine.
Okay ...
just sit down.
I WAS WORKING AS A LOCKPICK. MY DEXTERITY WAS THE ONLY SKILL I HAD. IT GOT ME THE JOB.

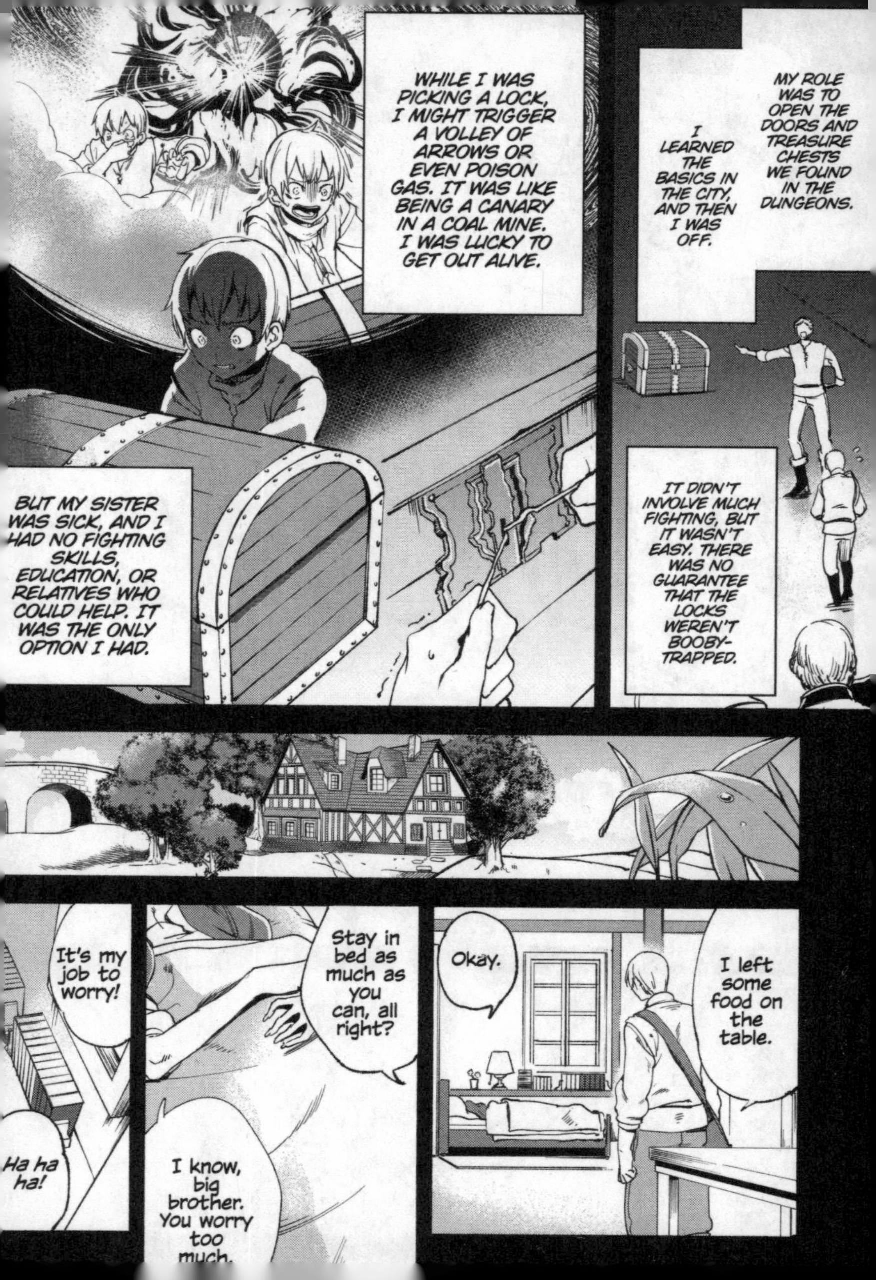
MY ROLE WAS TO OPEN THE DOORS AND TREASURE CHESTS WE FOUND IN THE DUNGEONS.
I LEARNED THE BASICS IN THE CITY, AND THEN I WAS OFF.
IT DIDN'T INVOLVE MUCH FIGHTING, BUT IT WASN'T EASY. THERE WAS NO GUARANTEE THAT THE LOCKS WEREN'T BOOBY-TRAPPED.
WHILE I WAS PICKING A LOCK, I MIGHT TRIGGER A VOLLEY OF ARROWS OR EVEN POISON GAS. IT WAS LIKE BEING A CANARY IN A COAL MINE. I WAS LUCKY TO GET OUT ALIVE.
BUT MY SISTER WAS SICK, AND I HAD NO FIGHTING SKILLS, EDUCATION, OR RELATIVES WHO COULD HELP. IT WAS THE ONLY OPTION I HAD.
I left some food on the table.
Okay.
Stay in bed as much as you can, all right?
I know, big brother. You worry too much.
It's my job to worry!
Ha ha ha!

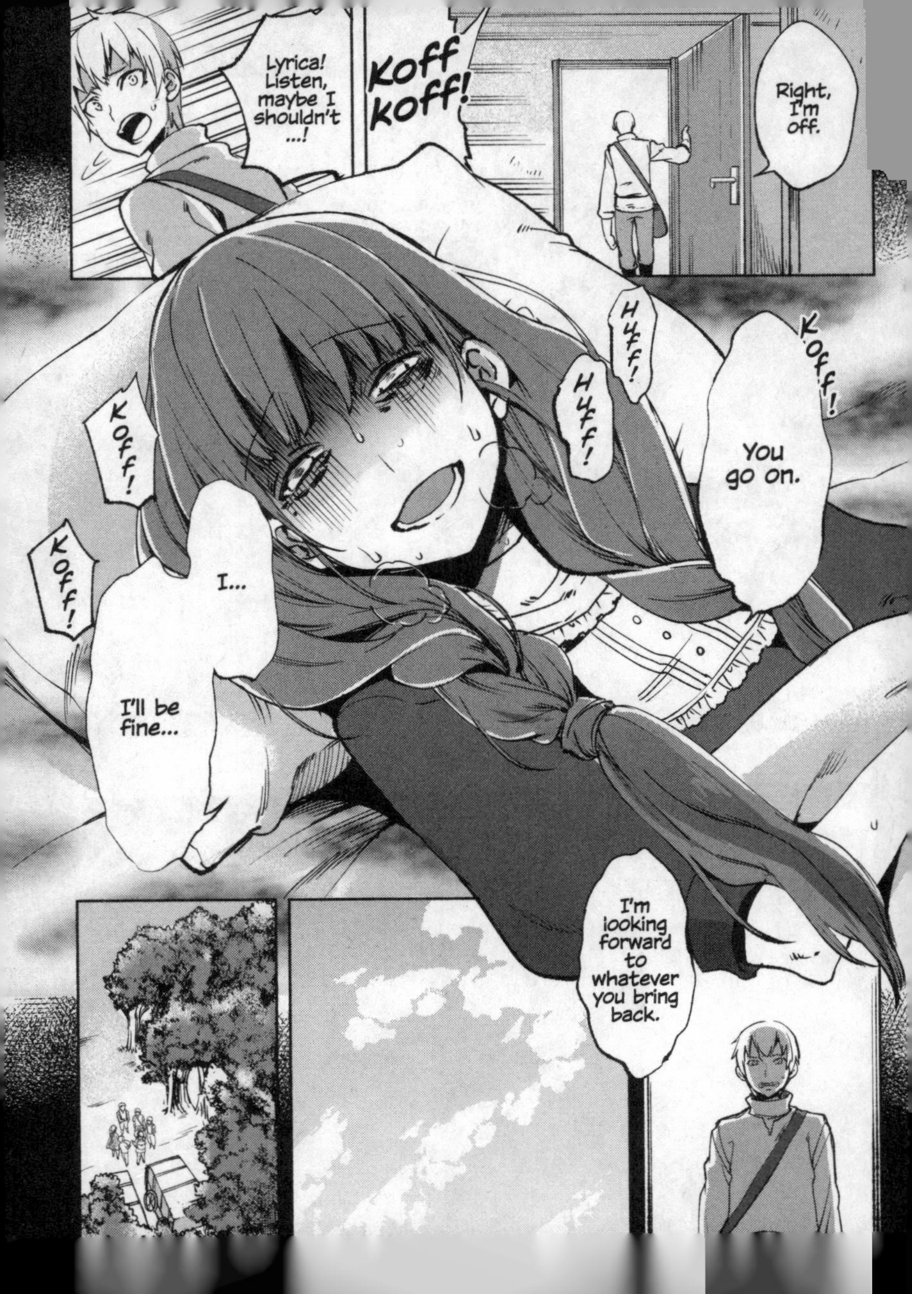
Right, I'm off.
Koff koff!
Lyrica! Listen, maybe I shouldn't ...!
Koff!
Huff! Huff!
You go on.
Koff!
Koff!
I...
I'll be fine...
I'm looking forward to whatever you bring back.

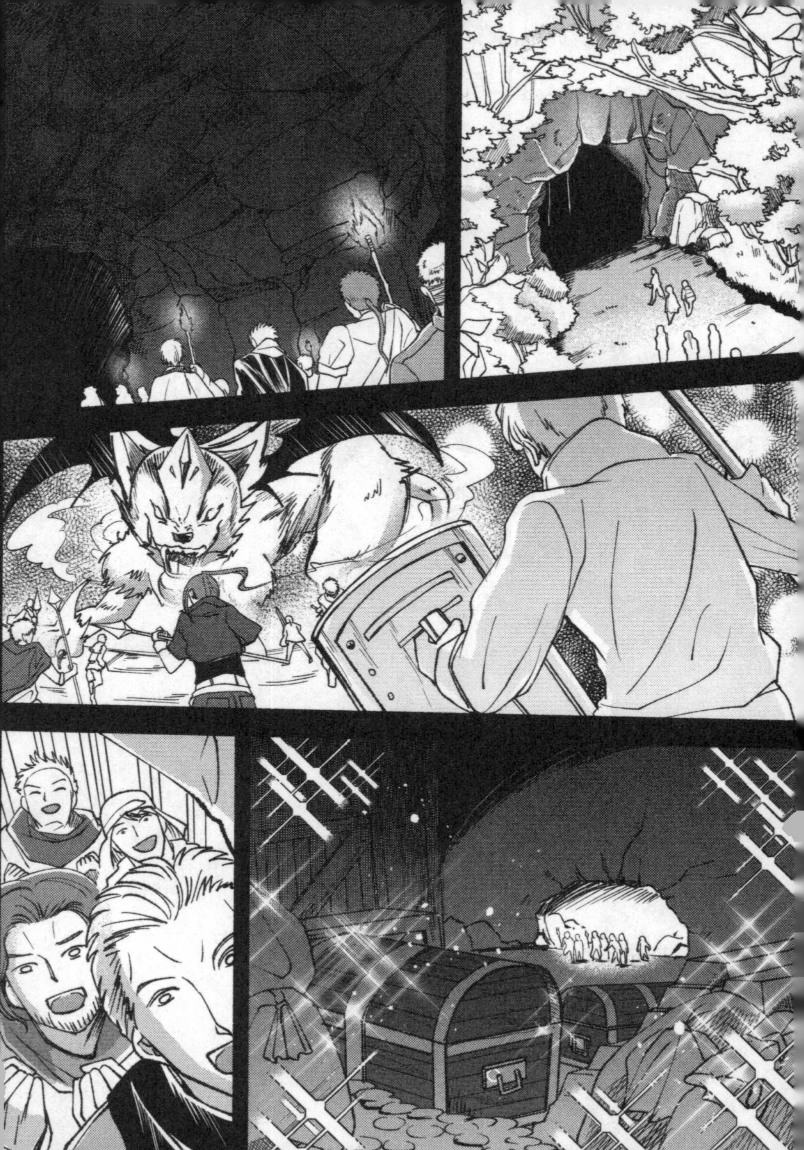

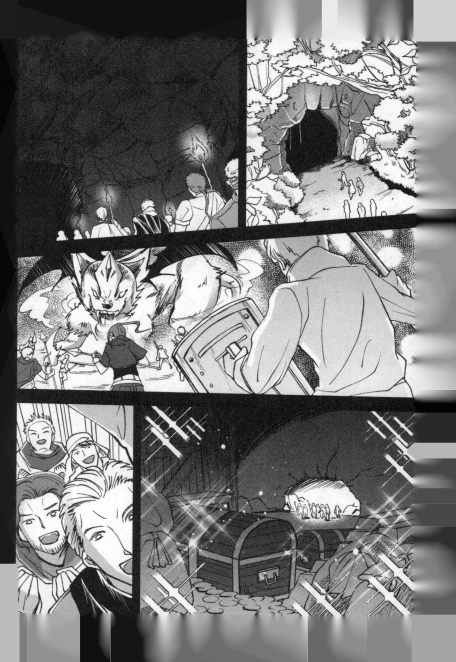

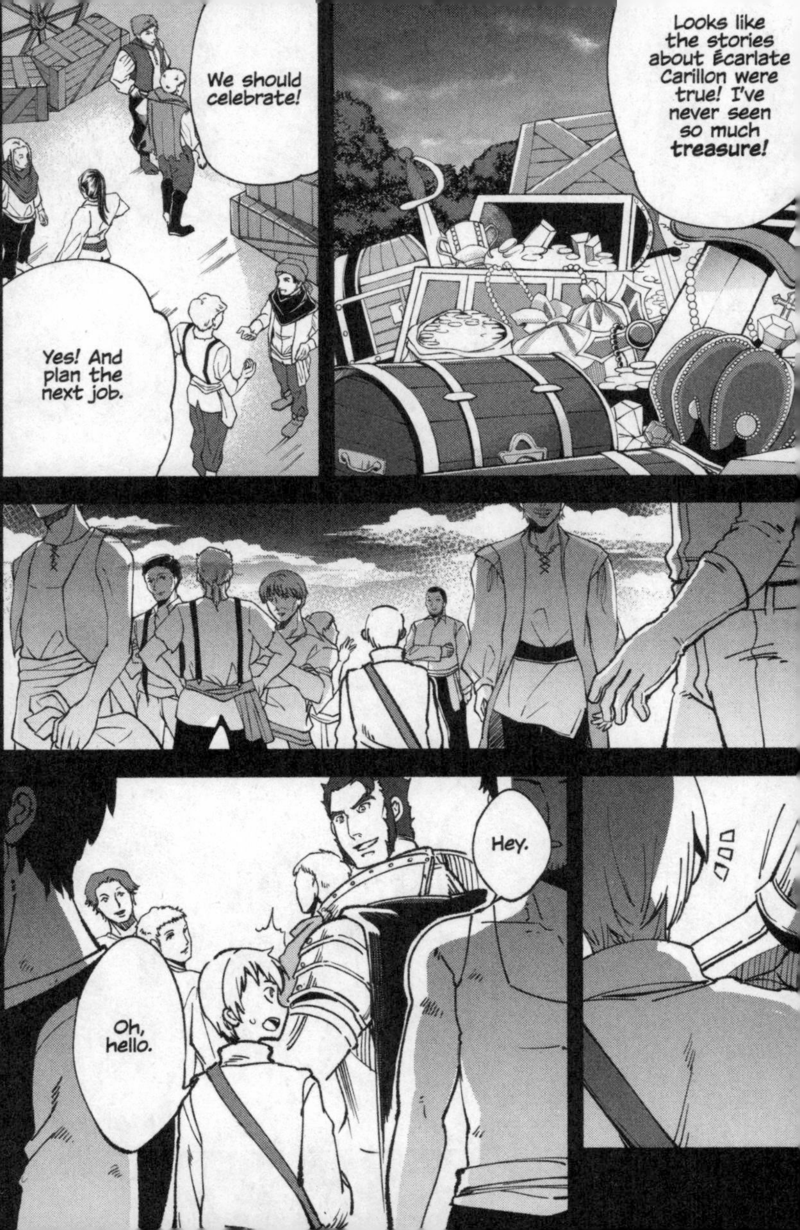
Looks like the stories about Écarlate Carillon were true! I've never seen so much treasure!
We should celebrate!
Yes! And plan the next job.
Hey.
Oh, hello.

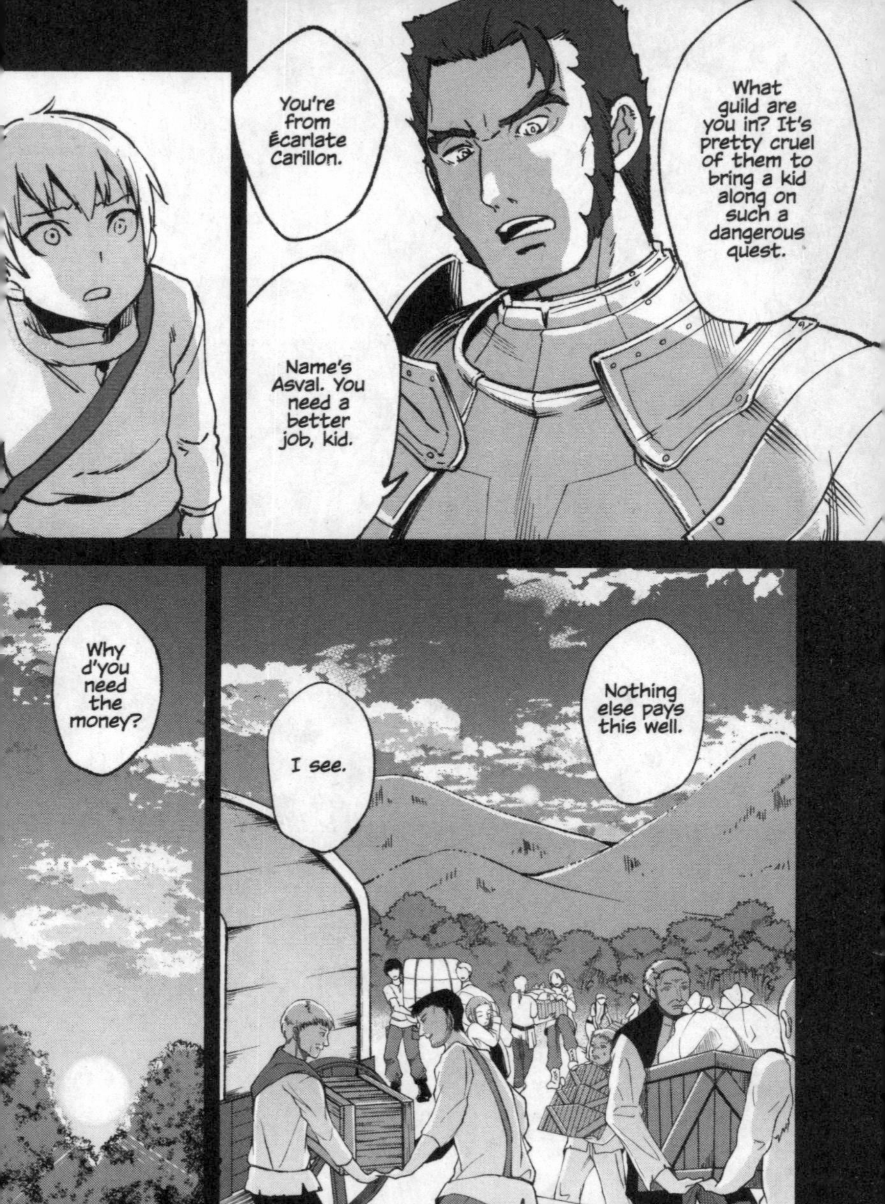
What guild are you in? It's pretty cruel of them to bring a kid along on such a dangerous quest.
You're from Écarlate Carillon.
Name's Asval. You need a better job, kid.
Nothing else pays this well.
I see.
Why d'you need the money?

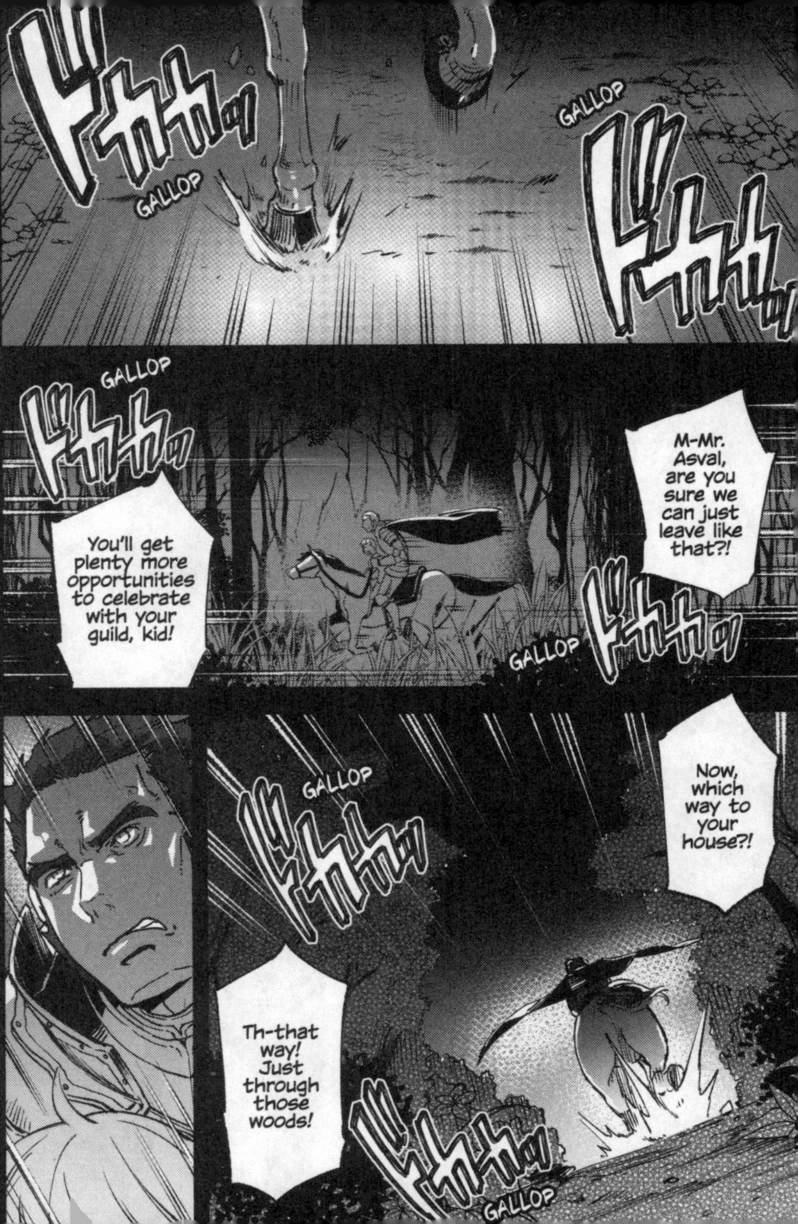
GALLOP
GALLOP
GALLOP
M-Mr. Asval, are you sure we can just leave like that?!
GALLOP
You'll get plenty more opportunities to celebrate with your guild, kid!
Now, which way to your house?!
GALLOP
Th-that way! Just through those woods!
GALLOP

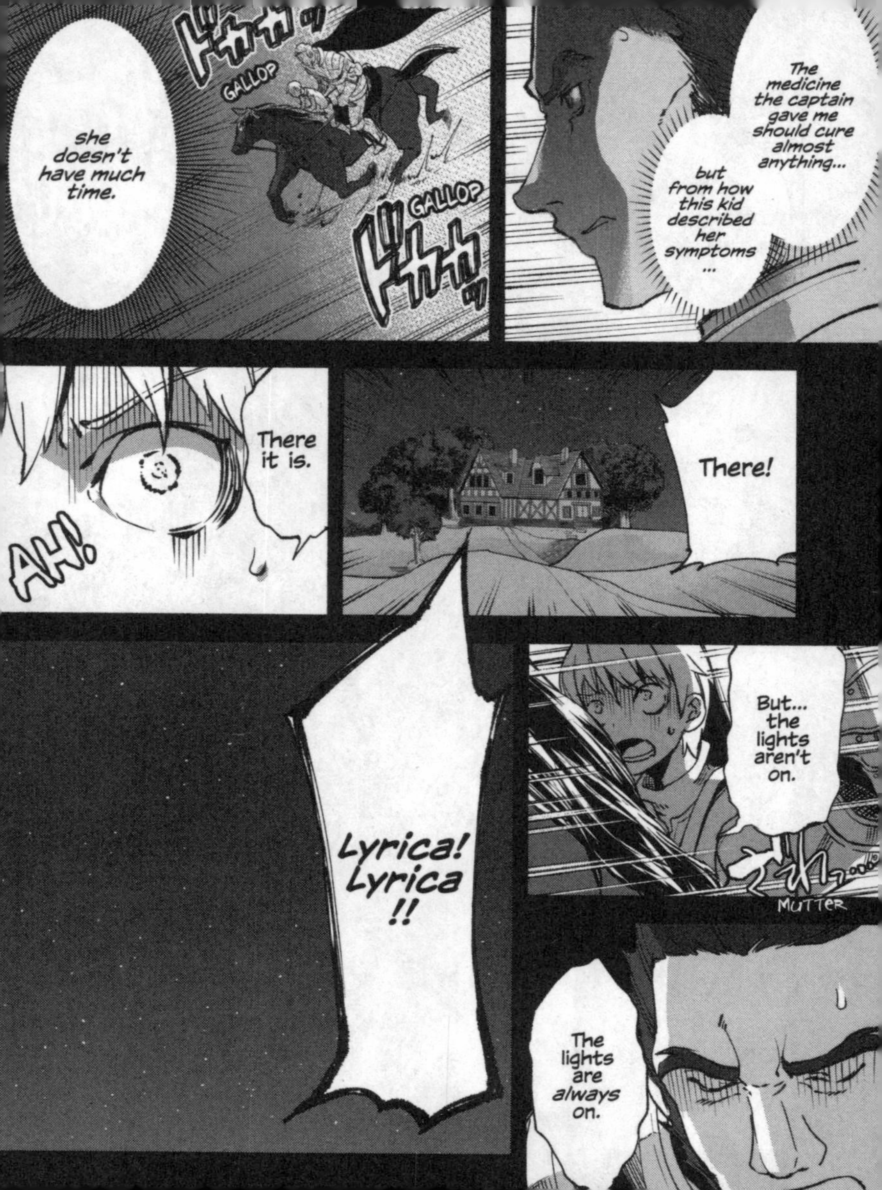
The medicine the captain gave me should cure almost anything...
but from how this kid described her symptoms...
GALLOP
GALLOP
she doesn't have much time.
There!
There it is.
AH!
But... the lights aren't on.
MUTTER
The lights are always on.
Lyrica! Lyrica!!

IF ONLY I'D BEEN SMARTER.

BROTHER.

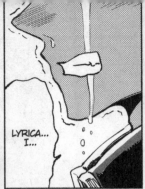

LYRICA... I...

I COULD HAVE...

IF ONLY I'D BEEN FASTER!

Haah....

BIG BROTHER!

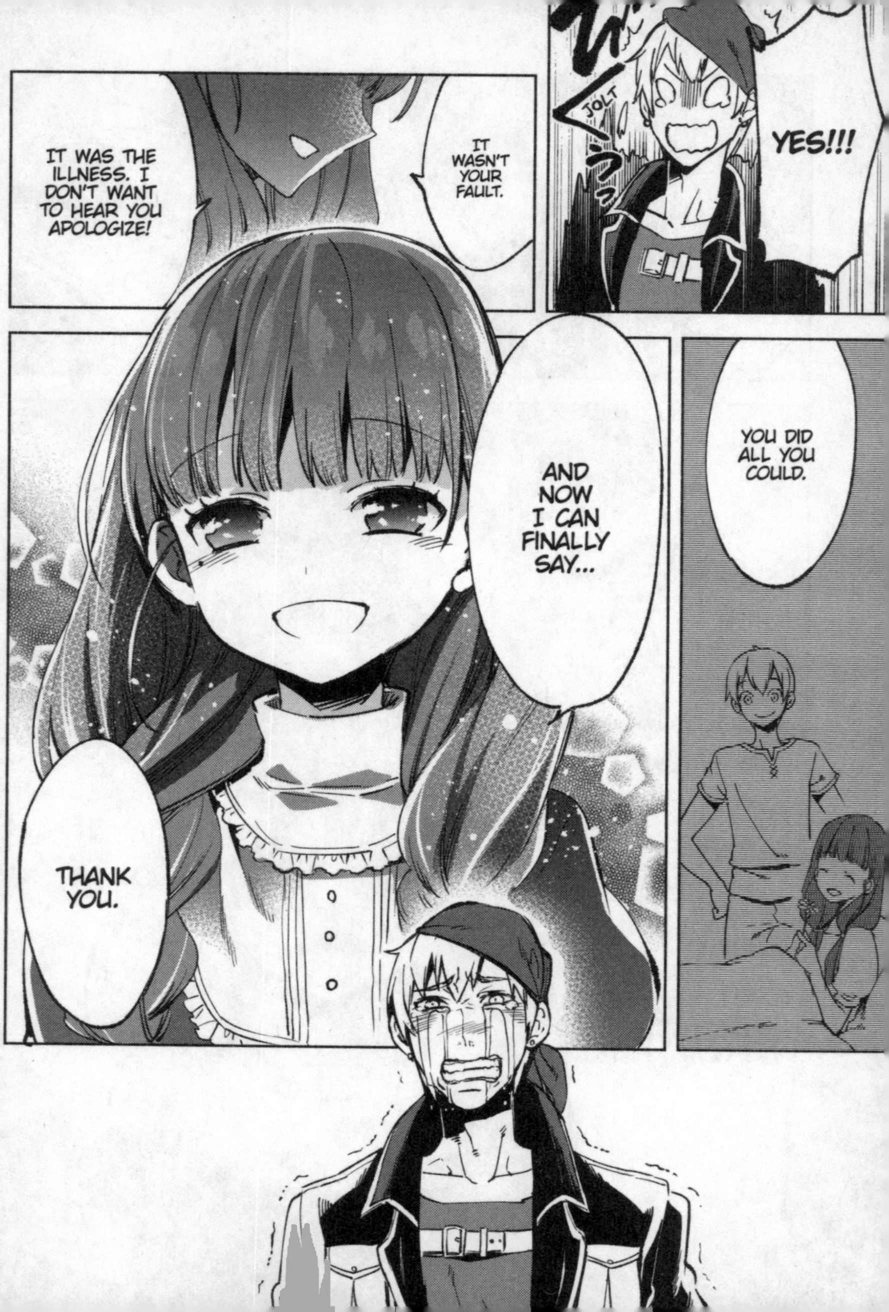
JOLT
YES!!!
IT WASN'T YOUR FAULT.
IT WAS THE ILLNESS. I DON'T WANT TO HEAR YOU APOLOGIZE!
YOU DID ALL YOU COULD.
AND NOW I CAN FINALLY SAY...
THANK YOU.

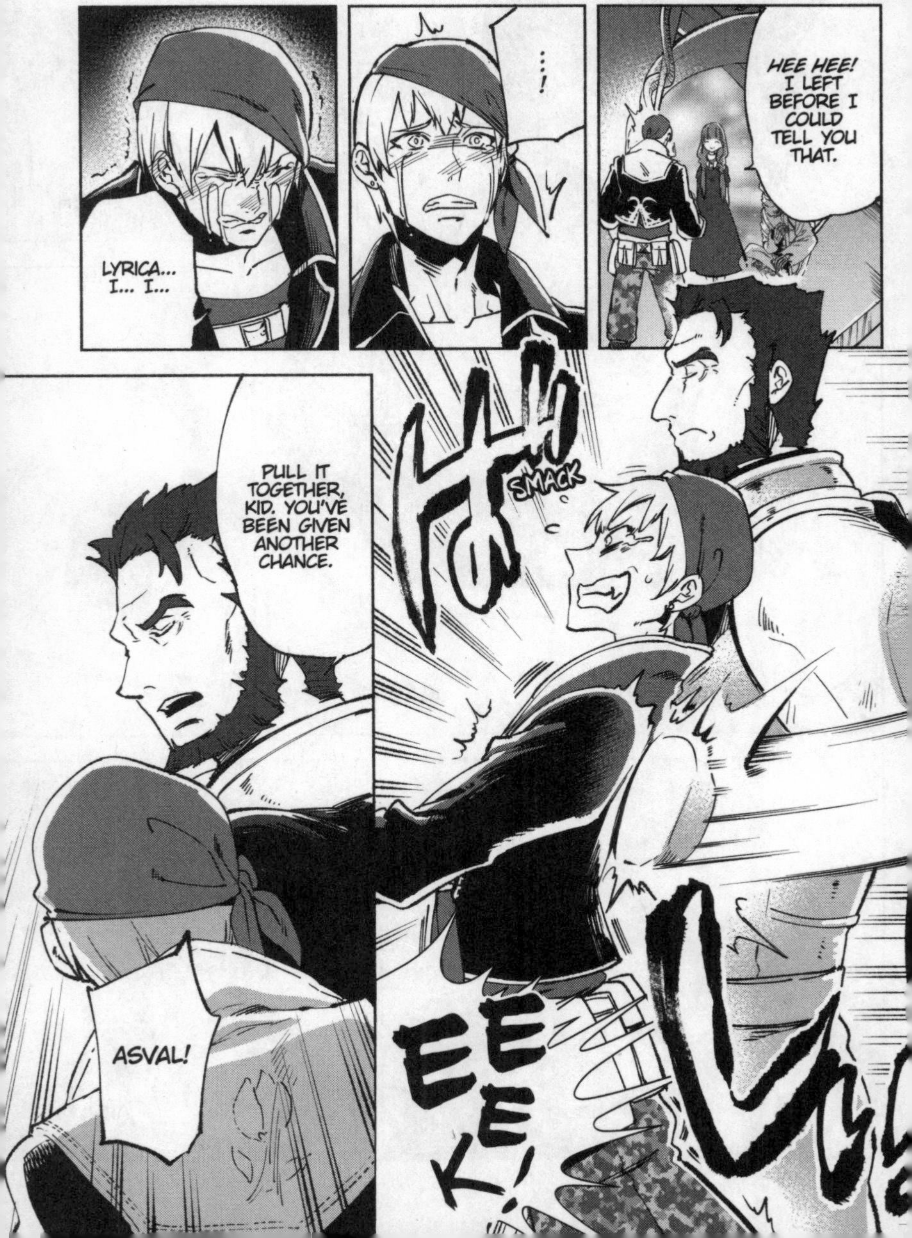
HEE HEE! I LEFT BEFORE I COULD TELL YOU THAT.
...!
LYRICA... I... I...
SMACK
EEEEK!
PULL IT TOGETHER, KID. YOU'VE BEEN GIVEN ANOTHER CHANCE.
ASVAL!

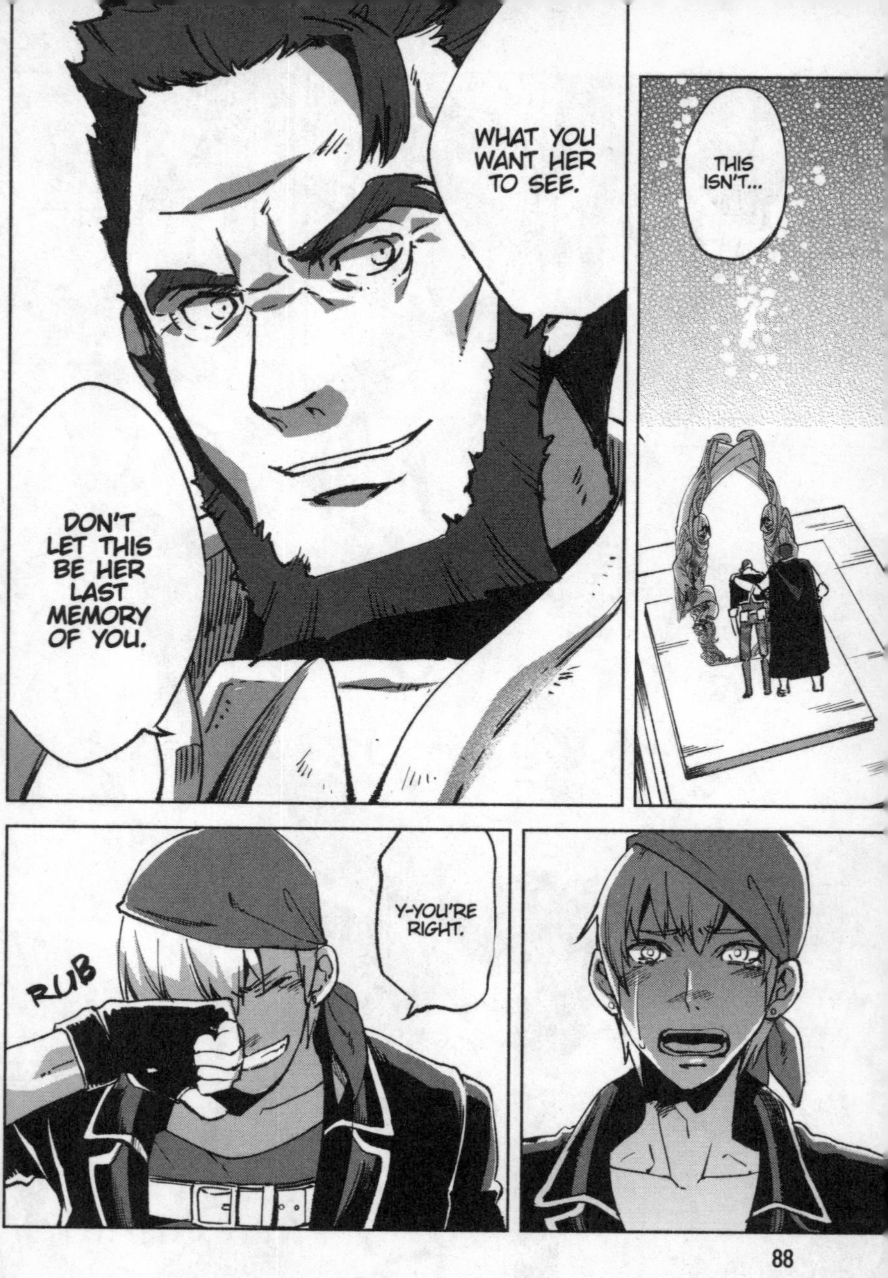
THIS ISN'T...
WHAT YOU WANT HER TO SEE.
DON'T LET THIS BE HER LAST MEMORY OF YOU.
Y-YOU'RE RIGHT.
RUB

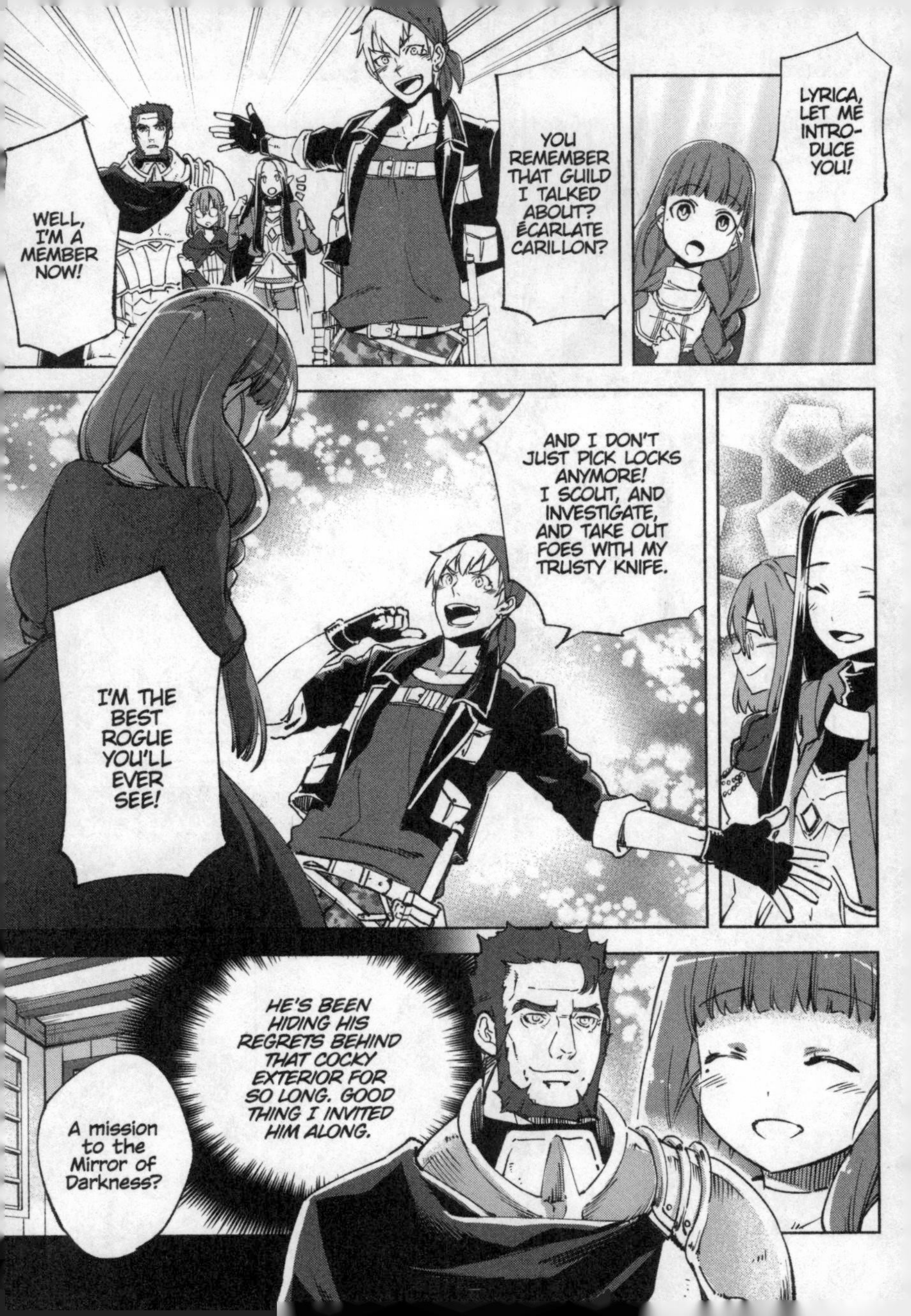
LYRICA, LET ME INTRODUCE YOU!
YOU REMEMBER THAT GUILD I TALKED ABOUT? ÉCARLATE CARILLON?
WELL, I'M A MEMBER NOW!
AND I DON'T JUST PICK LOCKS ANYMORE! I SCOUT, AND INVESTIGATE, AND TAKE OUT FOES WITH MY TRUSTY KNIFE.
I'M THE BEST ROGUE YOU'LL EVER SEE!
HE'S BEEN HIDING HIS REGRETS BEHIND THAT COCKY EXTERIOR FOR SO LONG. GOOD THING I INVITED HIM ALONG.
A mission to the Mirror of Darkness?

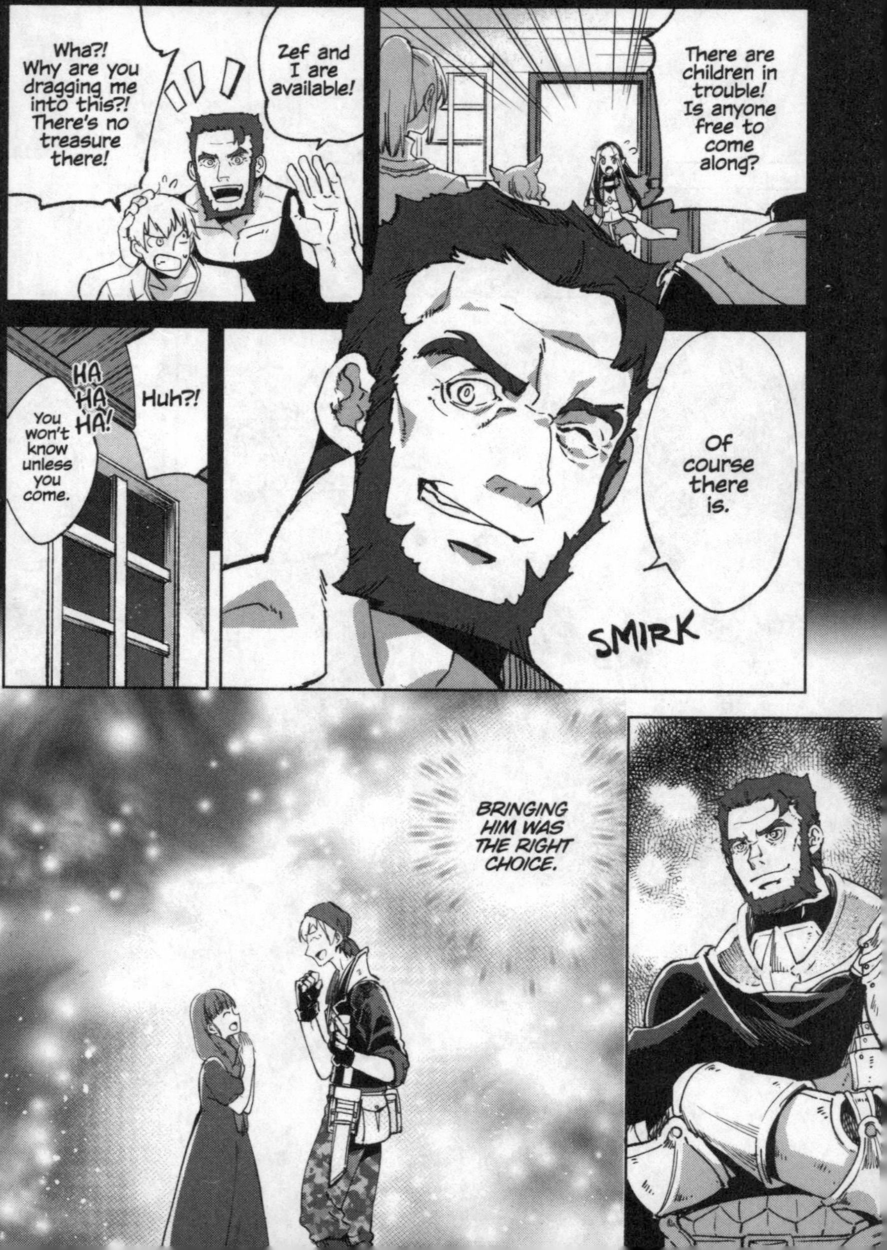
There are children in trouble! Is anyone free to come along?
Zef and I are available!
Wha?! Why are you dragging me into this?! There's no treasure there!
Of course there is.
SMIRK
Huh?!
HA HA HA!
You won't know unless you come.
BRINGING HIM WAS THE RIGHT CHOICE.

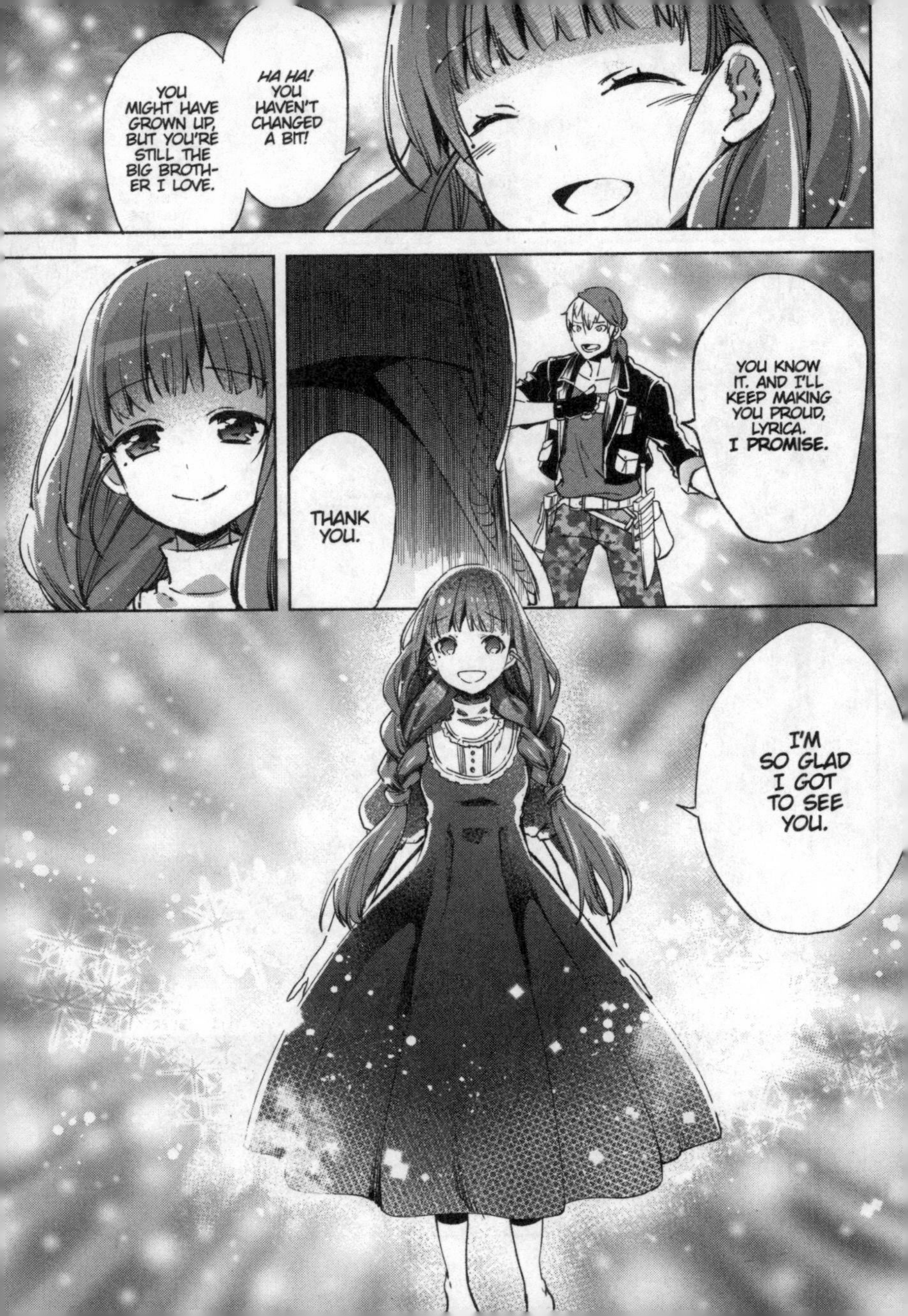
HA HA! YOU HAVEN'T CHANGED A BIT!
YOU MIGHT HAVE GROWN UP, BUT YOU'RE STILL THE BIG BROTH-ER I LOVE.
YOU KNOW IT. AND I'LL KEEP MAKING YOU PROUD, LYRICA. I PROMISE.
THANK YOU.
I'M SO GLAD I GOT TO SEE YOU.

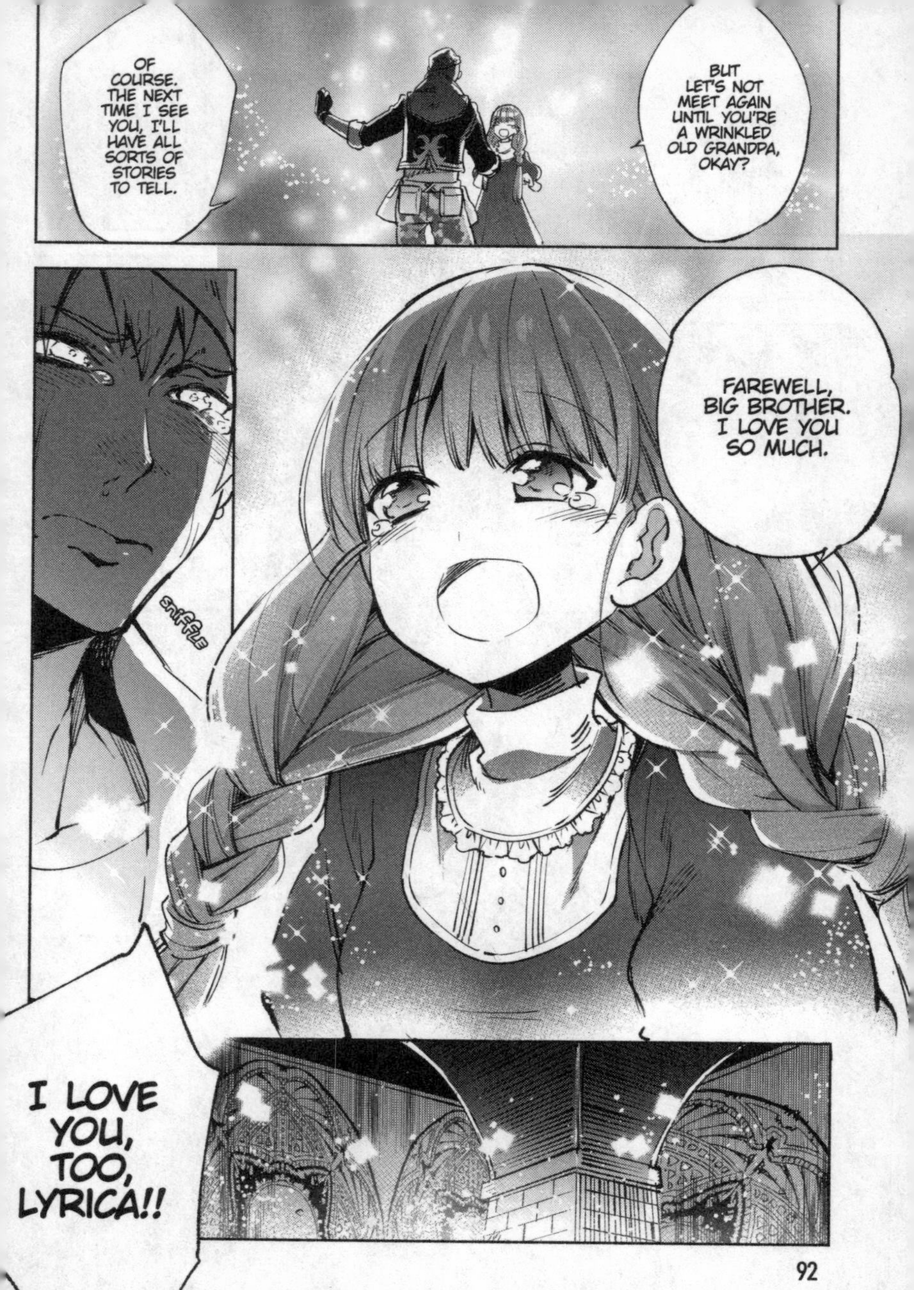
BUT LET'S NOT MEET AGAIN UNTIL YOU'RE A WRINKLED OLD GRANDPA, OKAY?
OF COURSE. THE NEXT TIME I SEE YOU, I'LL HAVE ALL SORTS OF STORIES TO TELL.
FAREWELL, BIG BROTHER. I LOVE YOU SO MUCH.
sniffle
I LOVE YOU, TOO, LYRICA!!

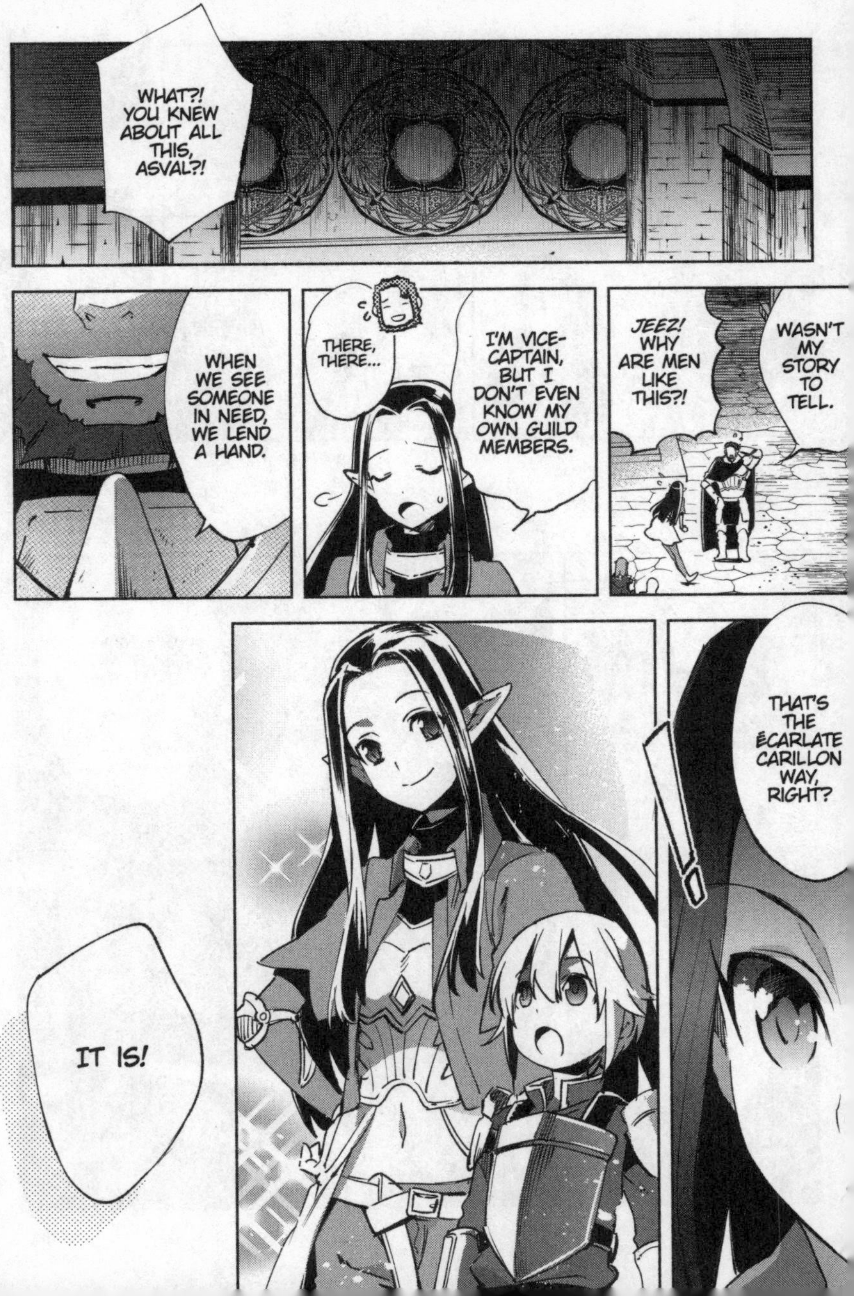
WHAT?! YOU KNEW ABOUT ALL THIS, ASVAL?!
WASN'T MY STORY TO TELL.
JEEZ! WHY ARE MEN LIKE THIS?!
I'M VICE-CAPTAIN, BUT I DON'T EVEN KNOW MY OWN GUILD MEMBERS.
THERE, THERE...
WHEN WE SEE SOMEONE IN NEED, WE LEND A HAND.
THAT'S THE ÉCARLATE CARILLON WAY, RIGHT?
IT IS!

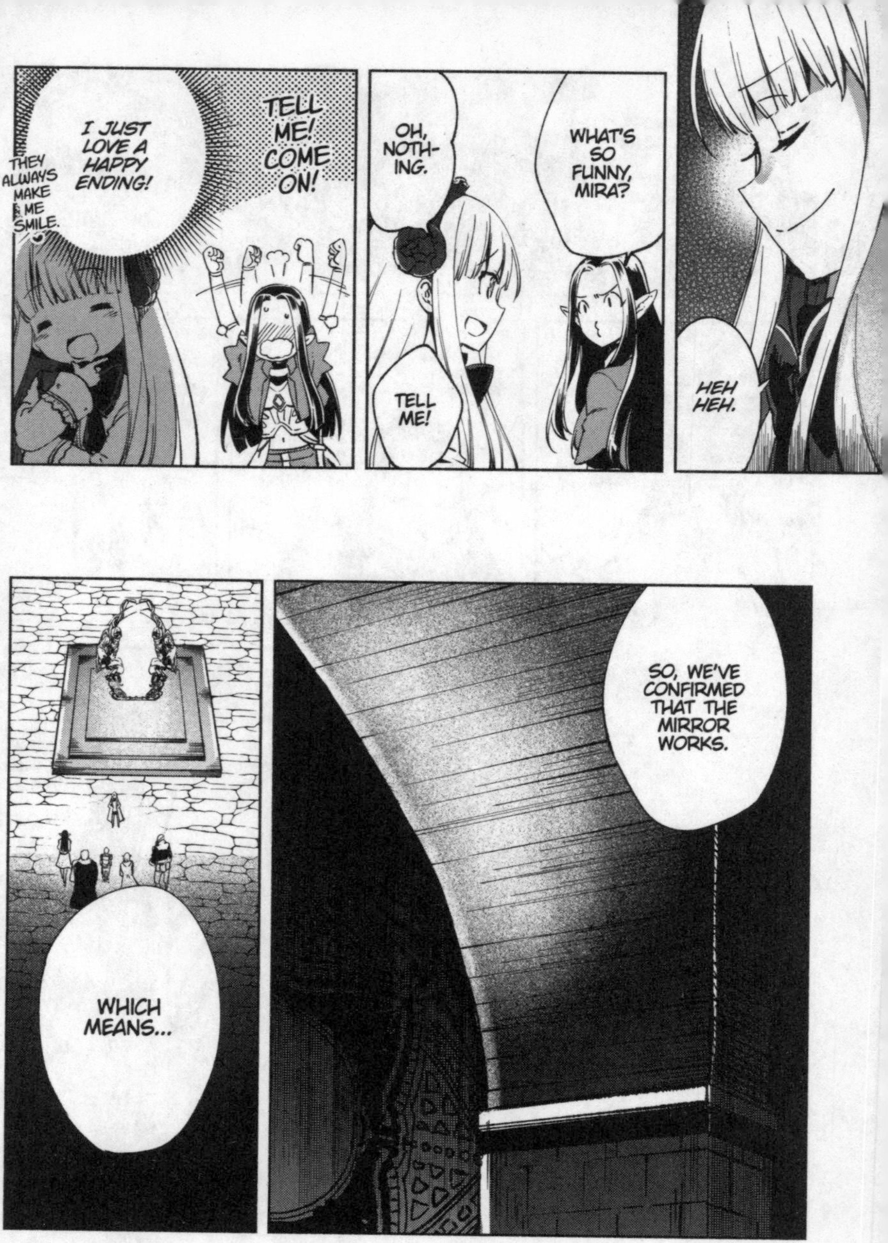
HEH HEH.
WHAT'S SO FUNNY, MIRA?
OH, NOTHING.
TELL ME!
TELL ME! COME ON!
I JUST LOVE A HAPPY ENDING!
THEY ALWAYS MAKE ME SMILE.
SO, WE'VE CONFIRMED THAT THE MIRROR WORKS.
WHICH MEANS...

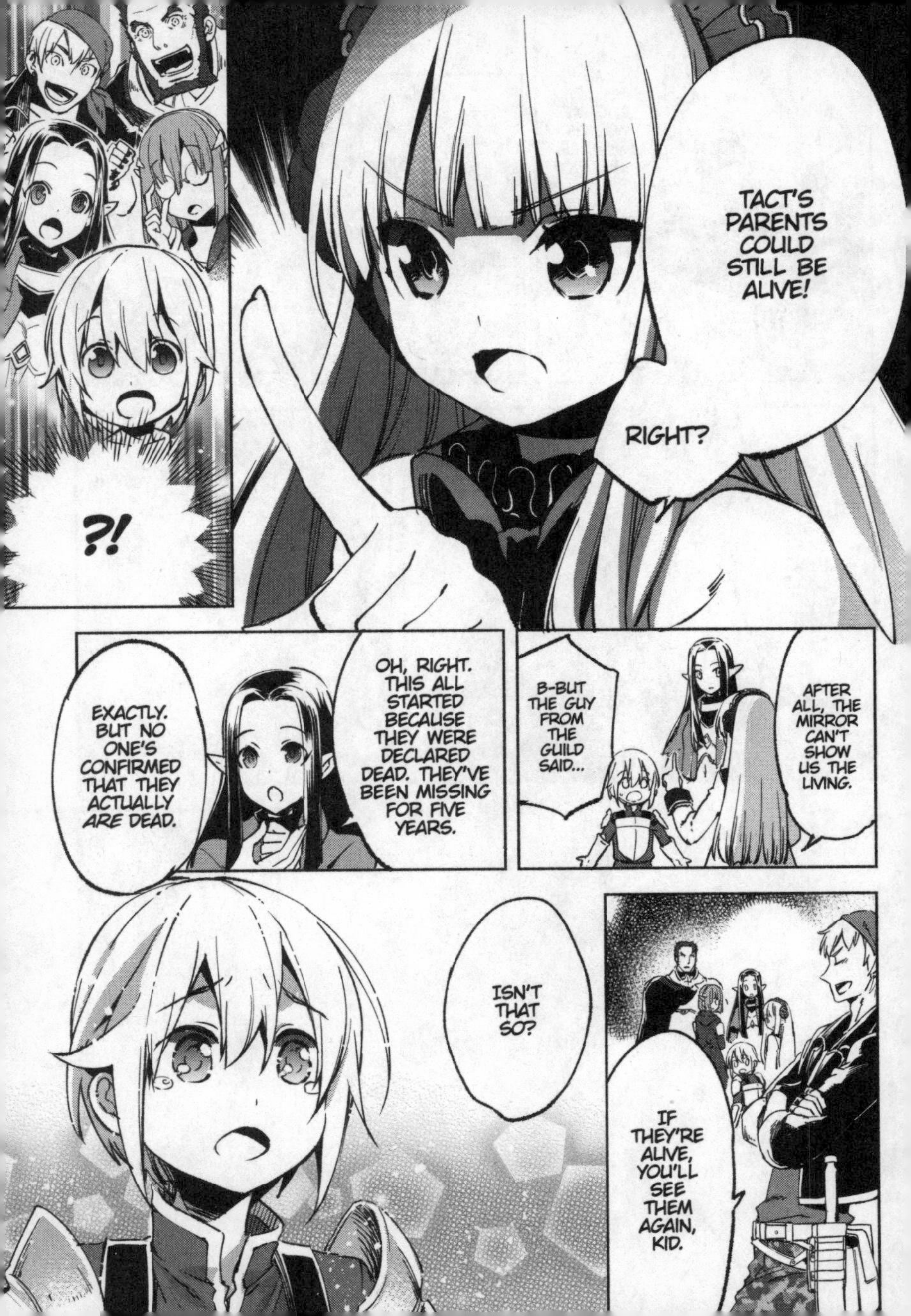
TACT'S PARENTS COULD STILL BE ALIVE!
RIGHT?
?!
AFTER ALL, THE MIRROR CAN'T SHOW US THE LIVING.
B-BUT THE GUY FROM THE GUILD SAID...
OH, RIGHT. THIS ALL STARTED BECAUSE THEY WERE DECLARED DEAD. THEY'VE BEEN MISSING FOR FIVE YEARS.
EXACTLY. BUT NO ONE'S CONFIRMED THAT THEY ACTUALLY ARE DEAD.
IF THEY'RE ALIVE, YOU'LL SEE THEM AGAIN, KID.
ISN'T THAT SO?

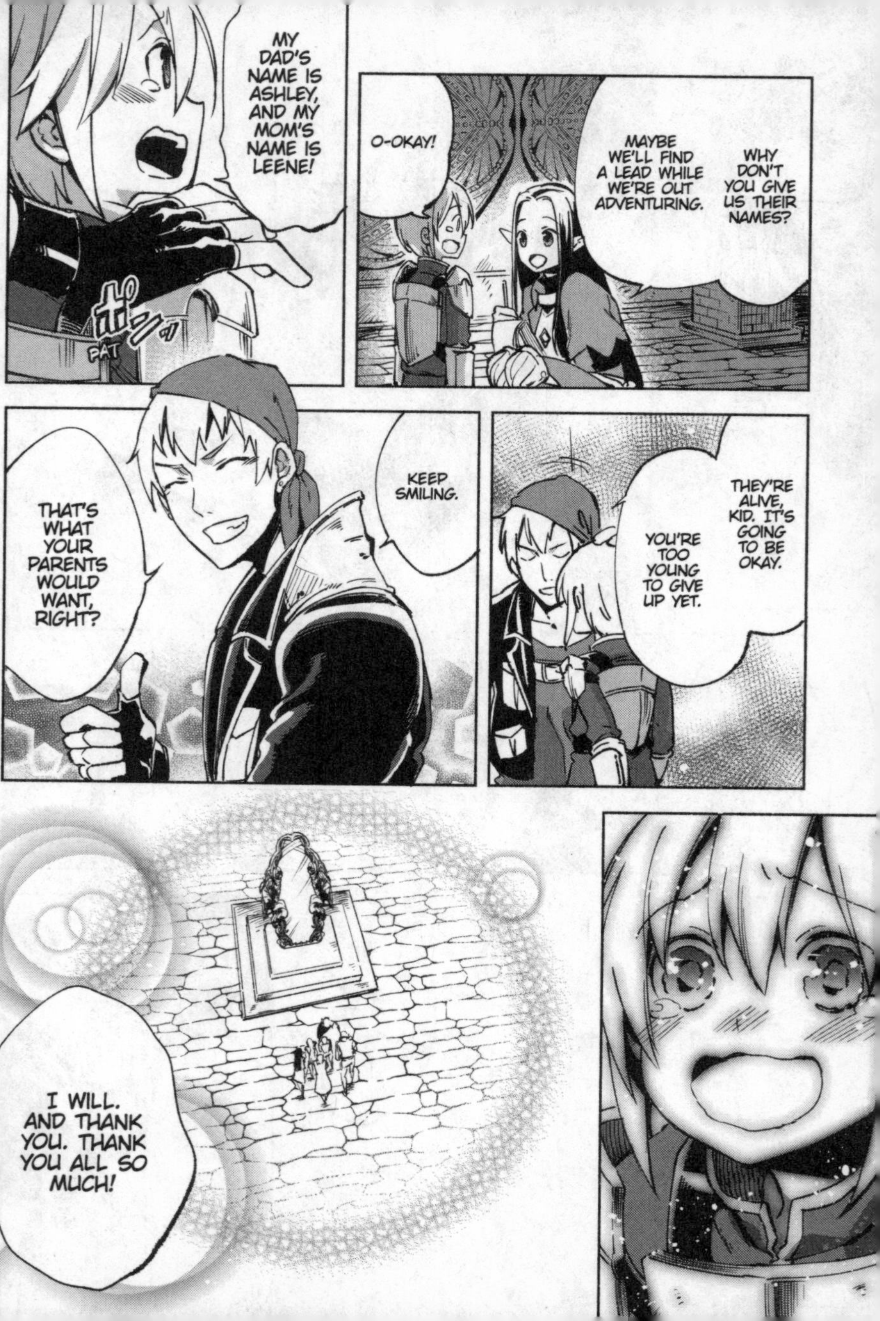
WHY DON'T YOU GIVE US THEIR NAMES?
MAYBE WE'LL FIND A LEAD WHILE WE'RE OUT ADVENTURING.
O-OKAY!
MY DAD'S NAME IS ASHLEY, AND MY MOM'S NAME IS LEENE!
PAT
THEY'RE ALIVE, KID. IT'S GOING TO BE OKAY.
YOU'RE TOO YOUNG TO GIVE UP YET.
KEEP SMILING.
THAT'S WHAT YOUR PARENTS WOULD WANT, RIGHT?
I WILL. AND THANK YOU. THANK YOU ALL SO MUCH!

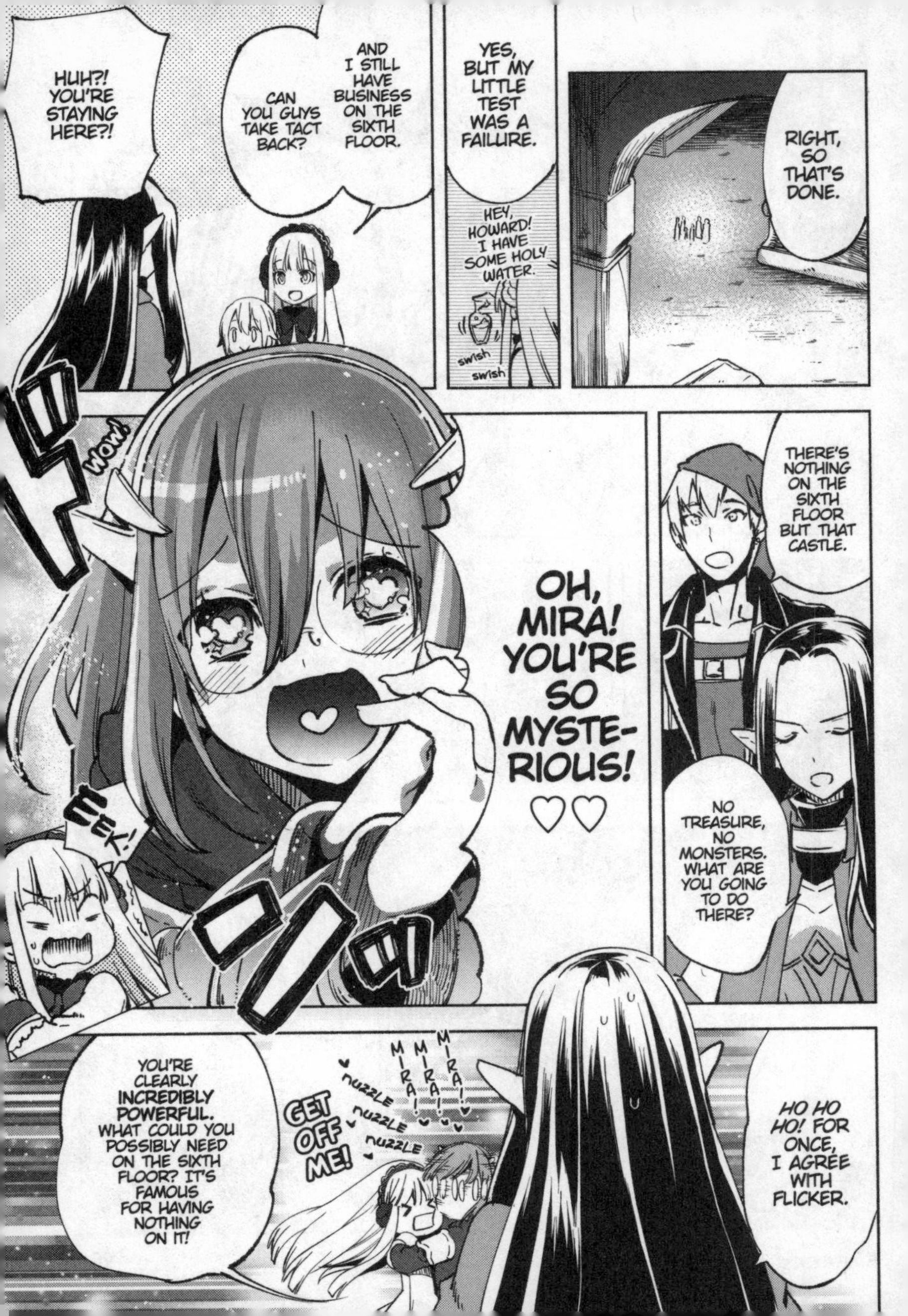
RIGHT, SO THAT'S DONE.
YES, BUT MY LITTLE TEST WAS A FAILURE.
HEY, HOWARD! I HAVE SOME HOLY WATER.
swish swish
AND I STILL HAVE BUSINESS ON THE SIXTH FLOOR.
CAN YOU GUYS TAKE TACT BACK?
HUH?! YOU'RE STAYING HERE?!
THERE'S NOTHING ON THE SIXTH FLOOR BUT THAT CASTLE.
NO TREASURE, NO MONSTERS. WHAT ARE YOU GOING TO DO THERE?
OH, MIRA! YOU'RE SO MYSTERIOUS! ♡♡
WOW!
EEK!
HO HO HO! FOR ONCE, I AGREE WITH FLICKER.
MIRA! MIRA! MIRA!
nuzzle nuzzle nuzzle
GET OFF ME!
YOU'RE CLEARLY INCREDIBLY POWERFUL. WHAT COULD YOU POSSIBLY NEED ON THE SIXTH FLOOR? IT'S FAMOUS FOR HAVING NOTHING ON IT!

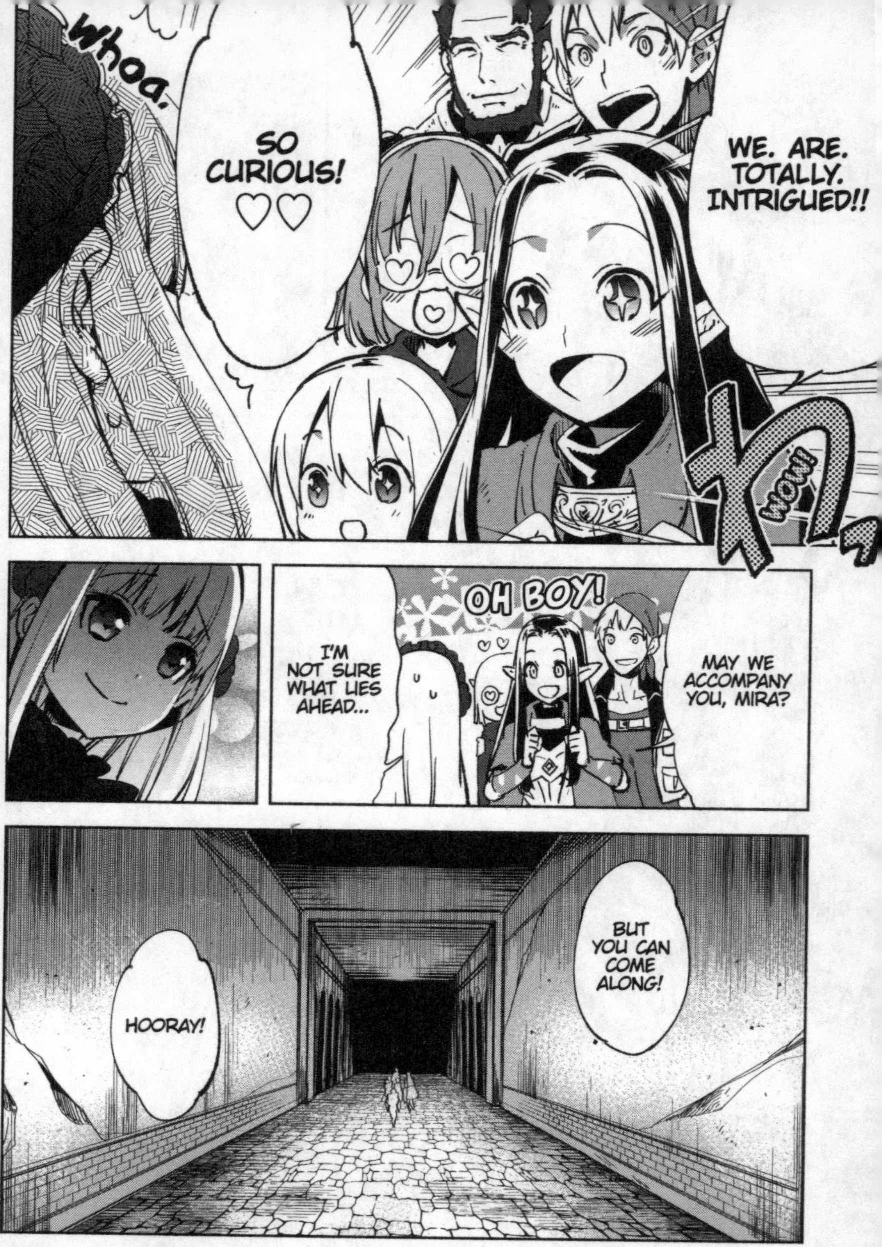
WE. ARE. TOTALLY. INTRIGUED!!
SO CURIOUS! ♡♡
Whoa.
WOW!
MAY WE ACCOMPANY YOU, MIRA?
OH BOY!
I'M NOT SURE WHAT LIES AHEAD...
BUT YOU CAN COME ALONG!
HOORAY!

Summon 11: END

She
Professed
Herself
Pupil of the
Wise Man

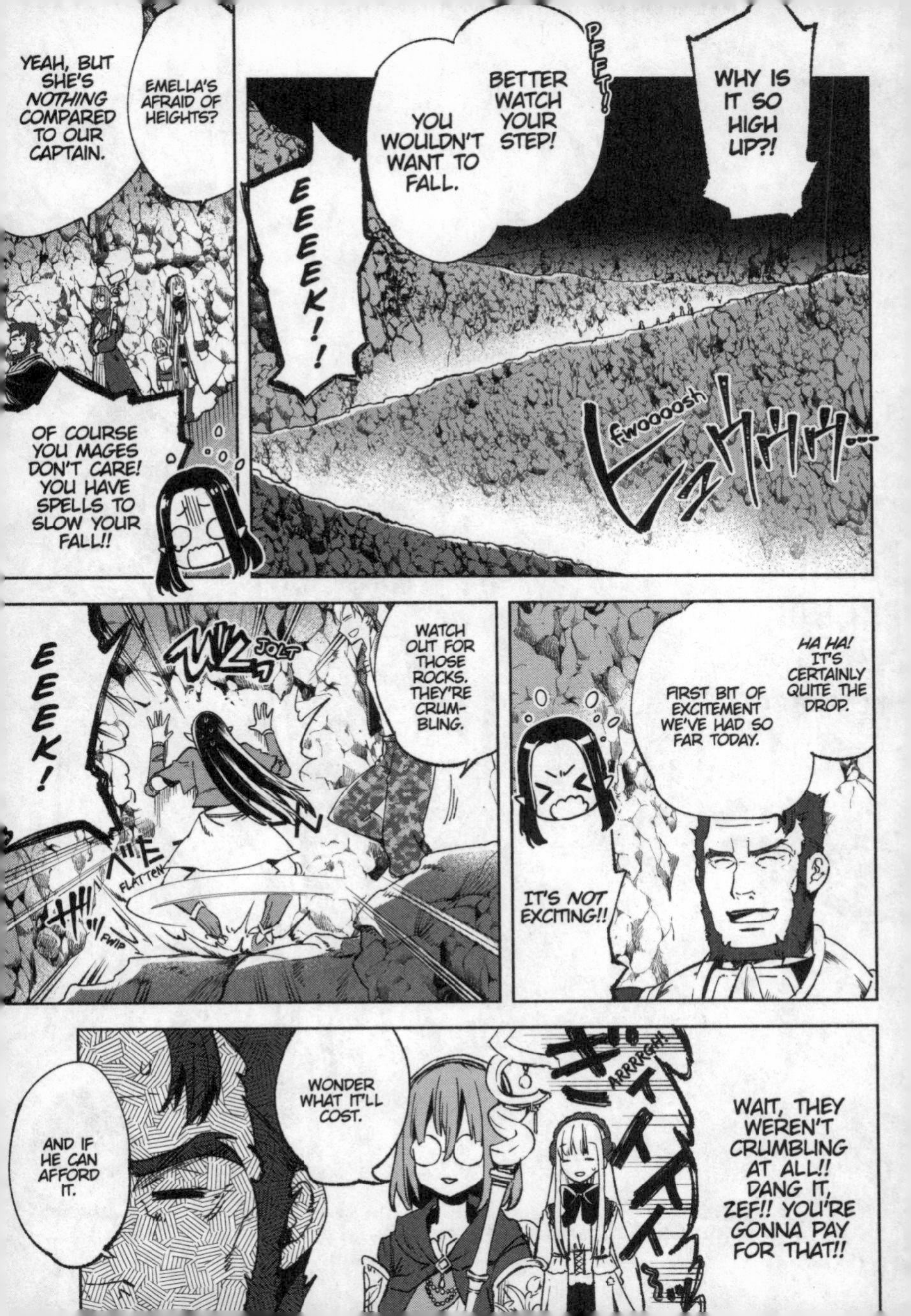
WHY IS IT SO HIGH UP?!
BETTER WATCH YOUR STEP!
YOU WOULDN'T WANT TO FALL.
PFFFT!
EEEEEK!!
fwoooosh
EMELLA'S AFRAID OF HEIGHTS?
YEAH, BUT SHE'S *NOTHING* COMPARED TO OUR CAPTAIN.
OF COURSE YOU MAGES DON'T CARE! YOU HAVE SPELLS TO SLOW YOUR FALL!!
HA HA! IT'S CERTAINLY QUITE THE DROP.
FIRST BIT OF EXCITEMENT WE'VE HAD SO FAR TODAY.
IT'S *NOT* EXCITING!!
WATCH OUT FOR THOSE ROCKS. THEY'RE CRUM-BLING.
JOLT
EEEEK!
FLATTEN
FWIP
WAIT, THEY WEREN'T CRUMBLING AT ALL!! DANG IT, ZEF!! YOU'RE GONNA PAY FOR THAT!!
ARRRRGH!
WONDER WHAT IT'LL COST.
AND IF HE CAN AFFORD IT.

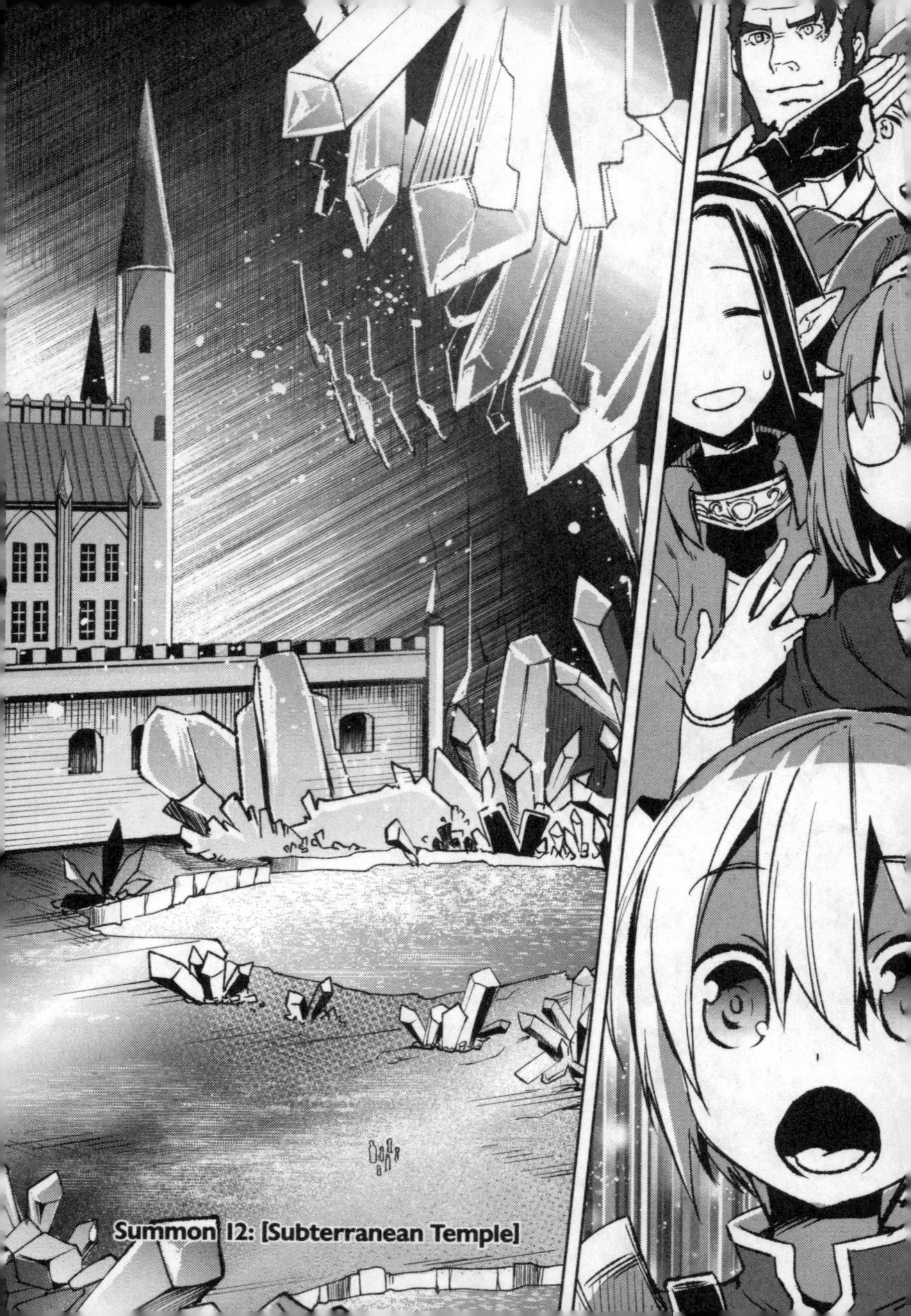
Summon 12: [Subterranean Temple]

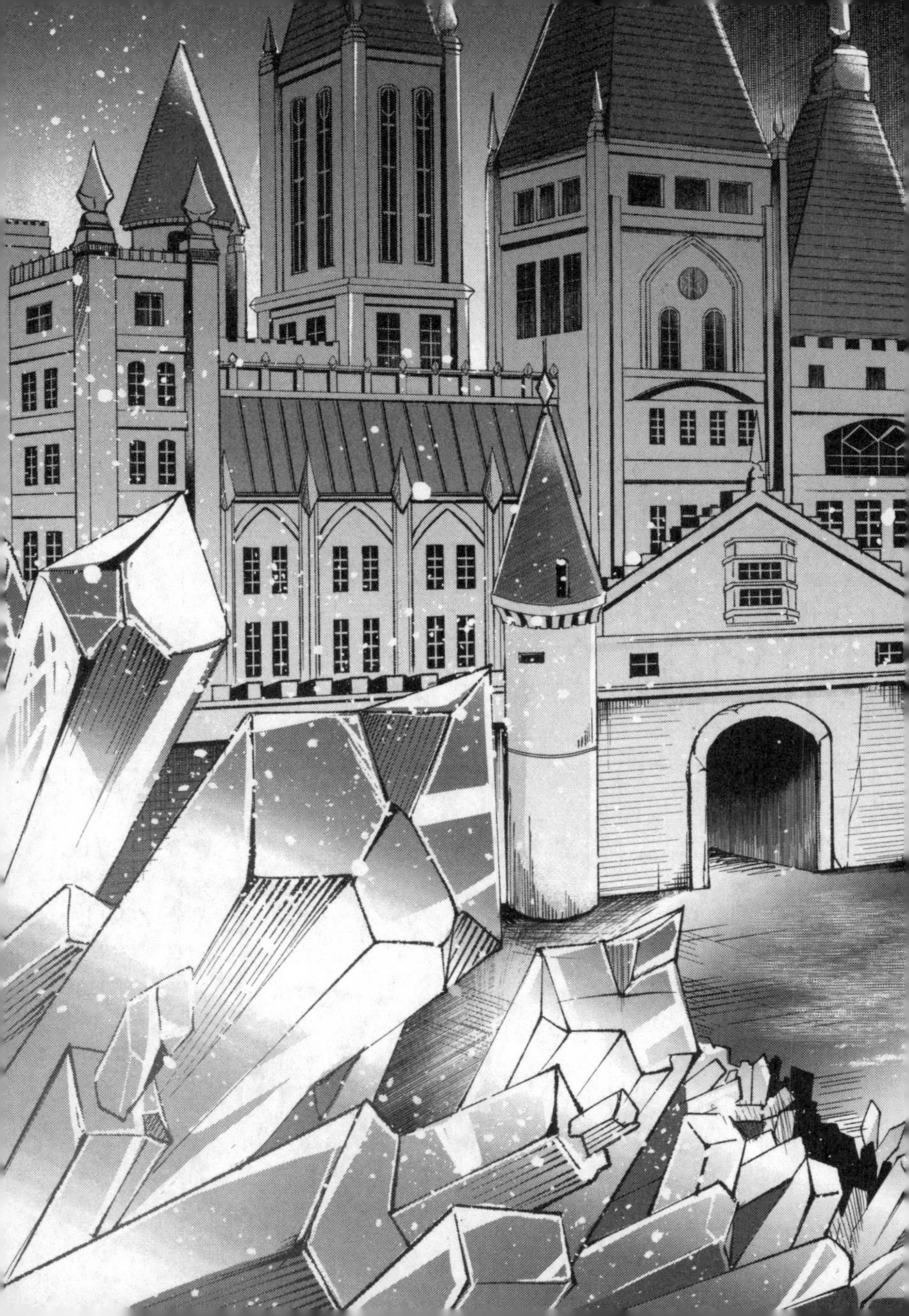

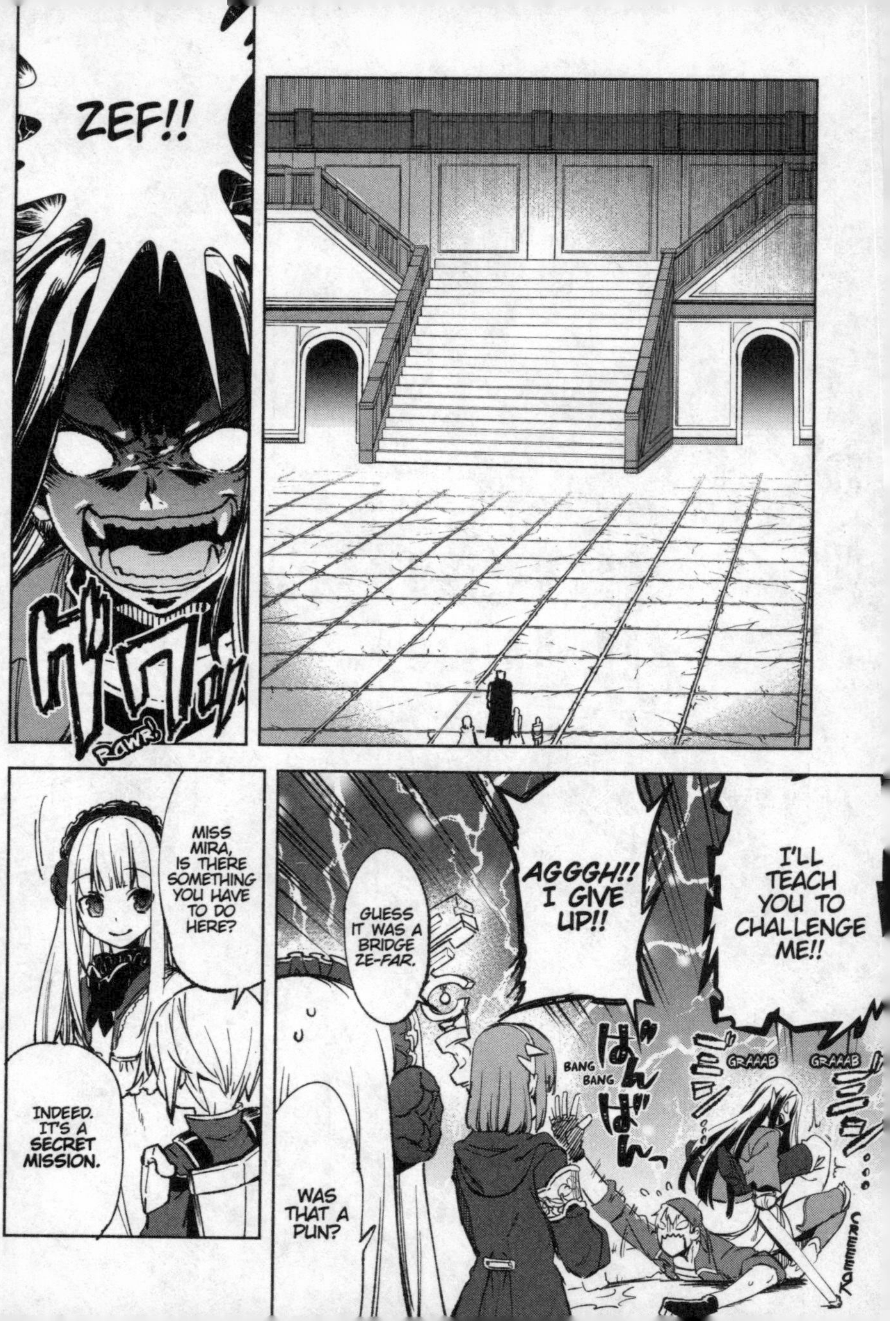
ZEF!!
RAWR!
I'LL TEACH YOU TO CHALLENGE ME!!
AGGGH!! I GIVE UP!!
GUESS IT WAS A BRIDGE ZE-FAR.
GRAAAB
GRAAAB
BANG BANG
WAS THAT A PUN?
MISS MIRA, IS THERE SOMETHING YOU HAVE TO DO HERE?
INDEED. IT'S A SECRET MISSION.

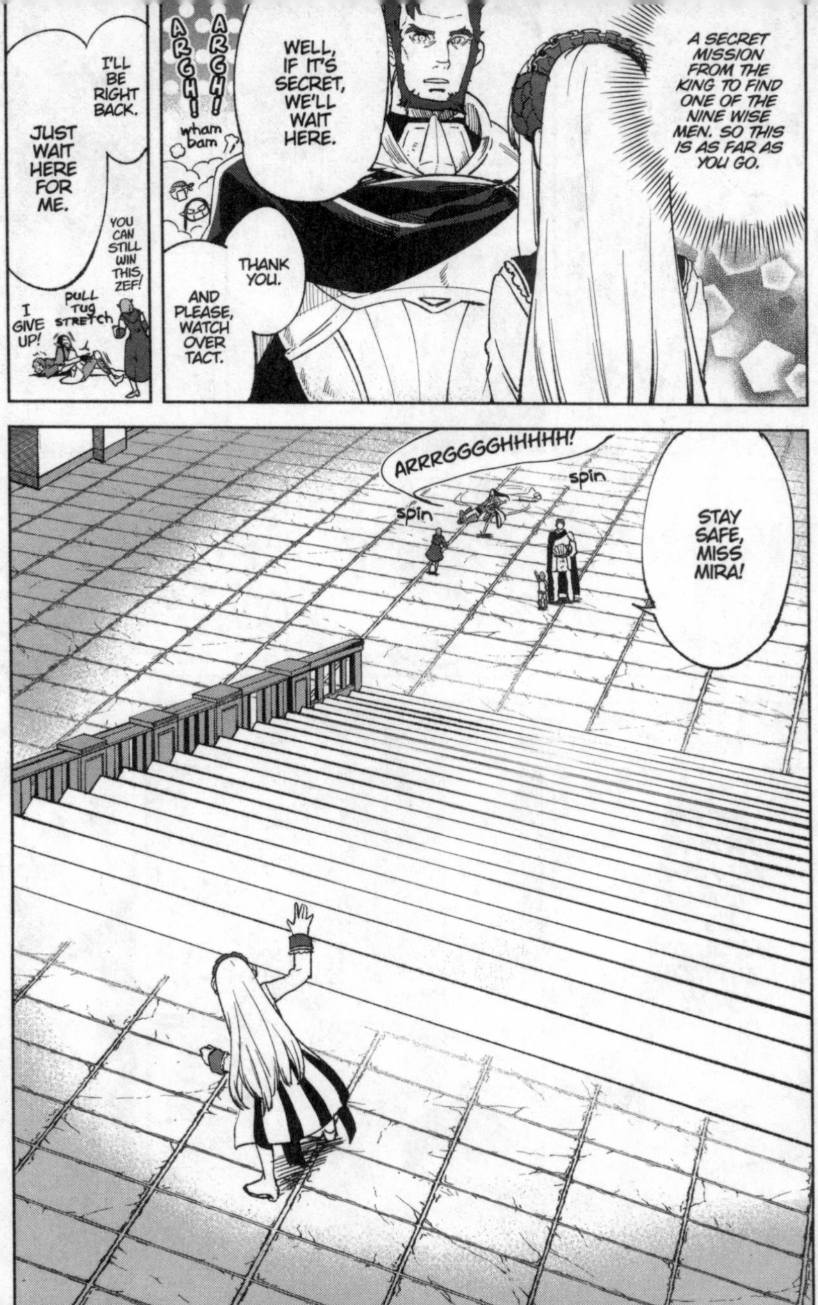
A SECRET MISSION FROM THE KING TO FIND ONE OF THE NINE WISE MEN. SO THIS IS AS FAR AS YOU GO.
WELL, IF IT'S SECRET, WE'LL WAIT HERE.
ARGH!
ARGH!
wham
bam
THANK YOU.
AND PLEASE, WATCH OVER TACT.
I'LL BE RIGHT BACK.
JUST WAIT HERE FOR ME.
YOU CAN STILL WIN THIS, ZEF!
PULL
TUG
STRETCH
I GIVE UP!
STAY SAFE, MISS MIRA!
ARRRGGGGHHHHH!
spin
spin

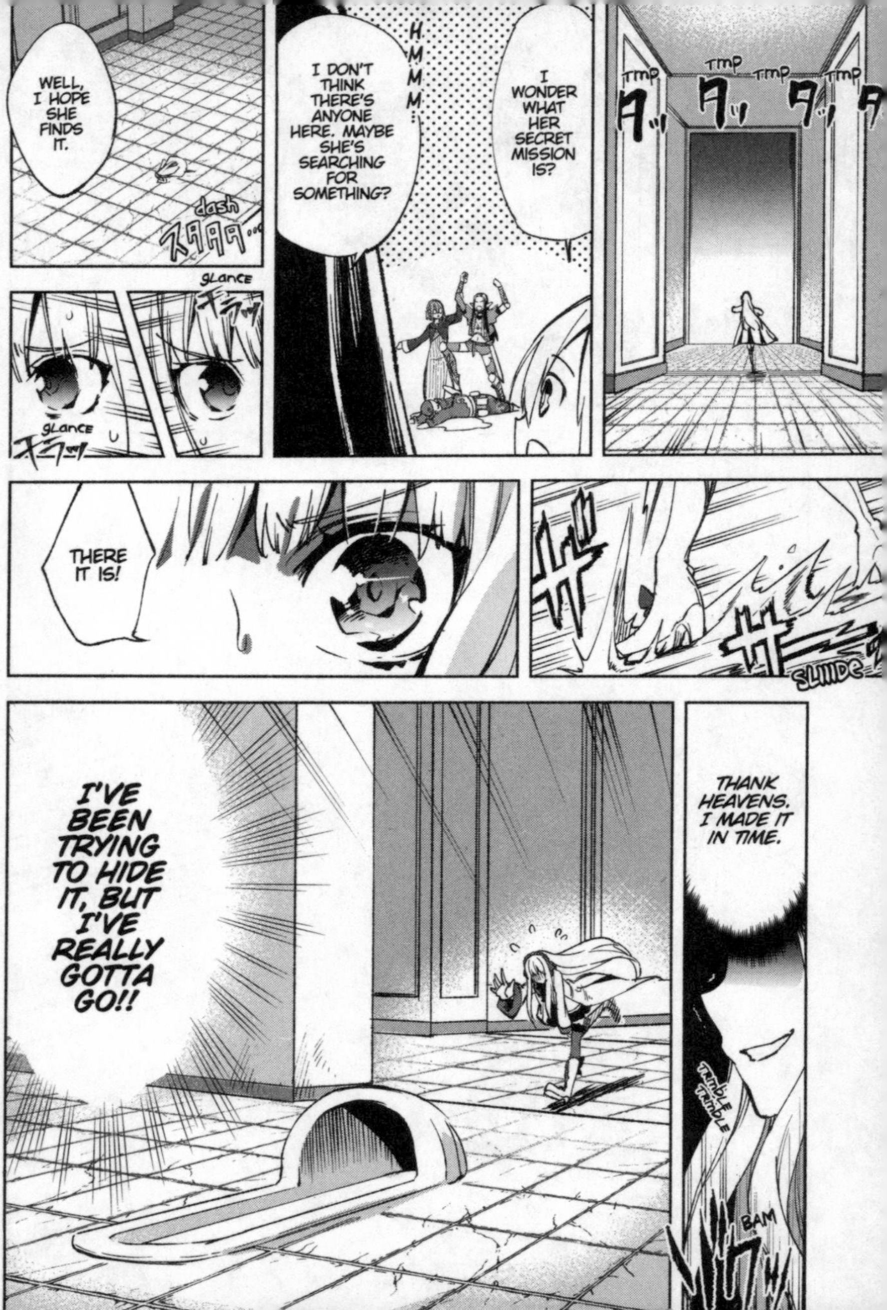
TMP TMP TMP TMP
I WONDER WHAT HER SECRET MISSION IS?
HMMM...
I DON'T THINK THERE'S ANYONE HERE. MAYBE SHE'S SEARCHING FOR SOMETHING?
WELL, I HOPE SHE FINDS IT.
dash
glance
glance
SLIIIDE
THERE IT IS!
THANK HEAVENS. I MADE IT IN TIME.
TRIMBLE TRIMBLE
BAM
I'VE BEEN TRYING TO HIDE IT, BUT I'VE REALLY GOTTA GO!!

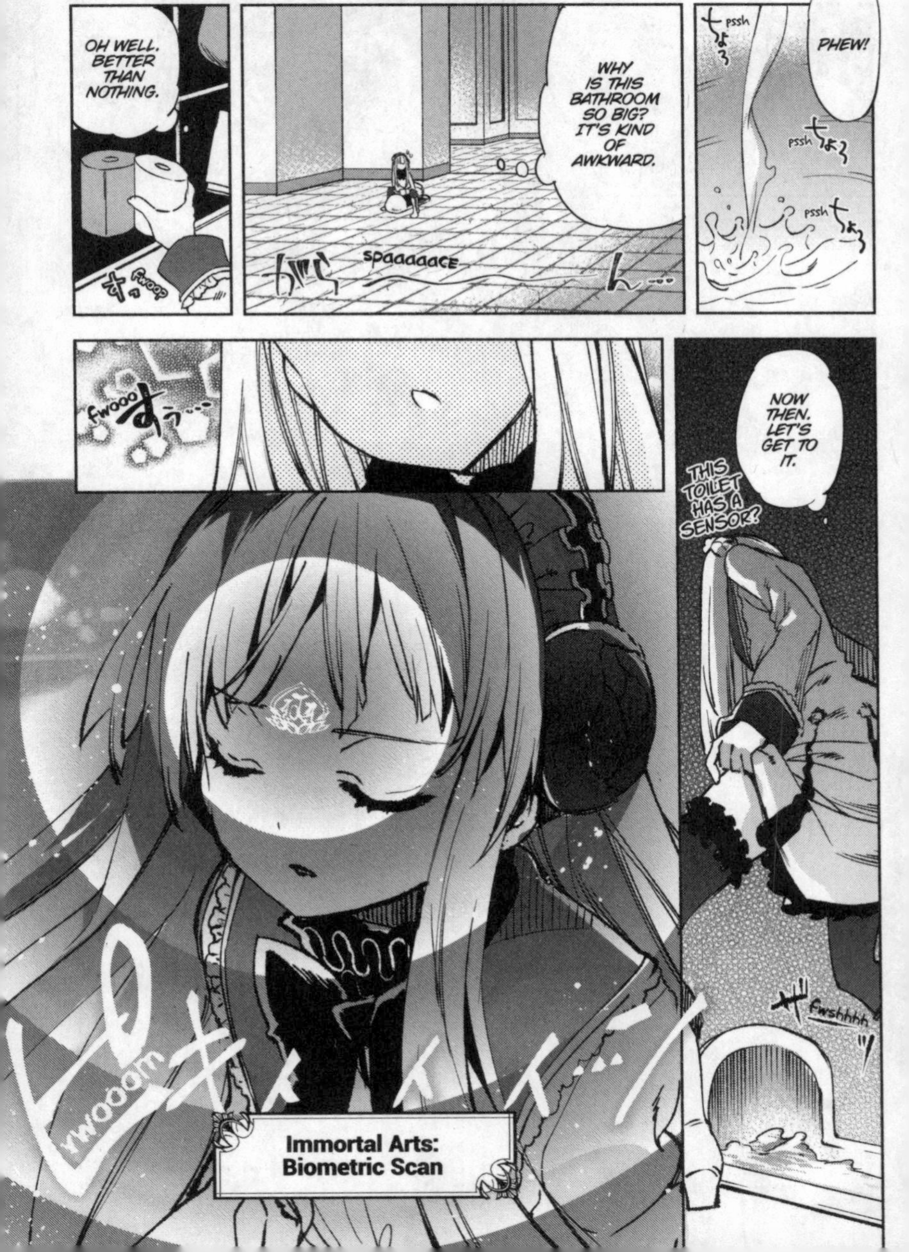
PHEW!
pssh
pssh
pssh
WHY IS THIS BATHROOM SO BIG? IT'S KIND OF AWKWARD.
spaaaaace
OH WELL. BETTER THAN NOTHING.
fwoop
NOW THEN. LET'S GET TO IT.
THIS TOILET HAS A SENSOR?
fwshhhh
fwooo
rwooom
Immortal Arts: Biometric Scan

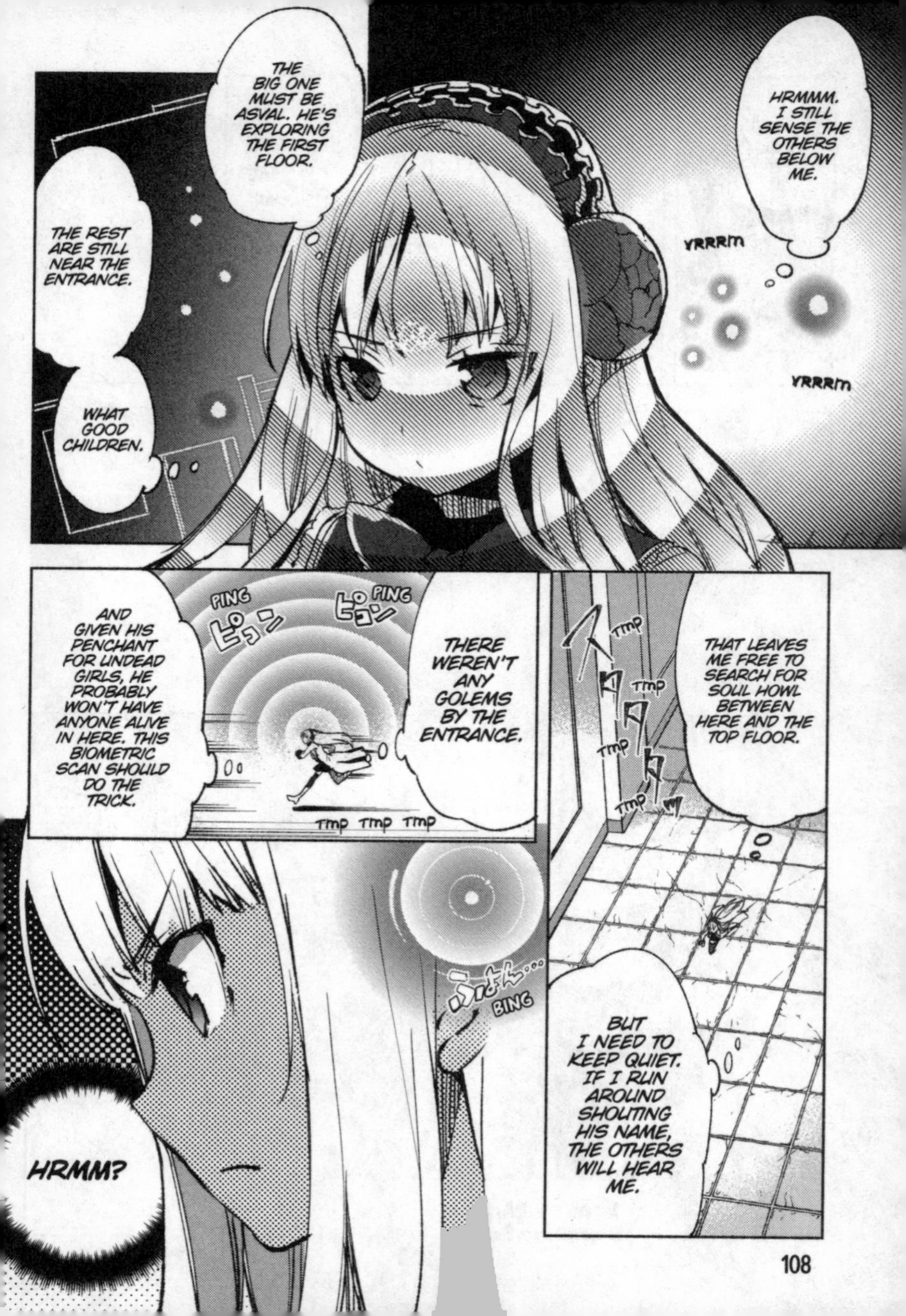
HRMMM. I STILL SENSE THE OTHERS BELOW ME.
YRRRM
YRRRM
THE BIG ONE MUST BE ASVAL. HE'S EXPLORING THE FIRST FLOOR.
THE REST ARE STILL NEAR THE ENTRANCE.
WHAT GOOD CHILDREN.
THAT LEAVES ME FREE TO SEARCH FOR SOUL HOWL BETWEEN HERE AND THE TOP FLOOR.
TMP
TMP
TMP
TMP
BUT I NEED TO KEEP QUIET. IF I RUN AROUND SHOUTING HIS NAME, THE OTHERS WILL HEAR ME.
PING
PING
THERE WEREN'T ANY GOLEMS BY THE ENTRANCE.
AND GIVEN HIS PENCHANT FOR UNDEAD GIRLS, HE PROBABLY WON'T HAVE ANYONE ALIVE IN HERE. THIS BIOMETRIC SCAN SHOULD DO THE TRICK.
TMP TMP TMP
BING
HRMM?

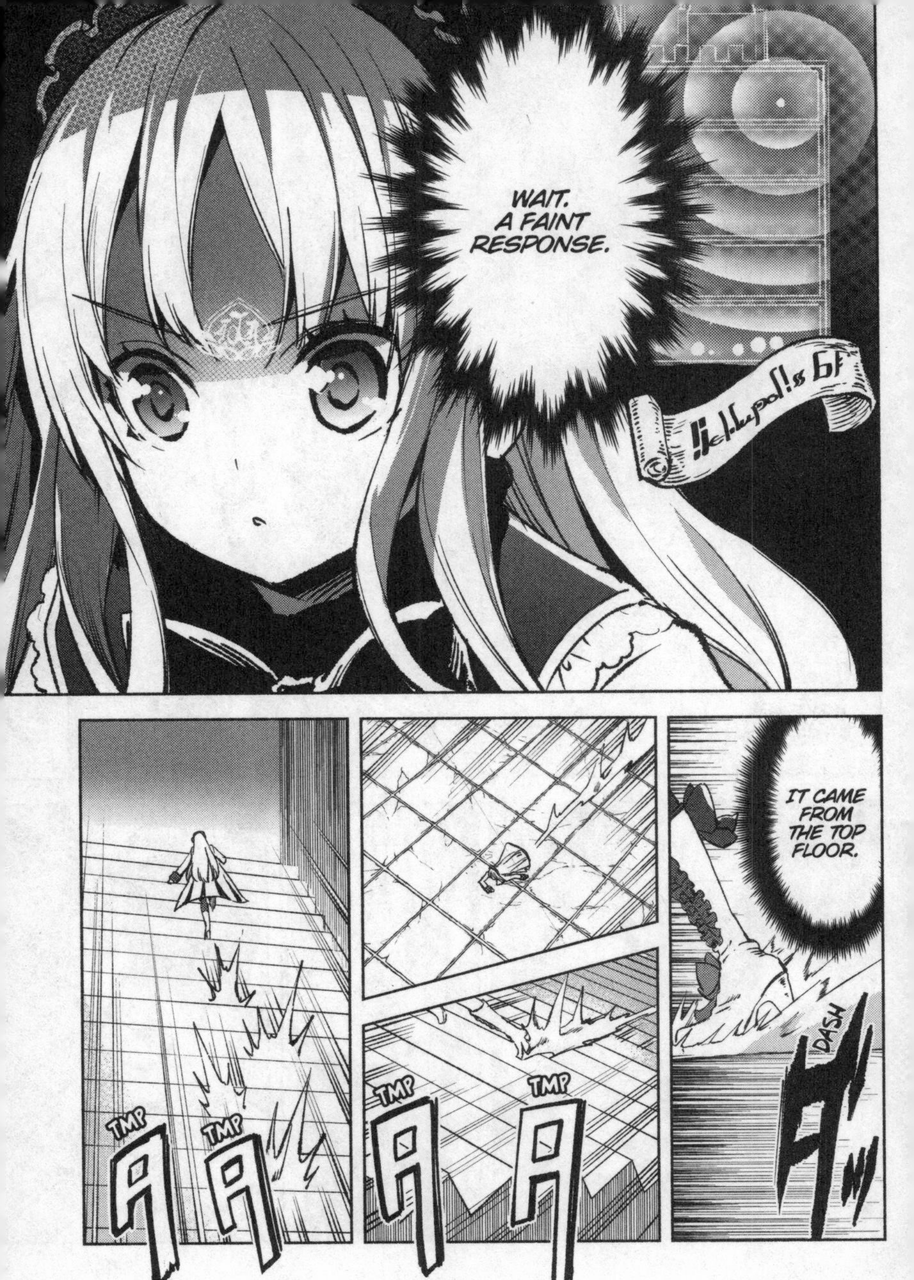
WAIT. A FAINT RESPONSE.
IT CAME FROM THE TOP FLOOR.
DASH
TMP
TMP
TMP
TMP

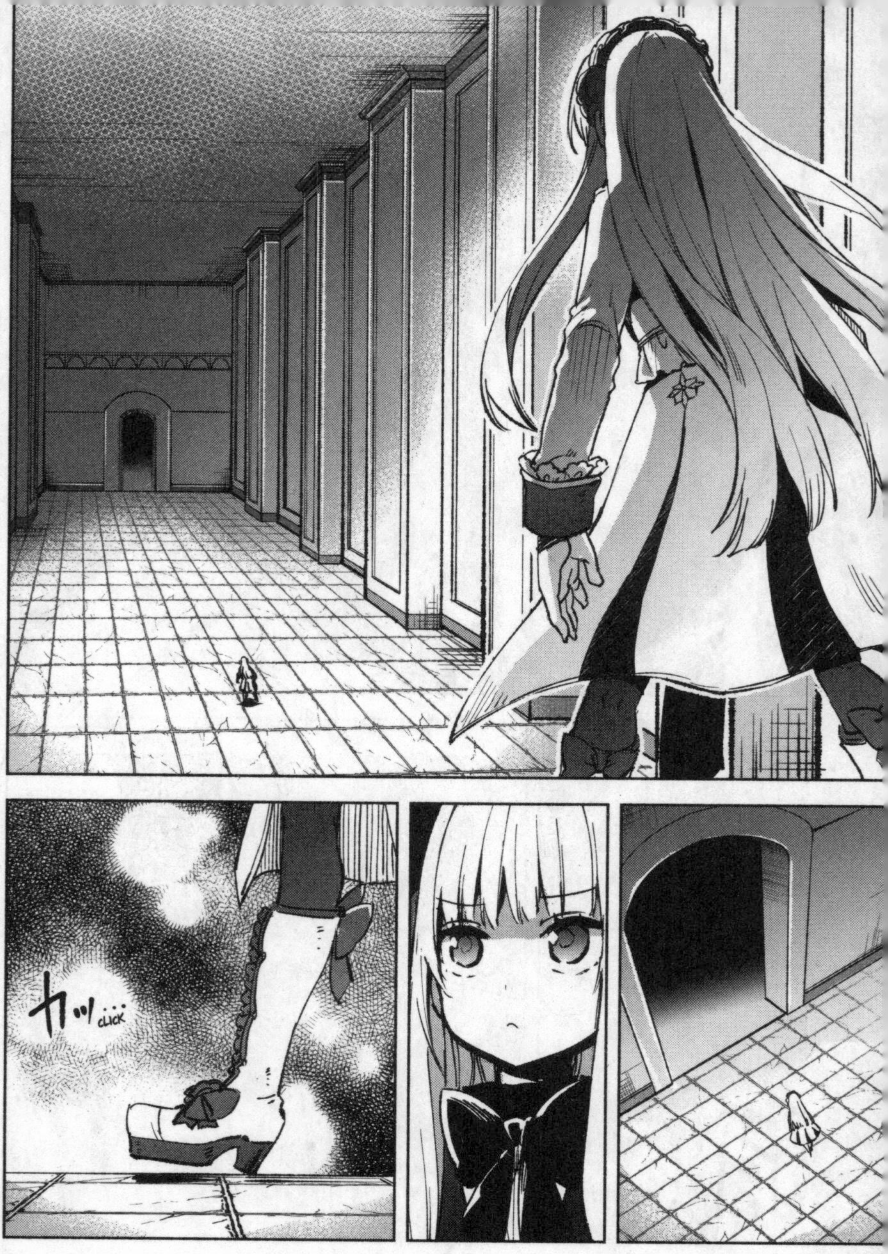
カッ
...
CLICK

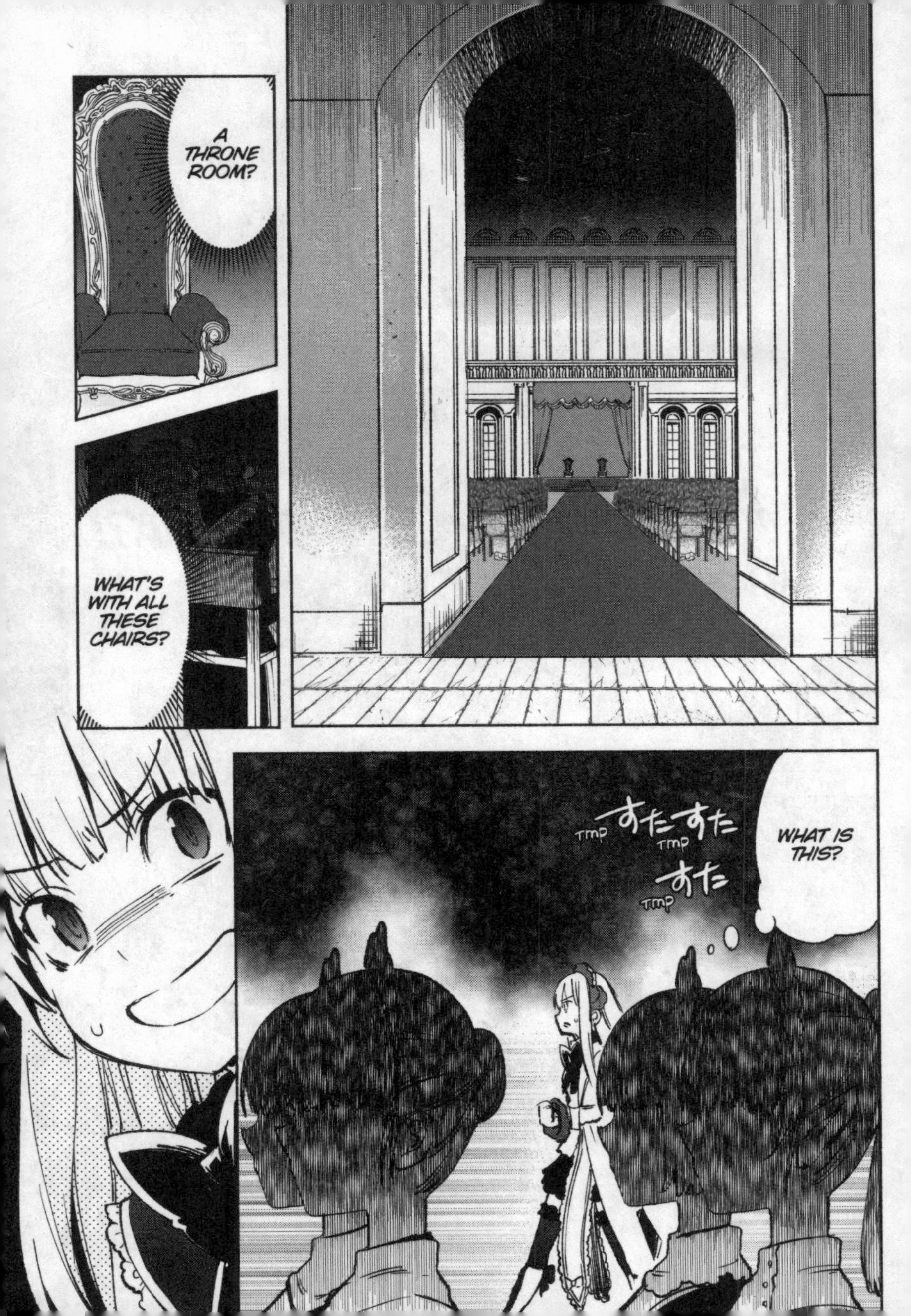
A THRONE ROOM?
WHAT'S WITH ALL THESE CHAIRS?
WHAT IS THIS?
TMP すたすた TMP
すた TMP

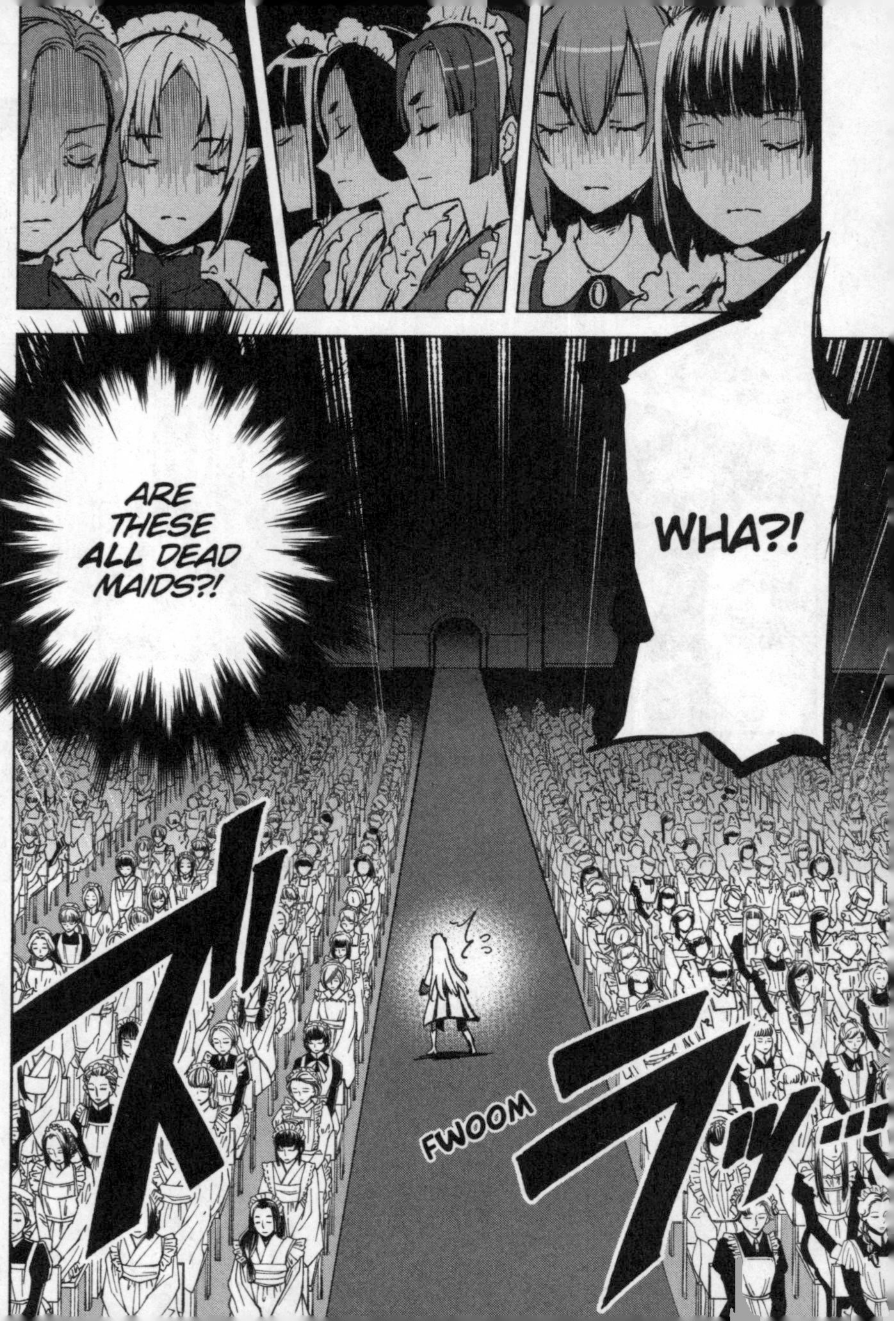
WHA?!
ARE THESE ALL DEAD MAIDS?!
FWOOM

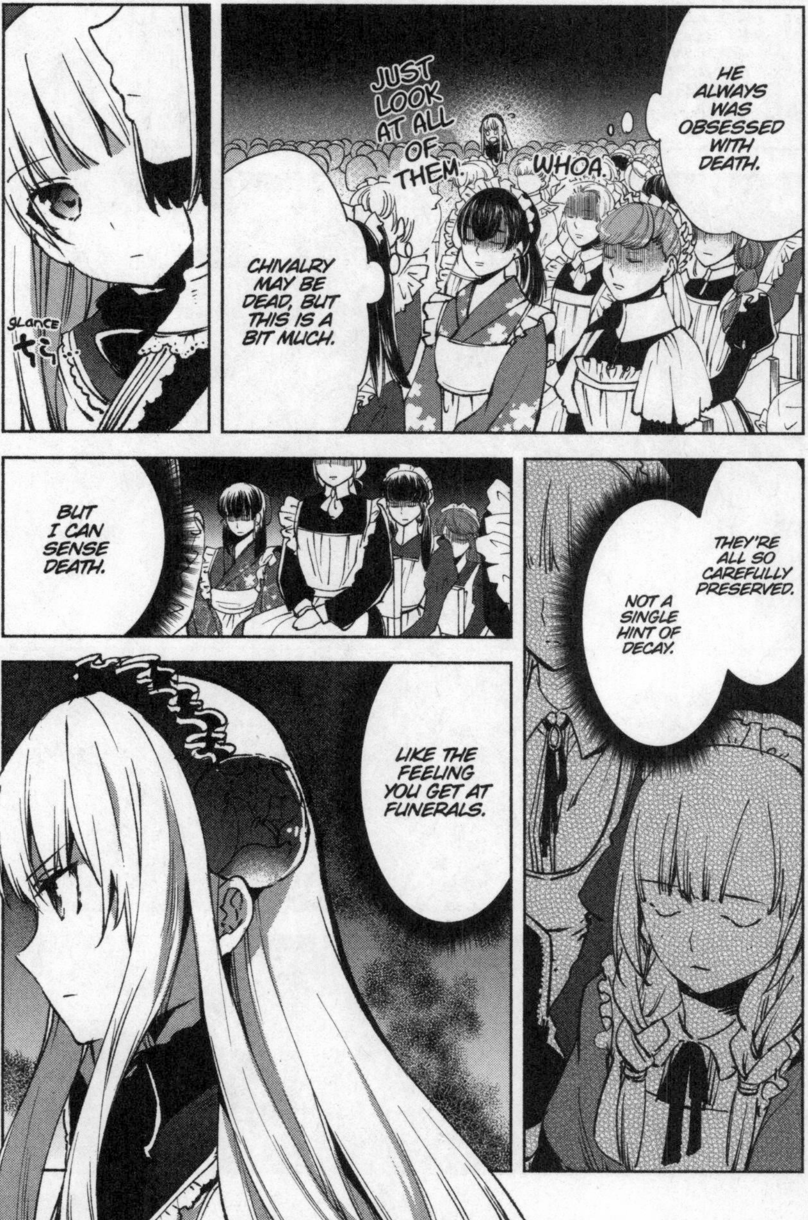
HE ALWAYS WAS OBSESSED WITH DEATH.
WHOA.
JUST LOOK AT ALL OF THEM.
CHIVALRY MAY BE DEAD, BUT THIS IS A BIT MUCH.
glance
THEY'RE ALL SO CAREFULLY PRESERVED.
NOT A SINGLE HINT OF DECAY.
BUT I CAN SENSE DEATH.
LIKE THE FEELING YOU GET AT FUNERALS.

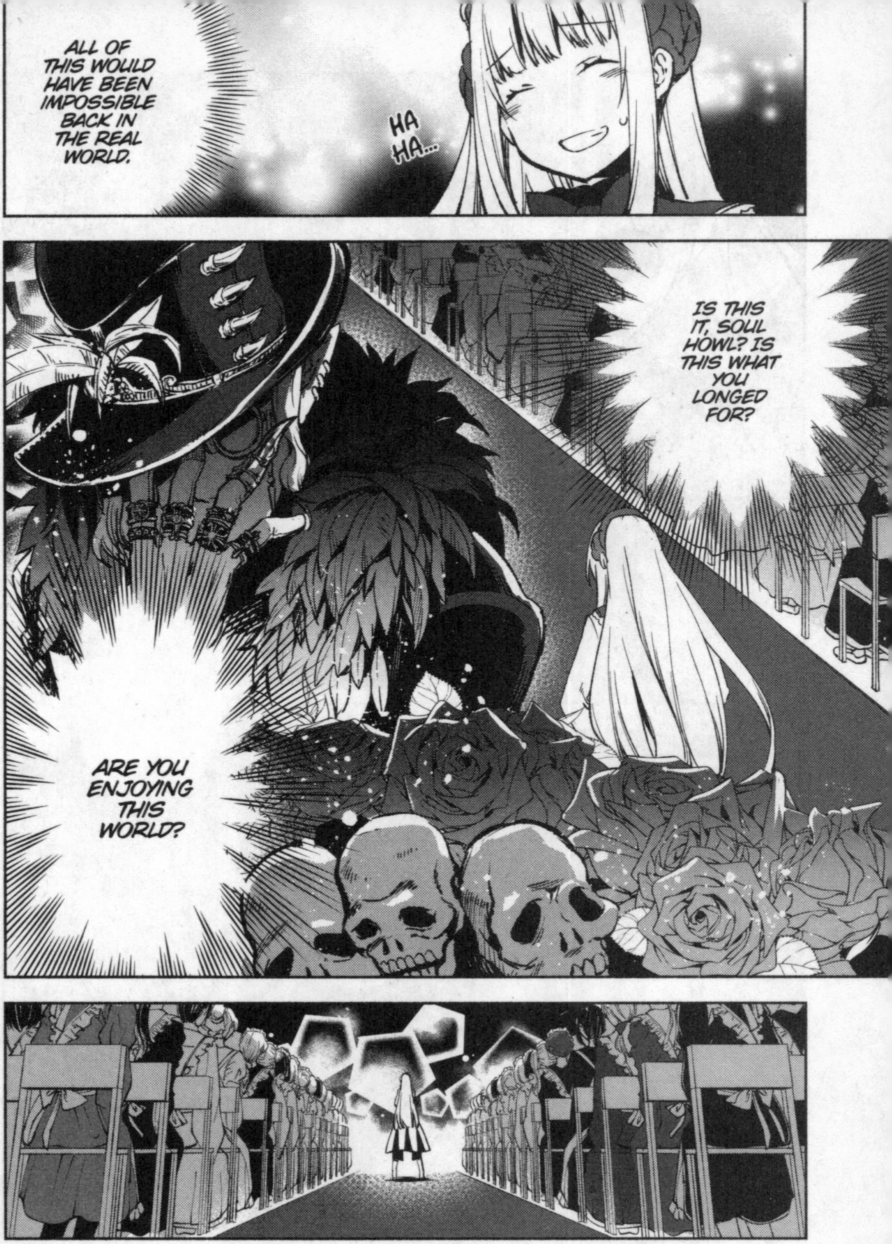
HA HA...
ALL OF THIS WOULD HAVE BEEN IMPOSSIBLE BACK IN THE REAL WORLD.
IS THIS IT, SOUL HOWL? IS THIS WHAT YOU LONGED FOR?
ARE YOU ENJOYING THIS WORLD?

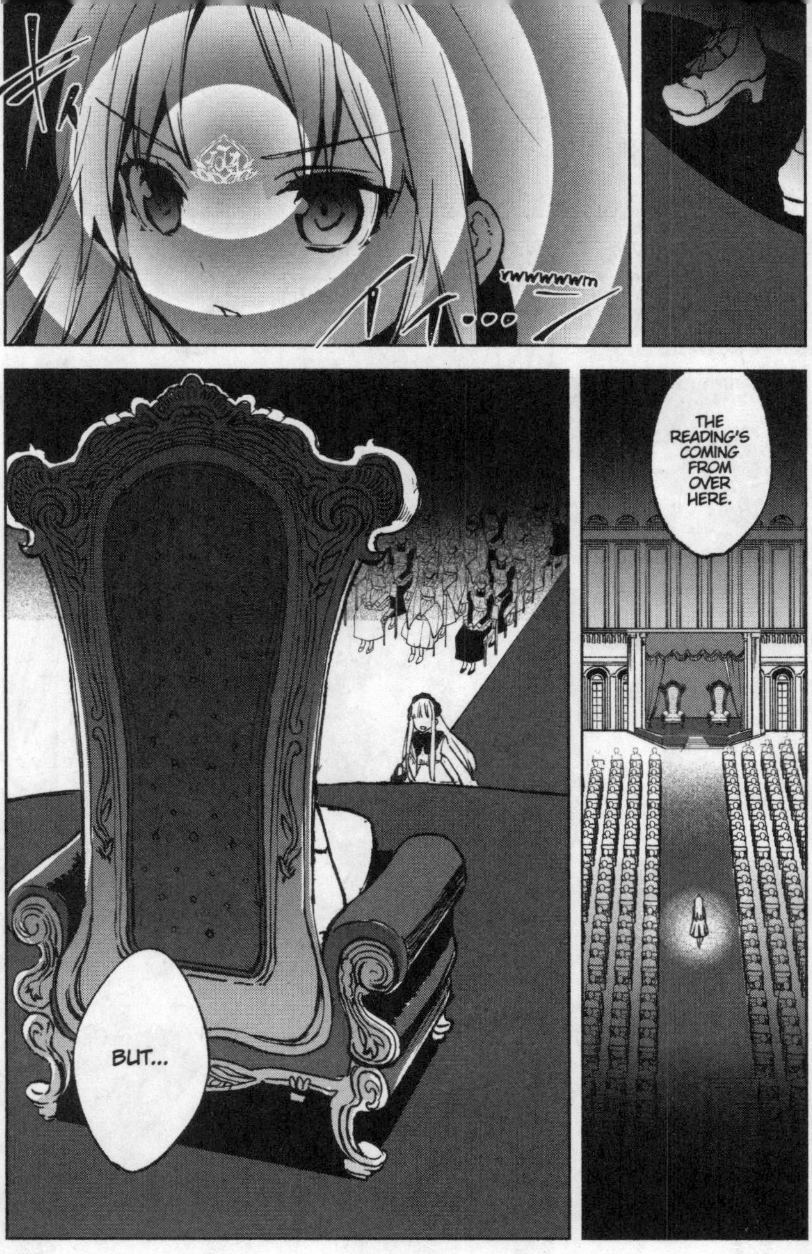
VWWWWWM
THE READING'S COMING FROM OVER HERE.
BUT...

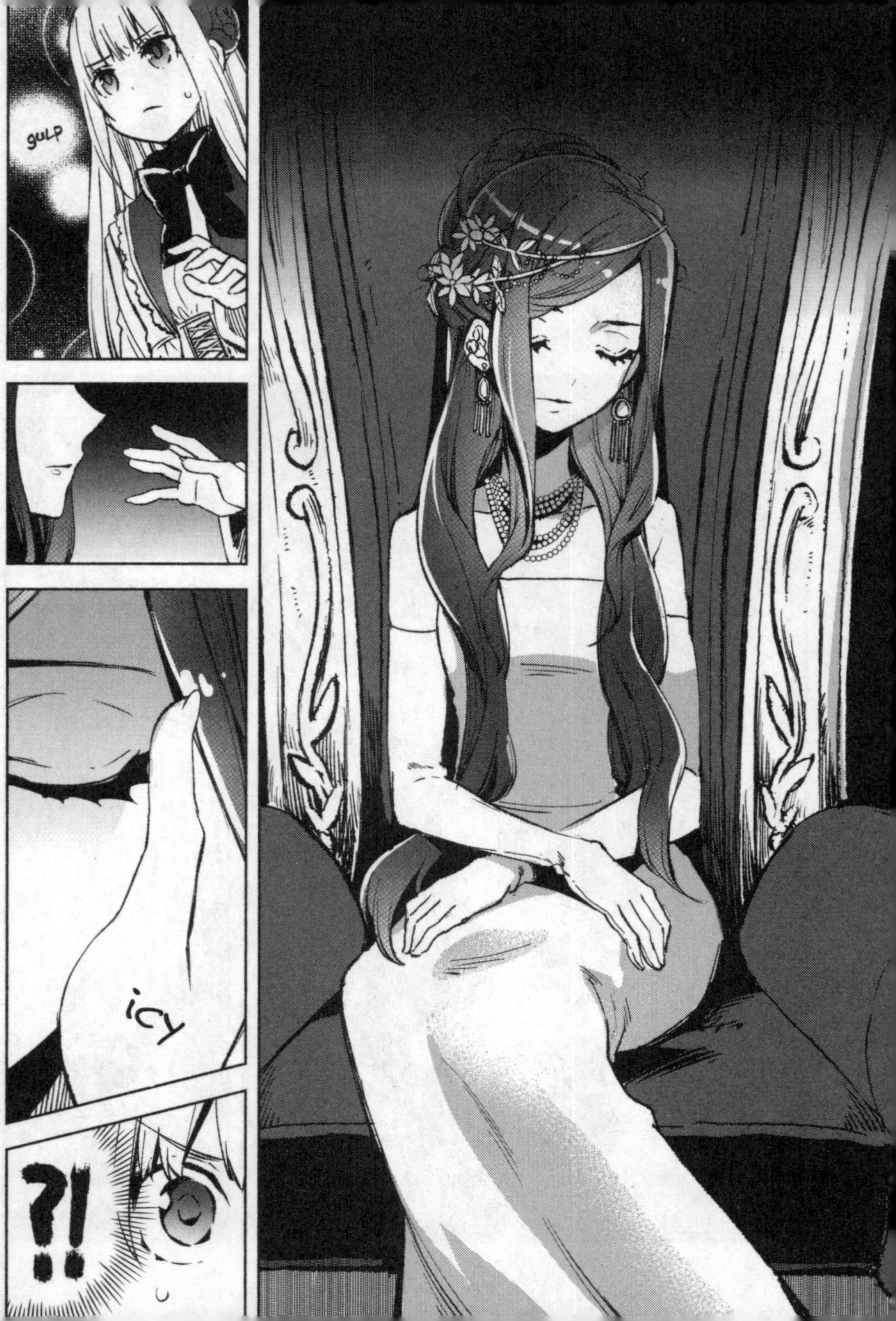
gulp
icy
?!!

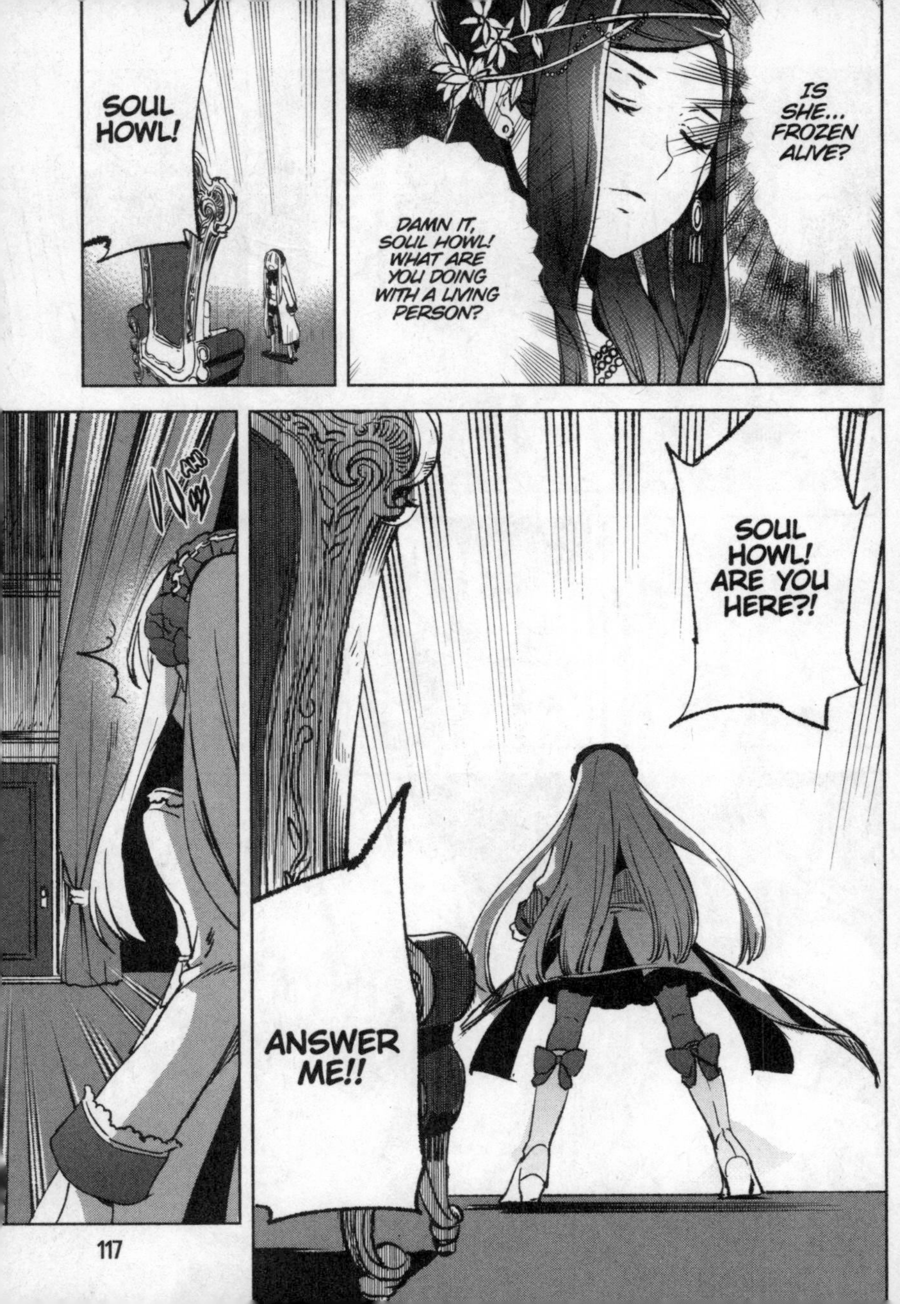
IS SHE... FROZEN ALIVE?
DAMN IT, SOUL HOWL! WHAT ARE YOU DOING WITH A LIVING PERSON?
SOUL HOWL!
SOUL HOWL! ARE YOU HERE?!
ANSWER ME!!

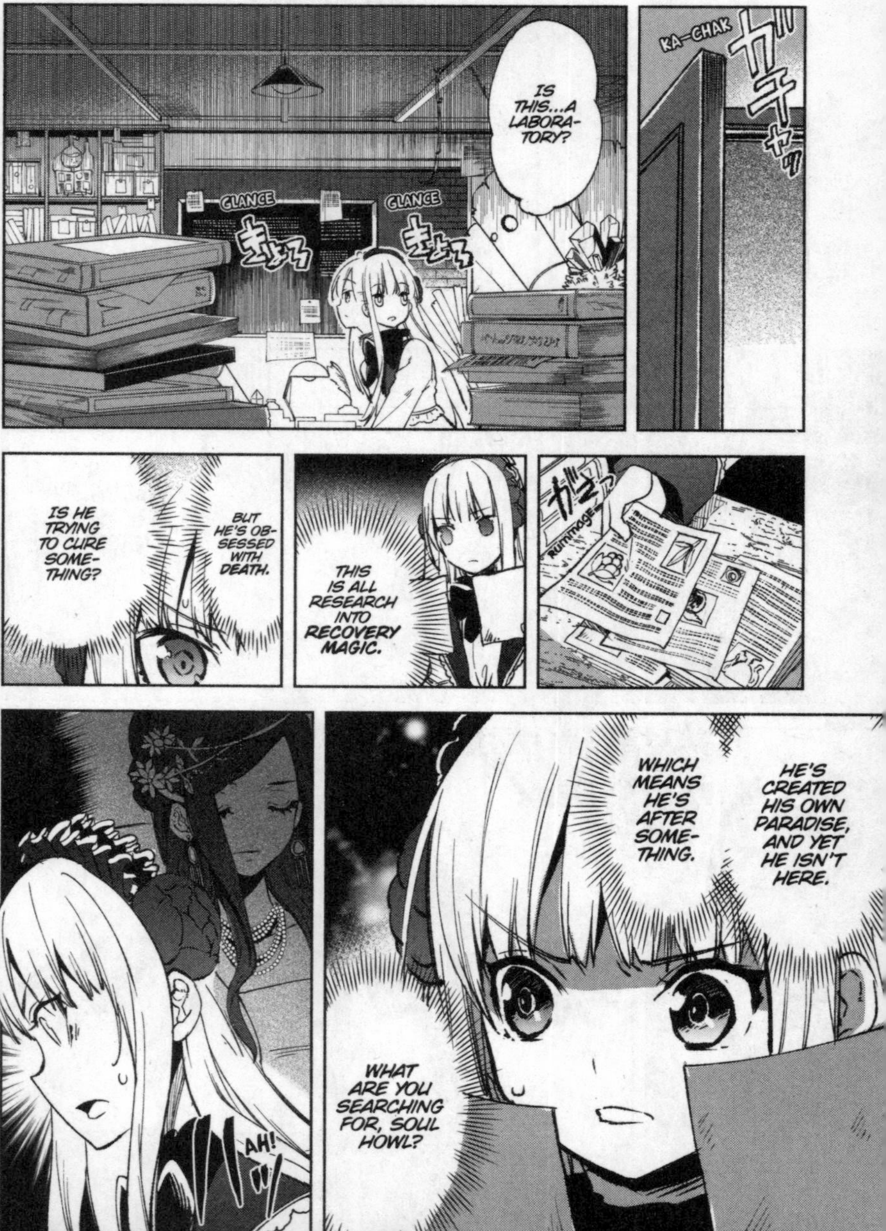
KA-CHAK
IS THIS...A LABORATORY?
GLANCE
GLANCE
RUMMAGE
THIS IS ALL RESEARCH INTO RECOVERY MAGIC.
IS HE TRYING TO CURE SOMETHING?
BUT HE'S OBSESSED WITH DEATH.
HE'S CREATED HIS OWN PARADISE, AND YET HE ISN'T HERE.
WHICH MEANS HE'S AFTER SOMETHING.
WHAT ARE YOU SEARCHING FOR, SOUL HOWL?
AH!

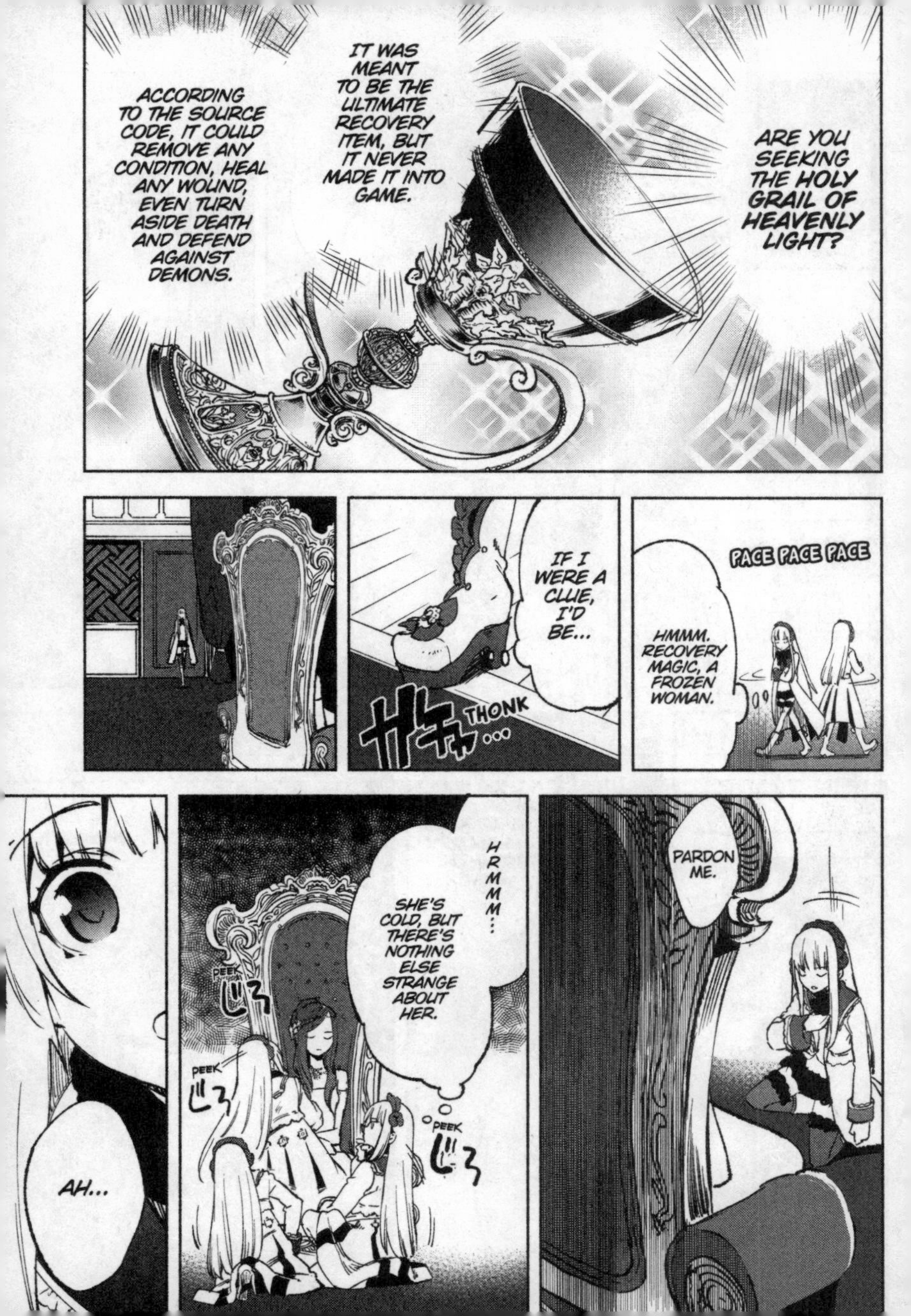
ARE YOU SEEKING THE HOLY GRAIL OF HEAVENLY LIGHT?
IT WAS MEANT TO BE THE ULTIMATE RECOVERY ITEM, BUT IT NEVER MADE IT INTO GAME.
ACCORDING TO THE SOURCE CODE, IT COULD REMOVE ANY CONDITION, HEAL ANY WOUND, EVEN TURN ASIDE DEATH AND DEFEND AGAINST DEMONS.
PACE PACE PACE
HMMM. RECOVERY MAGIC, A FROZEN WOMAN.
IF I WERE A CLUE, I'D BE...
THONK...
PARDON ME.
HRMMM...
SHE'S COLD, BUT THERE'S NOTHING ELSE STRANGE ABOUT HER.
PEEK
PEEK
PEEK
AH...

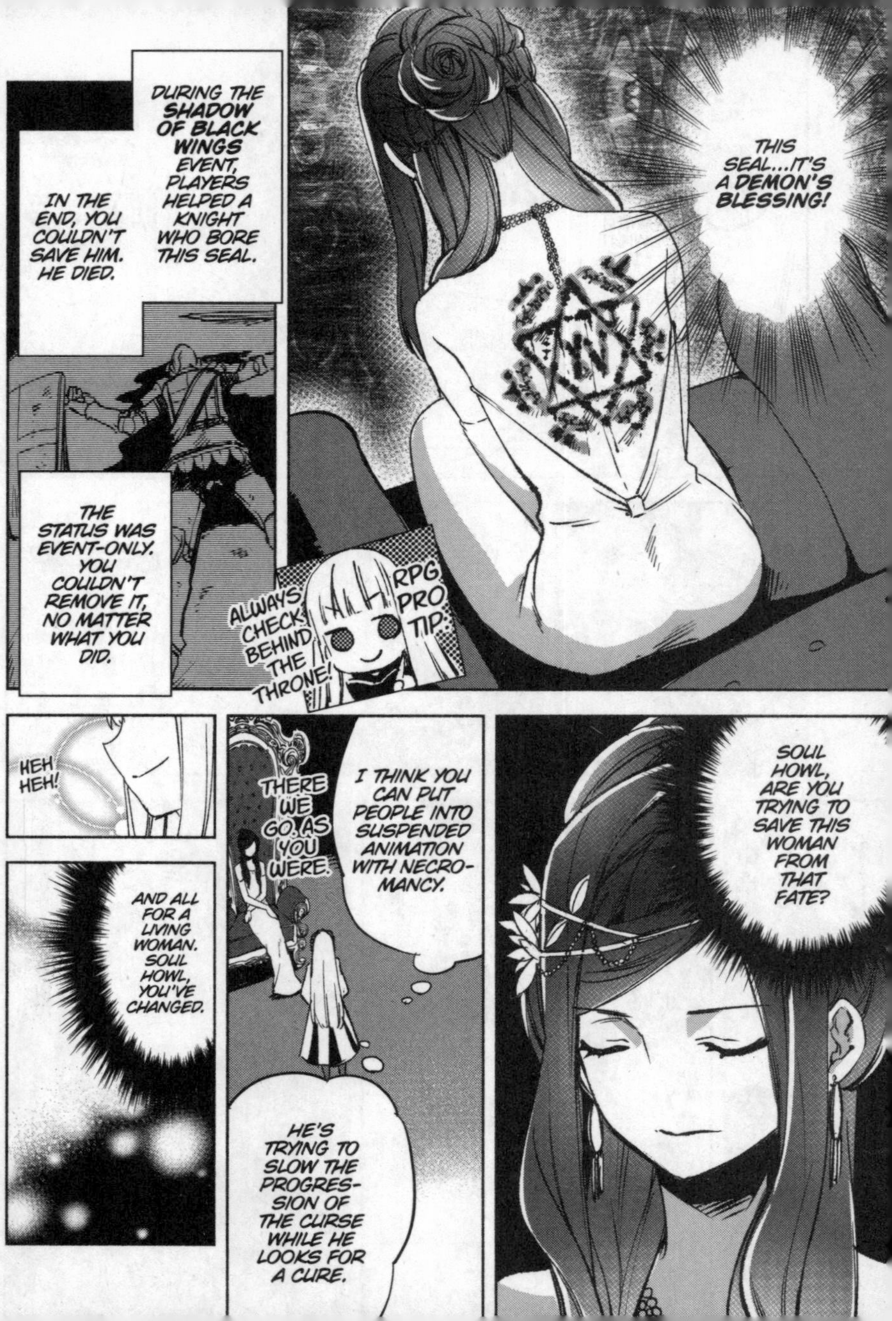
THIS SEAL...IT'S A DEMON'S BLESSING!
DURING THE SHADOW OF BLACK WINGS EVENT, PLAYERS HELPED A KNIGHT WHO BORE THIS SEAL.
IN THE END, YOU COULDN'T SAVE HIM. HE DIED.
RPG PRO TIP
ALWAYS CHECK BEHIND THE THRONE!
THE STATUS WAS EVENT-ONLY. YOU COULDN'T REMOVE IT, NO MATTER WHAT YOU DID.
SOUL HOWL, ARE YOU TRYING TO SAVE THIS WOMAN FROM THAT FATE?
I THINK YOU CAN PUT PEOPLE INTO SUSPENDED ANIMATION WITH NECRO-MANCY.
THERE WE GO. AS YOU WERE.
HE'S TRYING TO SLOW THE PROGRES-SION OF THE CURSE WHILE HE LOOKS FOR A CURE.
HEH HEH!
AND ALL FOR A LIVING WOMAN. SOUL HOWL, YOU'VE CHANGED.

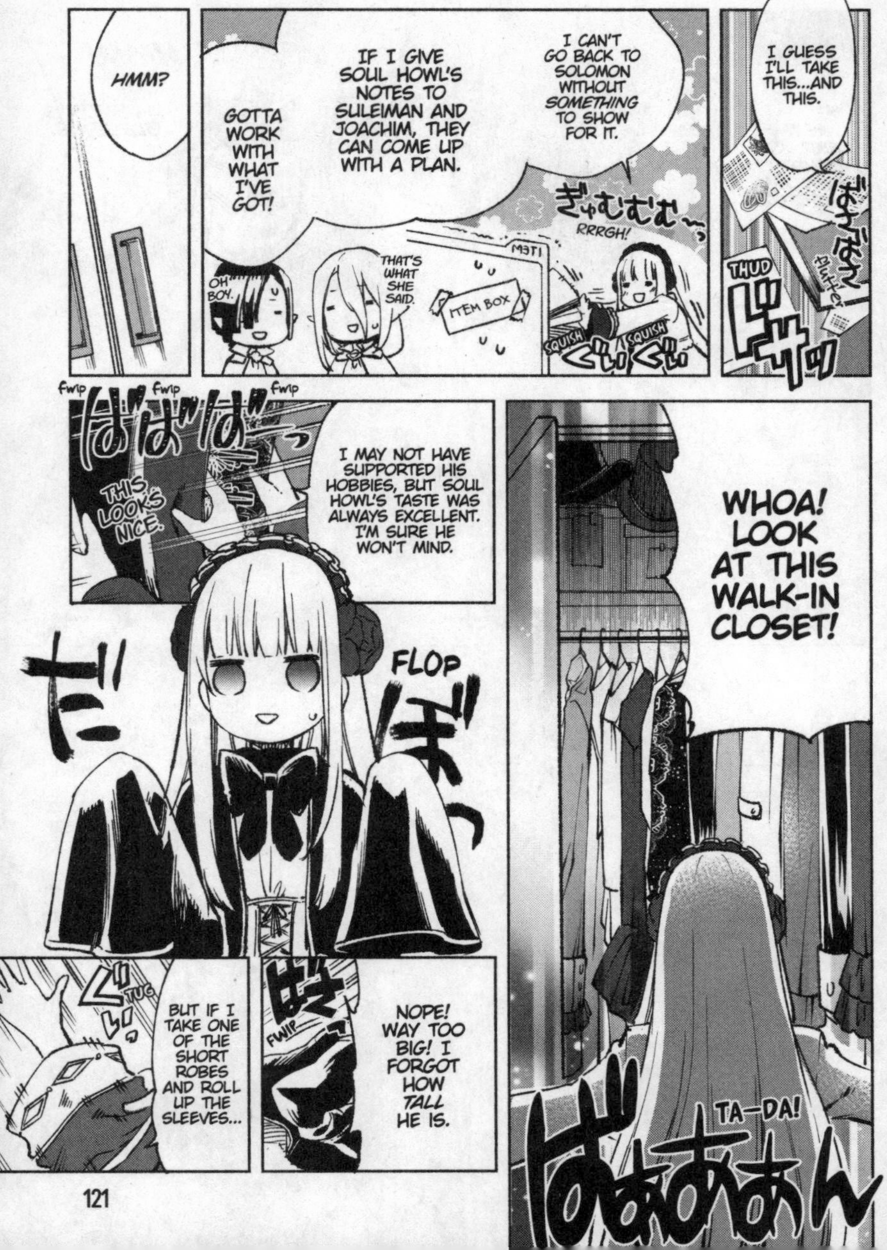
I GUESS I'LL TAKE THIS...AND THIS.
ばさばさ
THUD
ドサッ
I CAN'T GO BACK TO SOLOMON WITHOUT *SOMETHING* TO SHOW FOR IT.
ぎゅむむむ～
RRRGH!
ITEM BOX
SQUISH ぐい
SQUISH ぐい
IF I GIVE SOUL HOWL'S NOTES TO SULEIMAN AND JOACHIM, THEY CAN COME UP WITH A PLAN.
GOTTA WORK WITH WHAT I'VE GOT!
THAT'S WHAT SHE SAID.
OH BOY.
HMM?
WHOA! LOOK AT THIS WALK-IN CLOSET!
TA-DA!
ばあああん
fwip fwip fwip
ばばばっ
THIS LOOKS NICE.
I MAY NOT HAVE SUPPORTED HIS HOBBIES, BUT SOUL HOWL'S TASTE WAS ALWAYS EXCELLENT. I'M SURE HE WON'T MIND.
FLOP
だっ
ぼっ
NOPE! WAY TOO BIG! I FORGOT HOW *TALL* HE IS.
FWIP
ばさっ
BUT IF I TAKE ONE OF THE SHORT ROBES AND ROLL UP THE SLEEVES...
TUG
ぐいっ

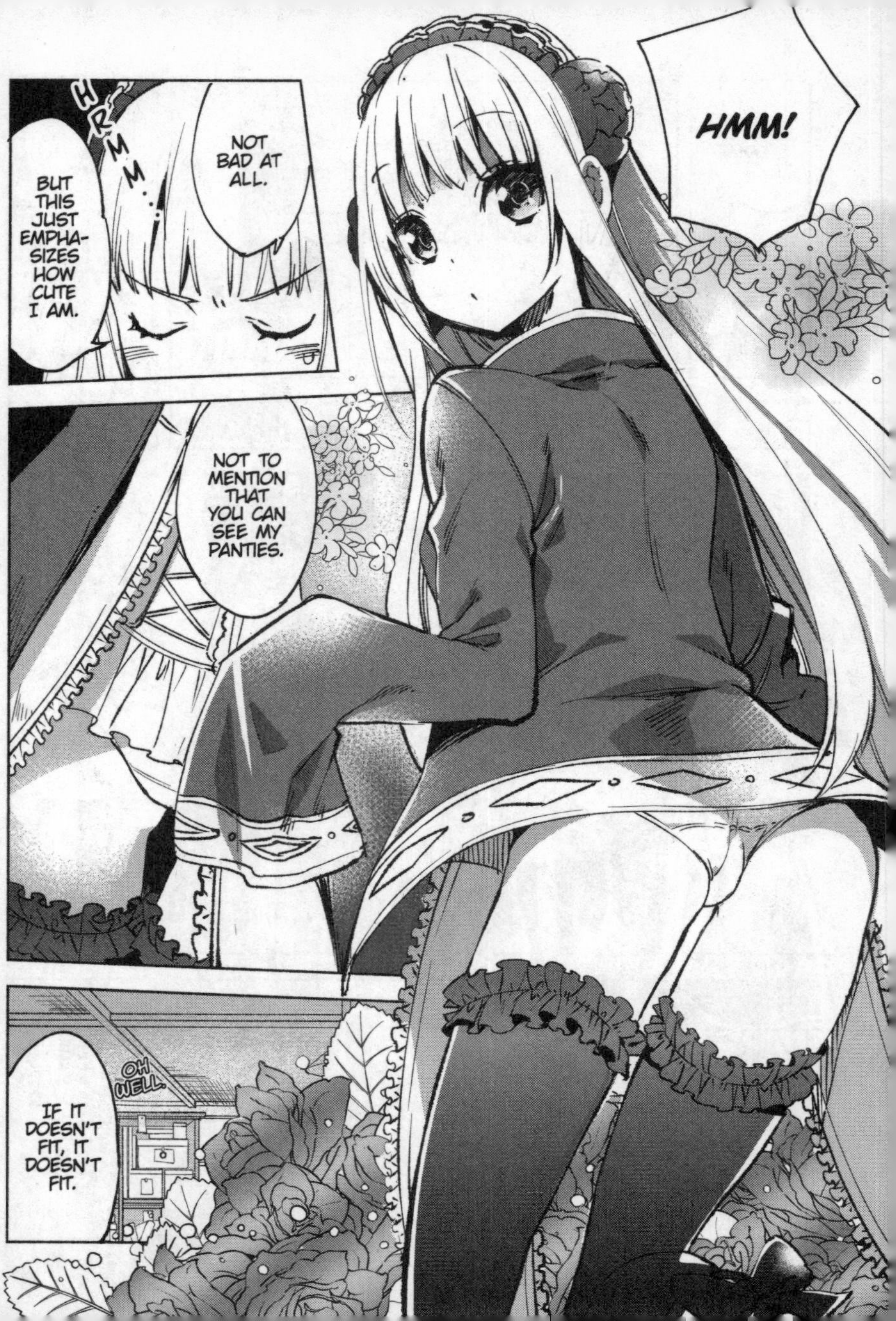
HMM!
NOT BAD AT ALL.
HRMM...
BUT THIS JUST EMPHASIZES HOW CUTE I AM.
NOT TO MENTION THAT YOU CAN SEE MY PANTIES.
OH WELL.
IF IT DOESN'T FIT, IT DOESN'T FIT.

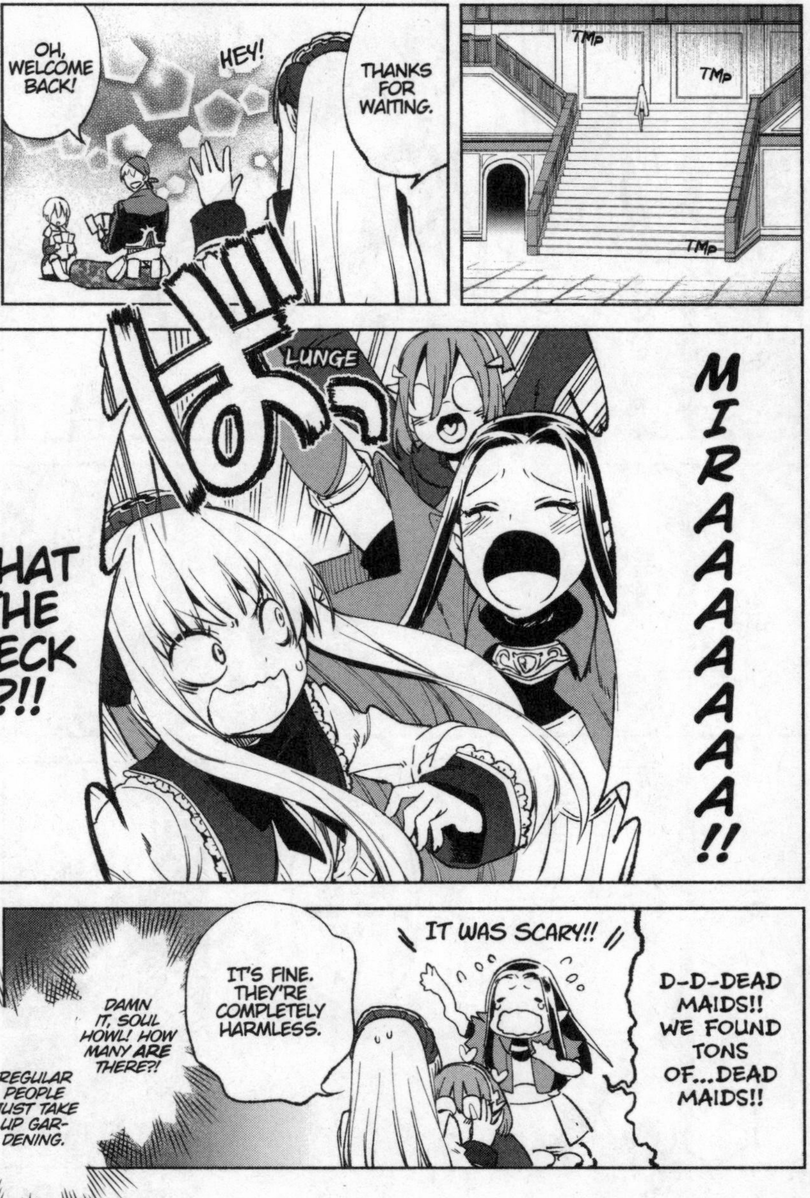
TMP
TMP
TMP
THANKS FOR WAITING.
HEY!
OH, WELCOME BACK!
MIRAAAAAAAAA!!
LUNGE
WHAT THE HECK?!!
D-D-DEAD MAIDS!! WE FOUND TONS OF...DEAD MAIDS!!
IT WAS SCARY!!
IT'S FINE. THEY'RE COMPLETELY HARMLESS.
DAMN IT, SOUL HOWL! HOW MANY ARE THERE?!
REGULAR PEOPLE JUST TAKE UP GAR-DENING.

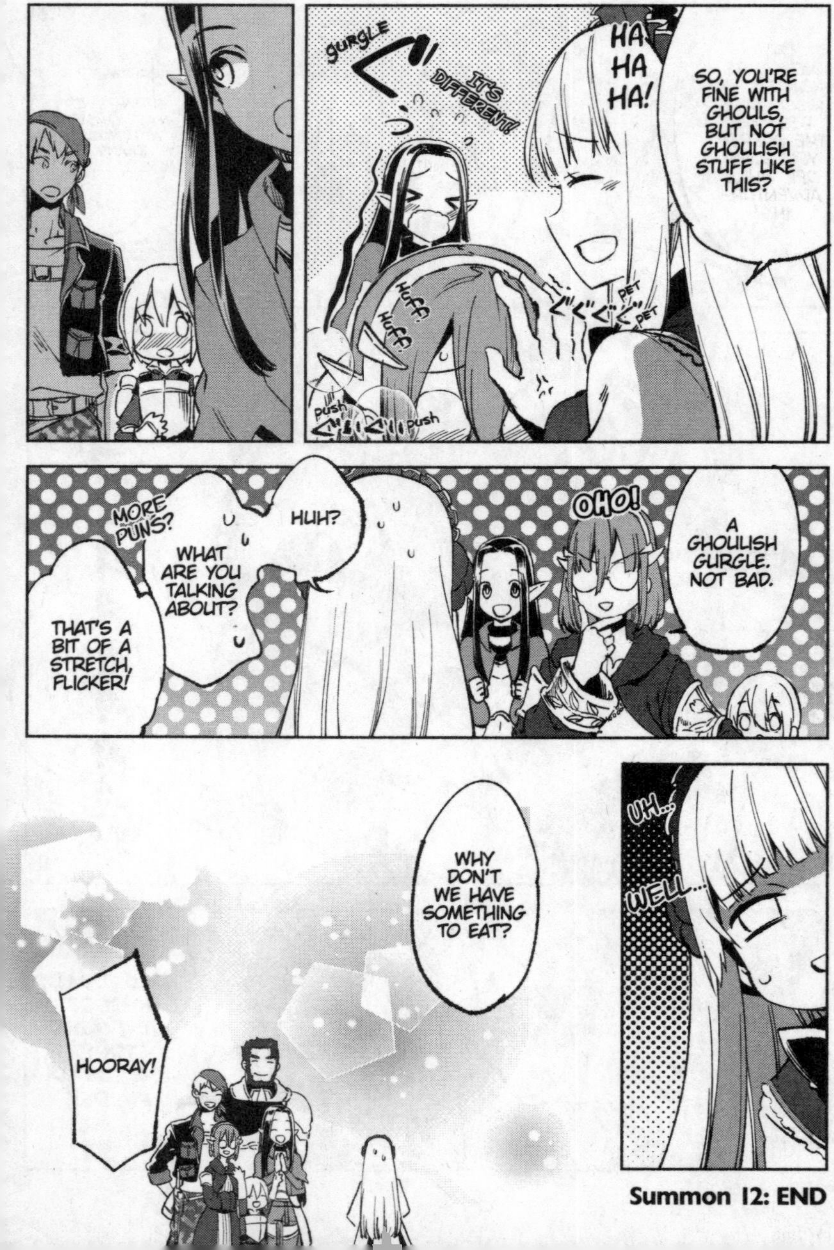
HA HA HA!
SO, YOU'RE FINE WITH GHOULS, BUT NOT GHOULISH STUFF LIKE THIS?
GURGLE
IT'S DIFFERENT!
PET PET
HUFF HUFF
PUSH PUSH
OHO!
A GHOULISH GURGLE. NOT BAD.
HUH?
WHAT ARE YOU TALKING ABOUT?
MORE PUNS?
THAT'S A BIT OF A STRETCH, FLICKER!
UH...
WELL...
WHY DON'T WE HAVE SOMETHING TO EAT?
HOORAY!

Summon 12: END

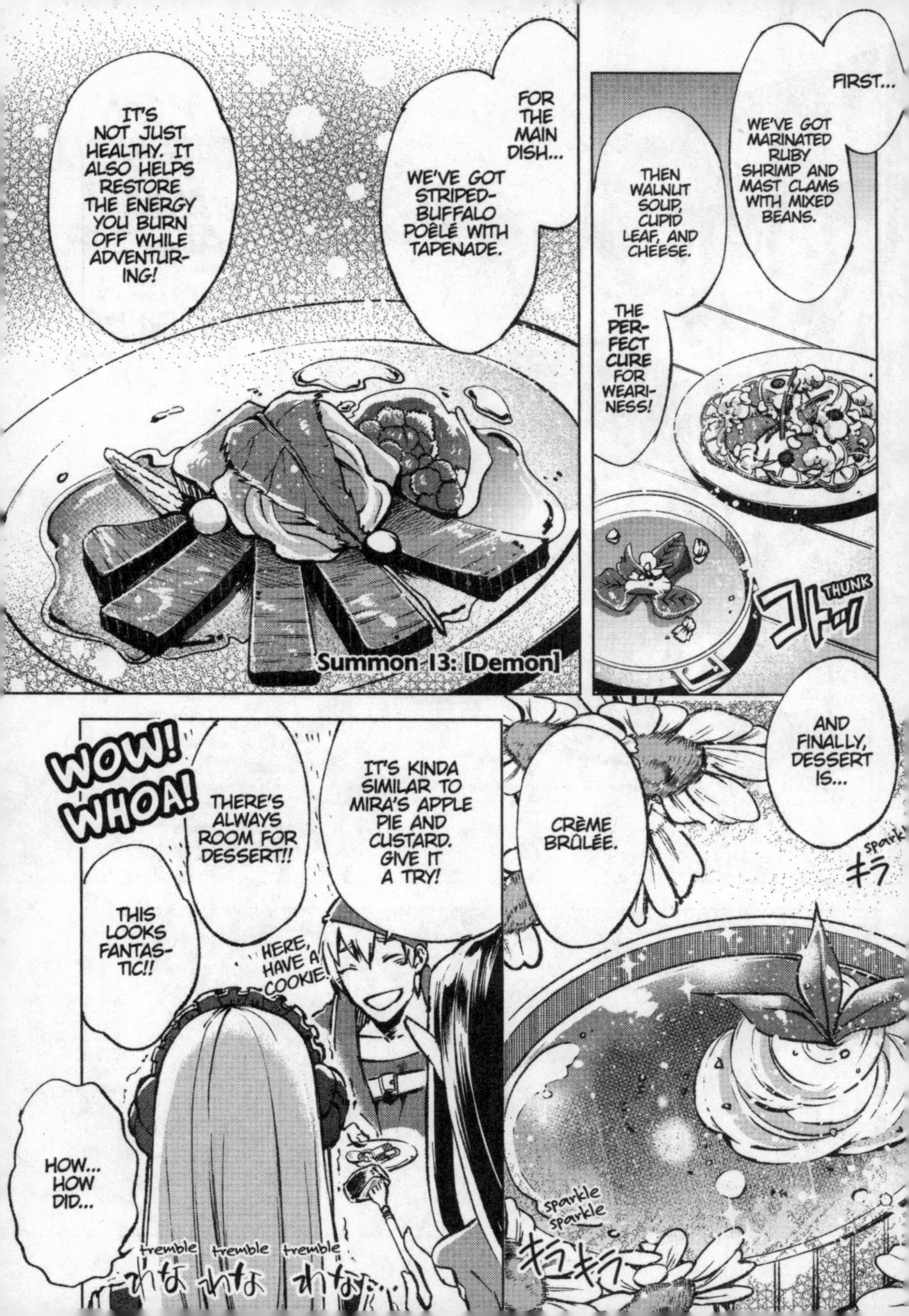
FIRST...
WE'VE GOT MARINATED RUBY SHRIMP AND MAST CLAMS WITH MIXED BEANS.
THEN WALNUT SOUP, CUPID LEAF, AND CHEESE.
THE PERFECT CURE FOR WEARINESS!
THUNK
FOR THE MAIN DISH...
WE'VE GOT STRIPED-BUFFALO POÊLÉ WITH TAPENADE.
IT'S NOT JUST HEALTHY. IT ALSO HELPS RESTORE THE ENERGY YOU BURN OFF WHILE ADVENTURING!
Summon 13: [Demon]
AND FINALLY, DESSERT IS...
CRÈME BRÛLÉE.
sparkle
sparkle sparkle
IT'S KINDA SIMILAR TO MIRA'S APPLE PIE AND CUSTARD. GIVE IT A TRY!
THERE'S ALWAYS ROOM FOR DESSERT!!
WOW! WHOA!
THIS LOOKS FANTASTIC!!
HERE, HAVE A COOKIE.
HOW... HOW DID...
tremble tremble tremble

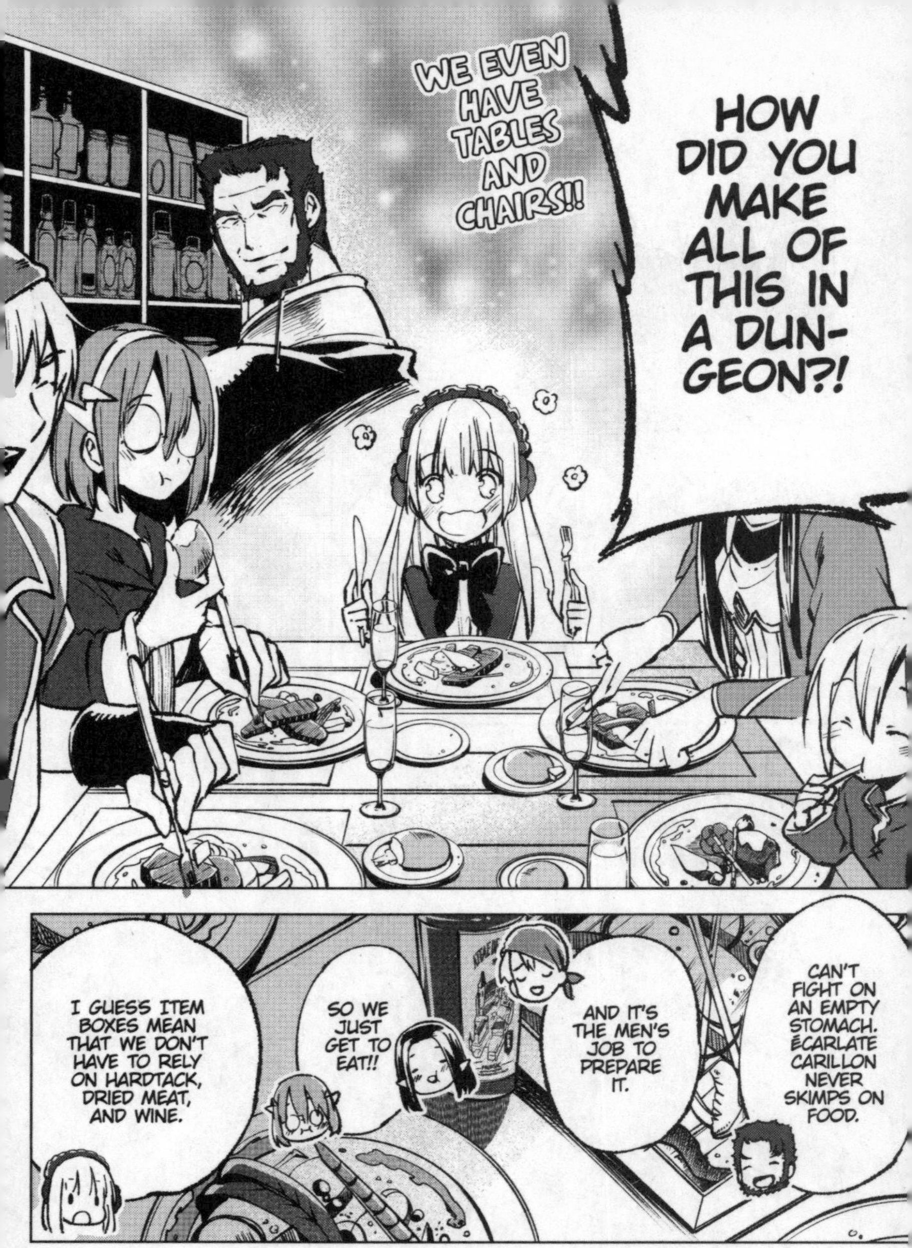
HOW DID YOU MAKE ALL OF THIS IN A DUN-GEON?!
WE EVEN HAVE TABLES AND CHAIRS!!
CAN'T FIGHT ON AN EMPTY STOMACH. ÉCARLATE CARILLON NEVER SKIMPS ON FOOD.
AND IT'S THE MEN'S JOB TO PREPARE IT.
SO WE JUST GET TO EAT!!
I GUESS ITEM BOXES MEAN THAT WE DON'T HAVE TO RELY ON HARDTACK, DRIED MEAT, AND WINE.

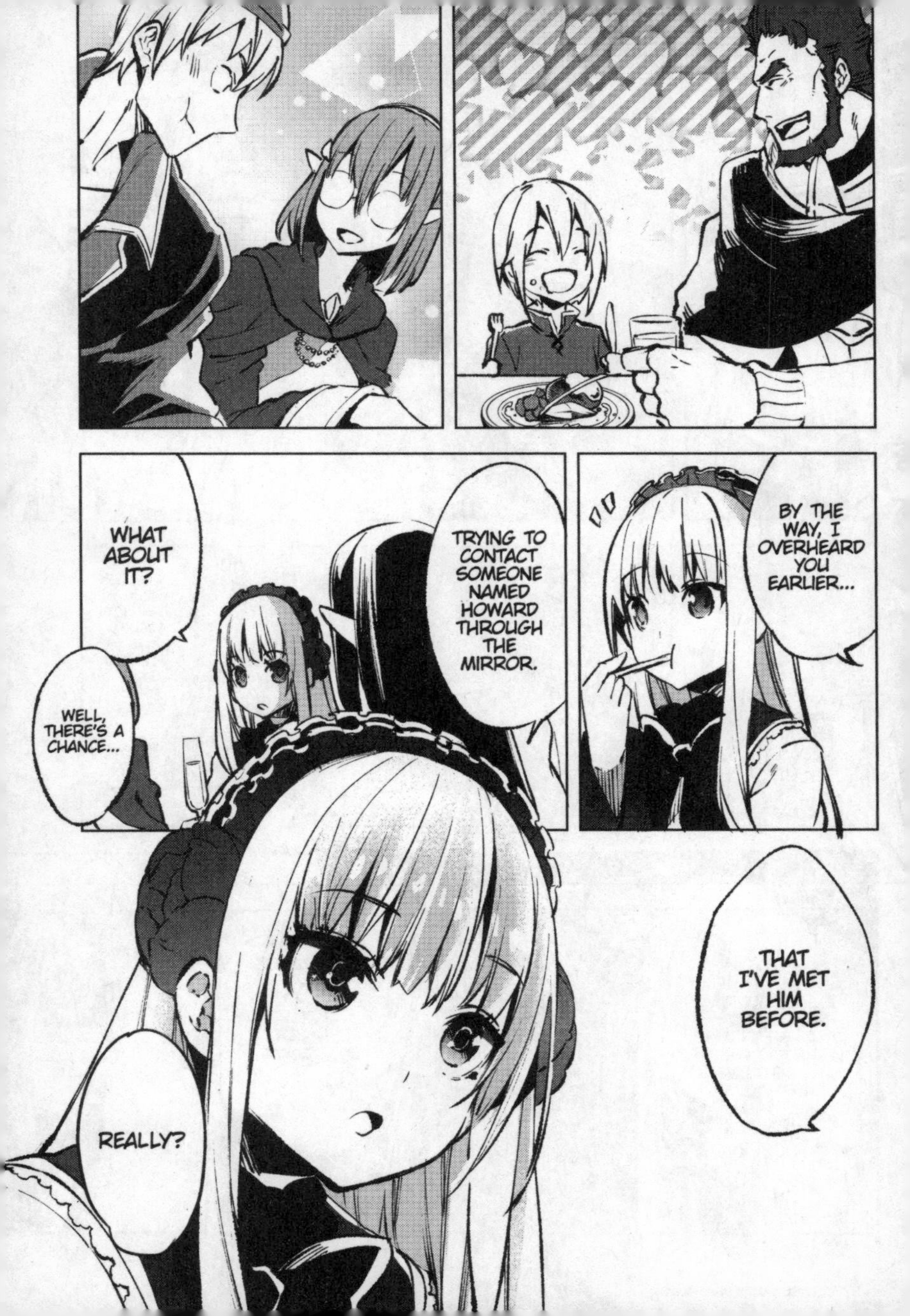
BY THE WAY, I OVERHEARD YOU EARLIER...
TRYING TO CONTACT SOMEONE NAMED HOWARD THROUGH THE MIRROR.
WHAT ABOUT IT?
WELL, THERE'S A CHANCE...
THAT I'VE MET HIM BEFORE.
REALLY?

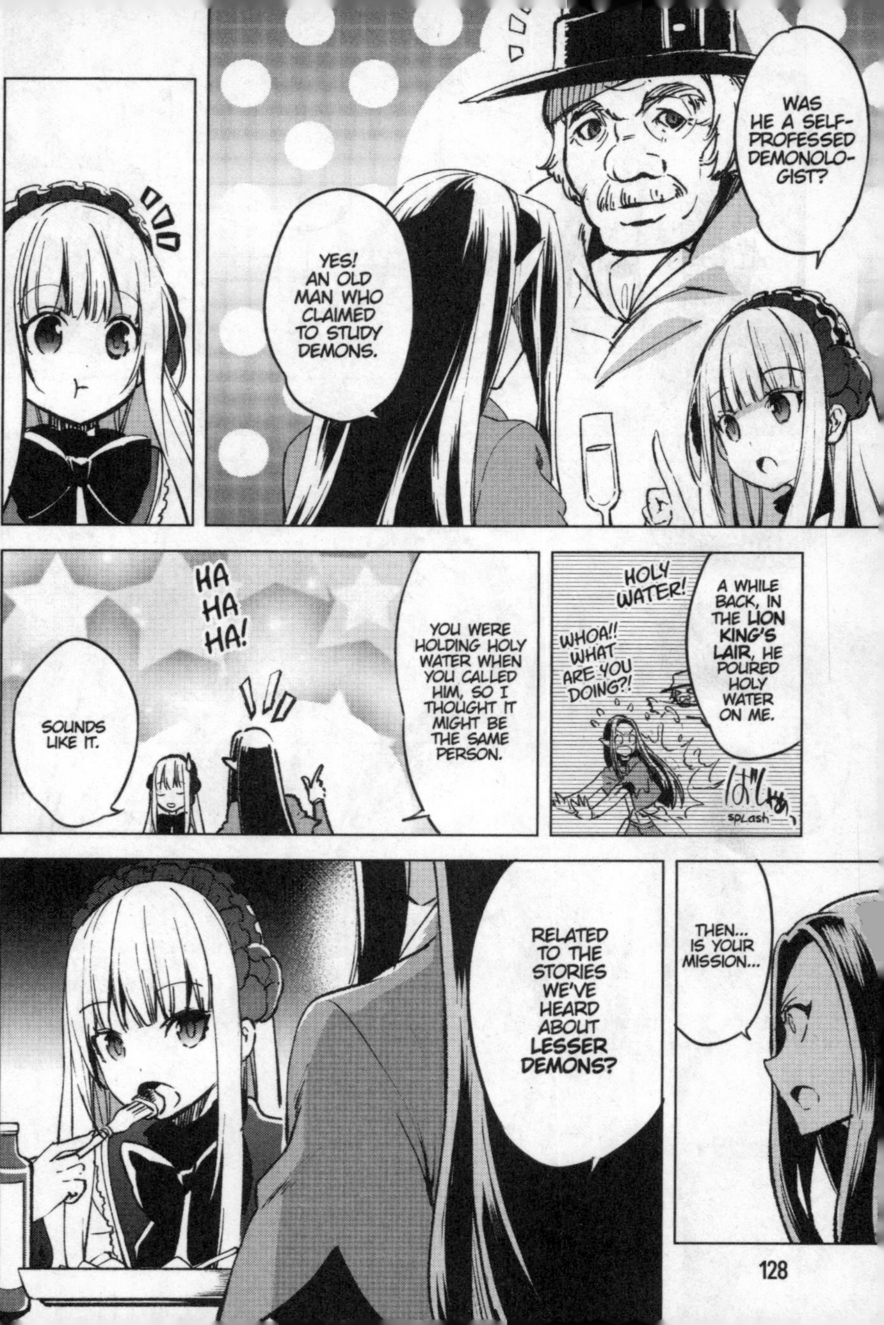

WAS HE A SELF-PROFESSED DEMONOLOGIST?
YES! AN OLD MAN WHO CLAIMED TO STUDY DEMONS.
A WHILE BACK, IN THE LION KING'S LAIR, HE POURED HOLY WATER ON ME.
HOLY WATER!
WHOA!! WHAT ARE YOU DOING?!
SPLASH
YOU WERE HOLDING HOLY WATER WHEN YOU CALLED HIM, SO I THOUGHT IT MIGHT BE THE SAME PERSON.
HA HA HA!
SOUNDS LIKE IT.
THEN... IS YOUR MISSION...
RELATED TO THE STORIES WE'VE HEARD ABOUT LESSER DEMONS?

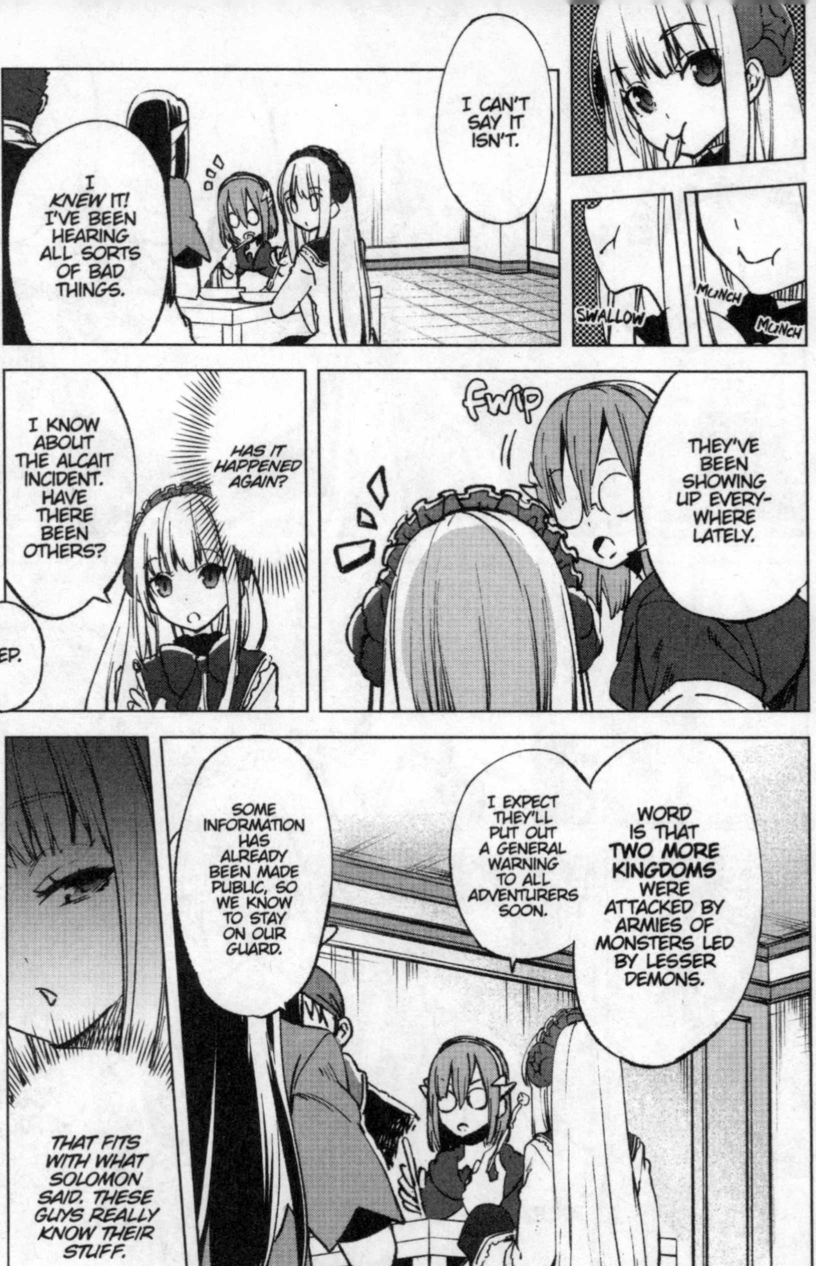
SWALLOW
MUNCH
MUNCH
I CAN'T SAY IT ISN'T.
I KNEW IT! I'VE BEEN HEARING ALL SORTS OF BAD THINGS.
fwip
THEY'VE BEEN SHOWING UP EVERYWHERE LATELY.
HAS IT HAPPENED AGAIN?
I KNOW ABOUT THE ALCAIT INCIDENT. HAVE THERE BEEN OTHERS?
YEP.
WORD IS THAT TWO MORE KINGDOMS WERE ATTACKED BY ARMIES OF MONSTERS LED BY LESSER DEMONS.
I EXPECT THEY'LL PUT OUT A GENERAL WARNING TO ALL ADVENTURERS SOON.
SOME INFORMATION HAS ALREADY BEEN MADE PUBLIC, SO WE KNOW TO STAY ON OUR GUARD.
THAT FITS WITH WHAT SOLOMON SAID. THESE GUYS REALLY KNOW THEIR STUFF.

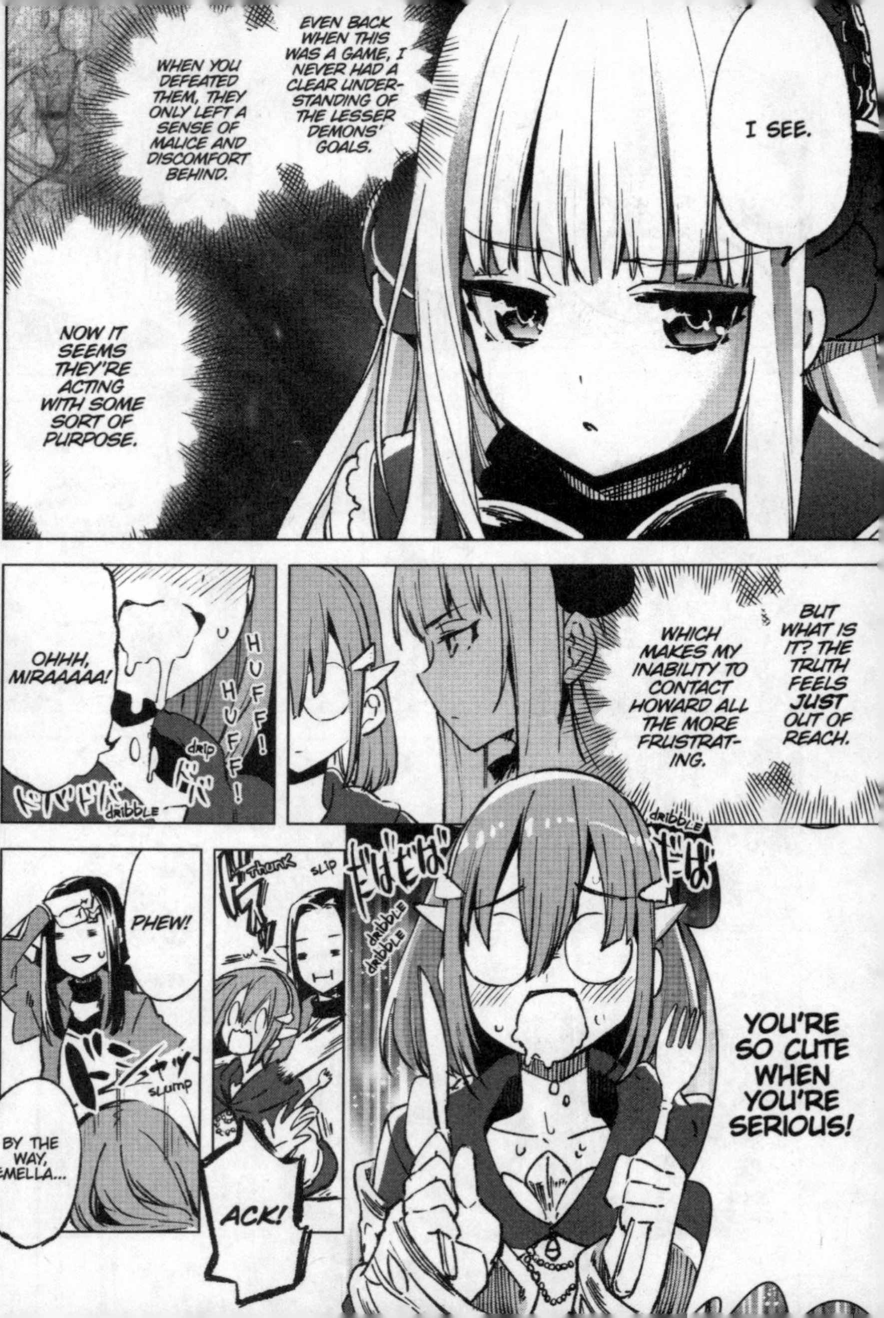

I SEE.
EVEN BACK WHEN THIS WAS A GAME, I NEVER HAD A CLEAR UNDERSTANDING OF THE LESSER DEMONS' GOALS.
WHEN YOU DEFEATED THEM, THEY ONLY LEFT A SENSE OF MALICE AND DISCOMFORT BEHIND.
NOW IT SEEMS THEY'RE ACTING WITH SOME SORT OF PURPOSE.
BUT WHAT IS IT? THE TRUTH FEELS JUST OUT OF REACH.
WHICH MAKES MY INABILITY TO CONTACT HOWARD ALL THE MORE FRUSTRATING.
OHHH, MIRAAAAA!
HUFF HUFF!
drip
dribble
dribble
dribble dribble
YOU'RE SO CUTE WHEN YOU'RE SERIOUS!
thunk
slip
ACK!
PHEW!
slump
BY THE WAY, EMELLA...

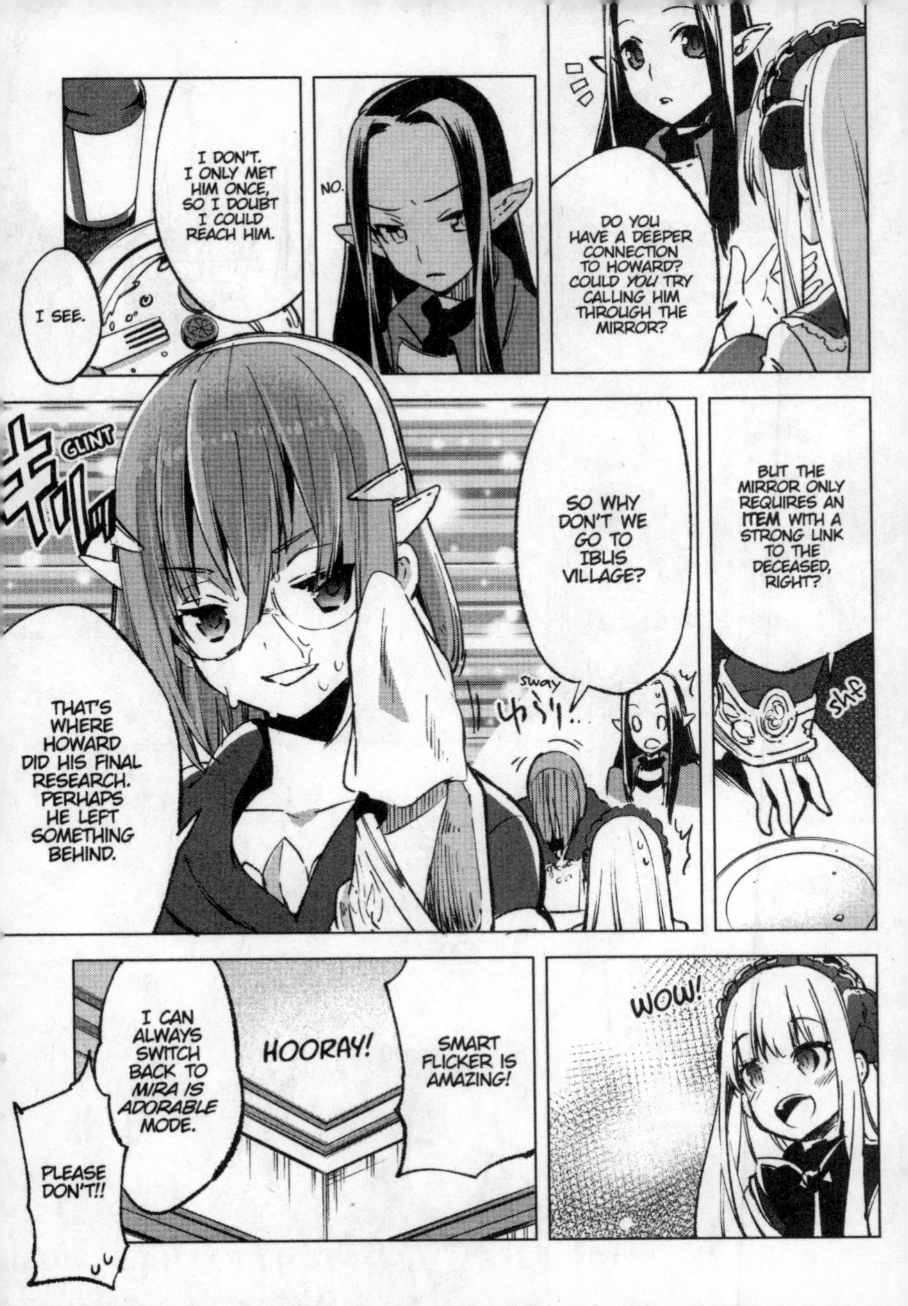
DO YOU HAVE A DEEPER CONNECTION TO HOWARD? COULD YOU TRY CALLING HIM THROUGH THE MIRROR?
NO.
I DON'T. I ONLY MET HIM ONCE, SO I DOUBT I COULD REACH HIM.
I SEE.
BUT THE MIRROR ONLY REQUIRES AN ITEM WITH A STRONG LINK TO THE DECEASED, RIGHT?
shf
SO WHY DON'T WE GO TO IBLIS VILLAGE?
sway
GLINT
THAT'S WHERE HOWARD DID HIS FINAL RESEARCH. PERHAPS HE LEFT SOMETHING BEHIND.
WOW!
SMART FLICKER IS AMAZING!
HOORAY!
I CAN ALWAYS SWITCH BACK TO *MIRA IS ADORABLE* MODE.
PLEASE DON'T!!

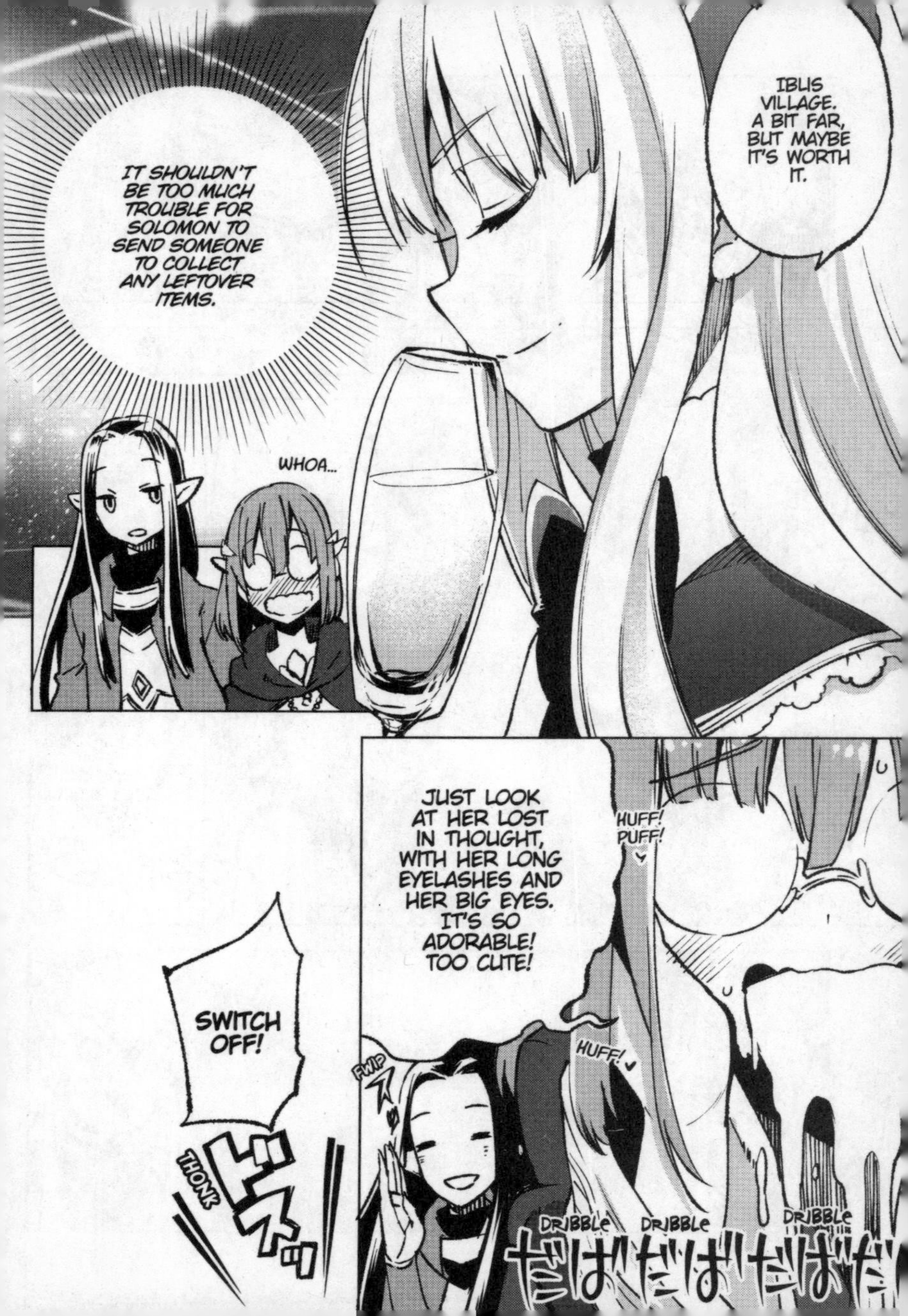
IBLIS VILLAGE. A BIT FAR, BUT MAYBE IT'S WORTH IT.
IT SHOULDN'T BE TOO MUCH TROUBLE FOR SOLOMON TO SEND SOMEONE TO COLLECT ANY LEFTOVER ITEMS.
WHOA...
JUST LOOK AT HER LOST IN THOUGHT, WITH HER LONG EYELASHES AND HER BIG EYES. IT'S SO ADORABLE! TOO CUTE!
HUFF! PUFF!
HUFF!
FWIP
DRIBBLE
DRIBBLE
DRIBBLE
SWITCH OFF!
THONK

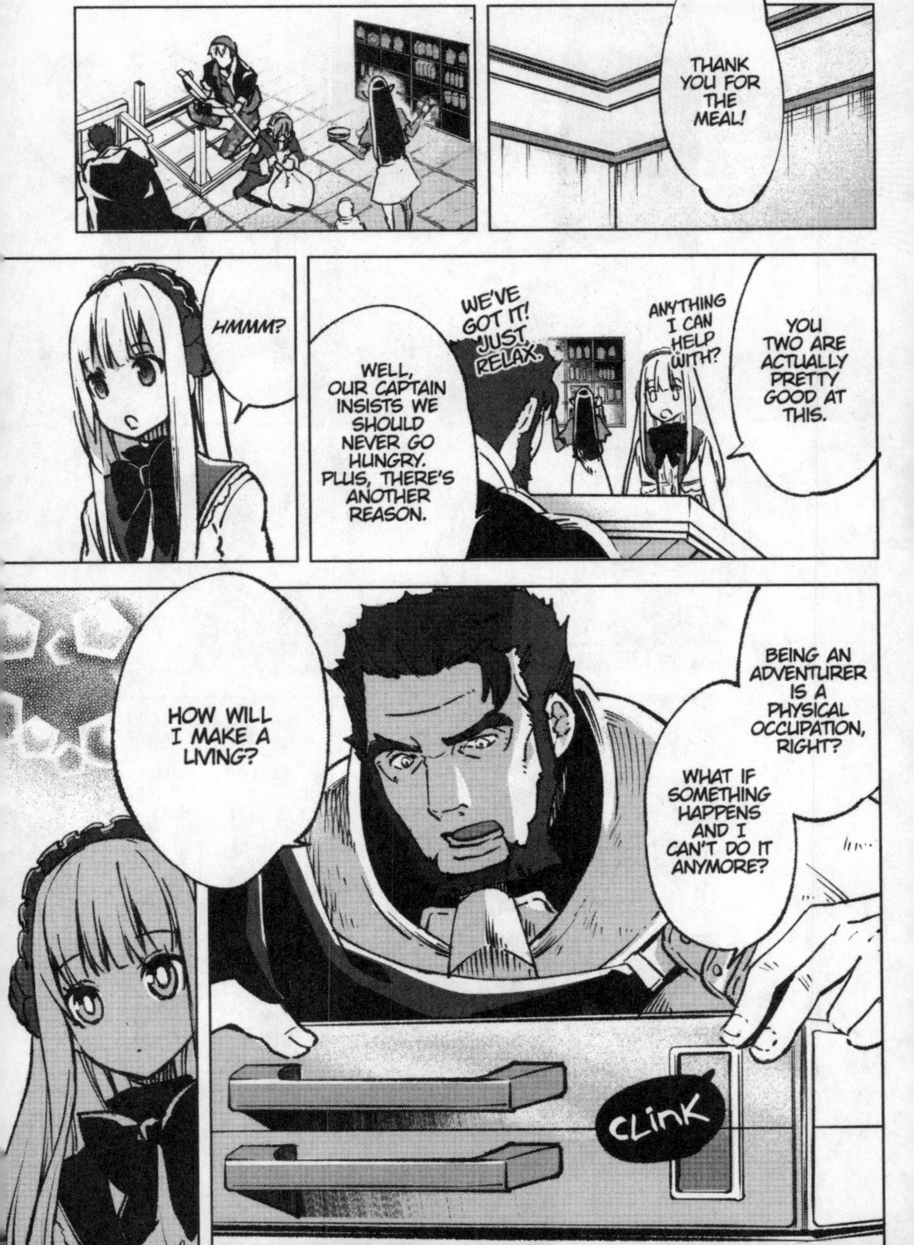
THANK YOU FOR THE MEAL!
YOU TWO ARE ACTUALLY PRETTY GOOD AT THIS.
ANYTHING I CAN HELP WITH?
WE'VE GOT IT! JUST RELAX.
WELL, OUR CAPTAIN INSISTS WE SHOULD NEVER GO HUNGRY. PLUS, THERE'S ANOTHER REASON.
HMMM?
BEING AN ADVENTURER IS A PHYSICAL OCCUPATION, RIGHT?
WHAT IF SOMETHING HAPPENS AND I CAN'T DO IT ANYMORE?
HOW WILL I MAKE A LIVING?
CLink

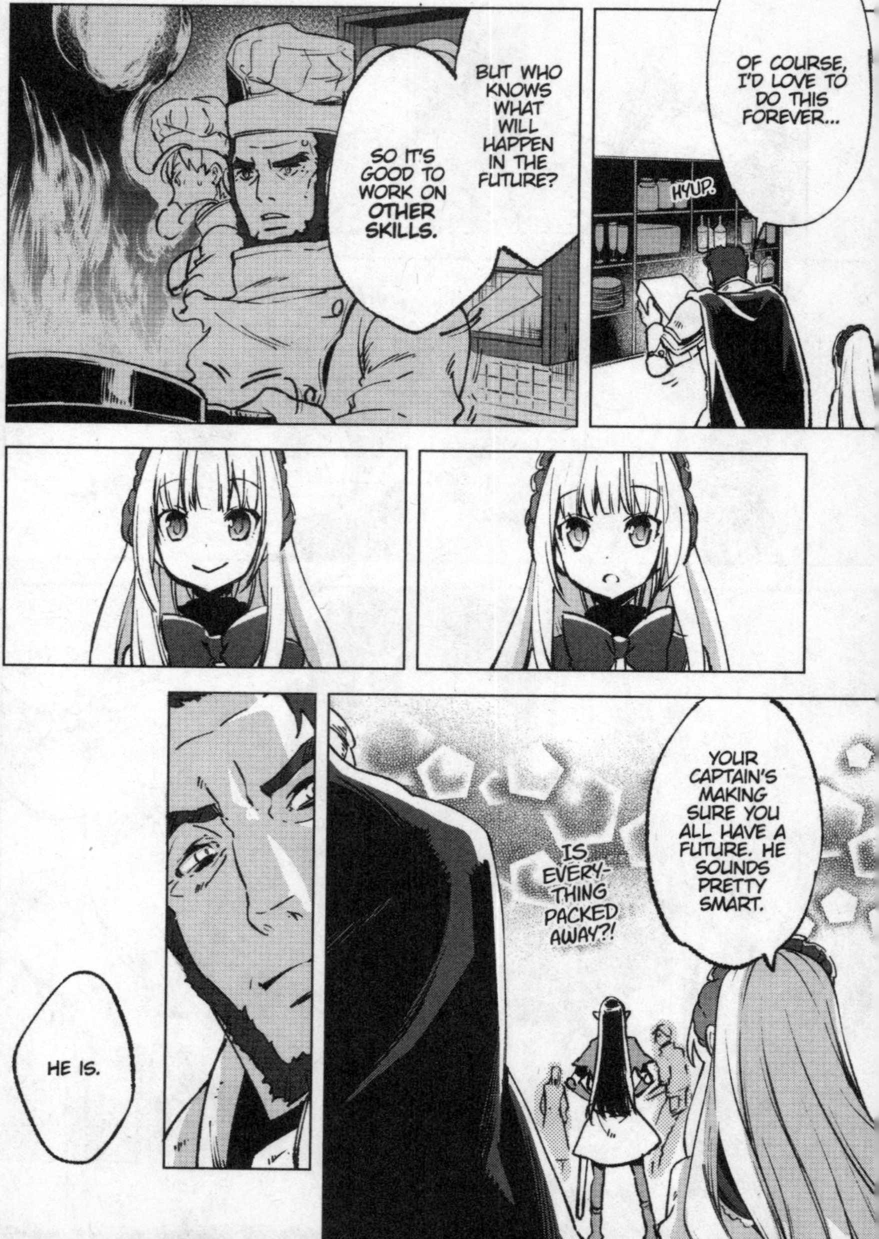
OF COURSE, I'D LOVE TO DO THIS FOREVER...
HYUP.
BUT WHO KNOWS WHAT WILL HAPPEN IN THE FUTURE?
SO IT'S GOOD TO WORK ON OTHER SKILLS.
YOUR CAPTAIN'S MAKING SURE YOU ALL HAVE A FUTURE. HE SOUNDS PRETTY SMART.
IS EVERY-THING PACKED AWAY?!
HE IS.

I GUESS IT'S TIME TO HEAD BACK.

SOUNDS GOOD.

LET'S BE OFF!

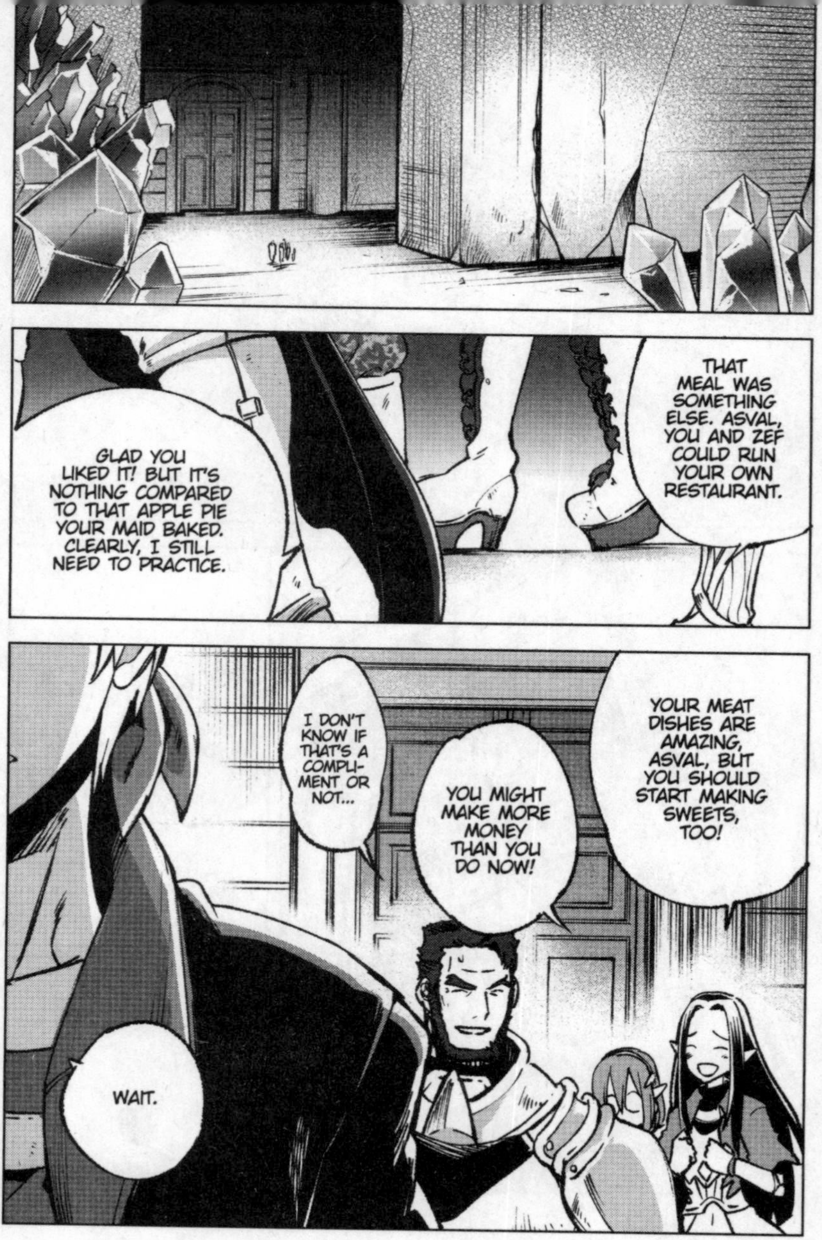
THAT MEAL WAS SOMETHING ELSE. ASVAL, YOU AND ZEF COULD RUN YOUR OWN RESTAURANT.
GLAD YOU LIKED IT! BUT IT'S NOTHING COMPARED TO THAT APPLE PIE YOUR MAID BAKED. CLEARLY, I STILL NEED TO PRACTICE.
YOUR MEAT DISHES ARE AMAZING, ASVAL, BUT YOU SHOULD START MAKING SWEETS, TOO!
YOU MIGHT MAKE MORE MONEY THAN YOU DO NOW!
I DON'T KNOW IF THAT'S A COMPLI-MENT OR NOT...
WAIT.

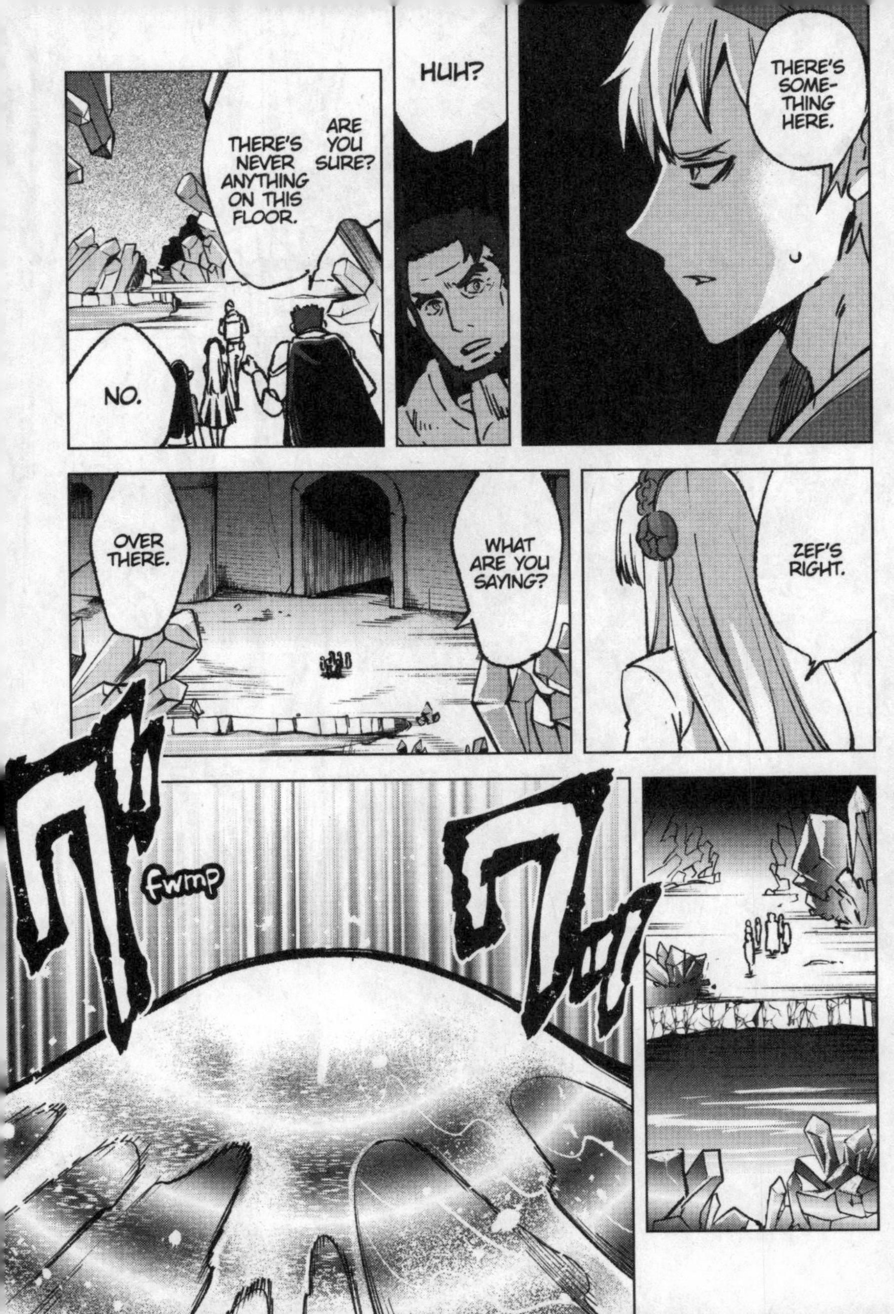
THERE'S SOMETHING HERE.
HUH?
ARE YOU SURE?
THERE'S NEVER ANYTHING ON THIS FLOOR.
NO.
ZEF'S RIGHT.
WHAT ARE YOU SAYING?
OVER THERE.
fwmp

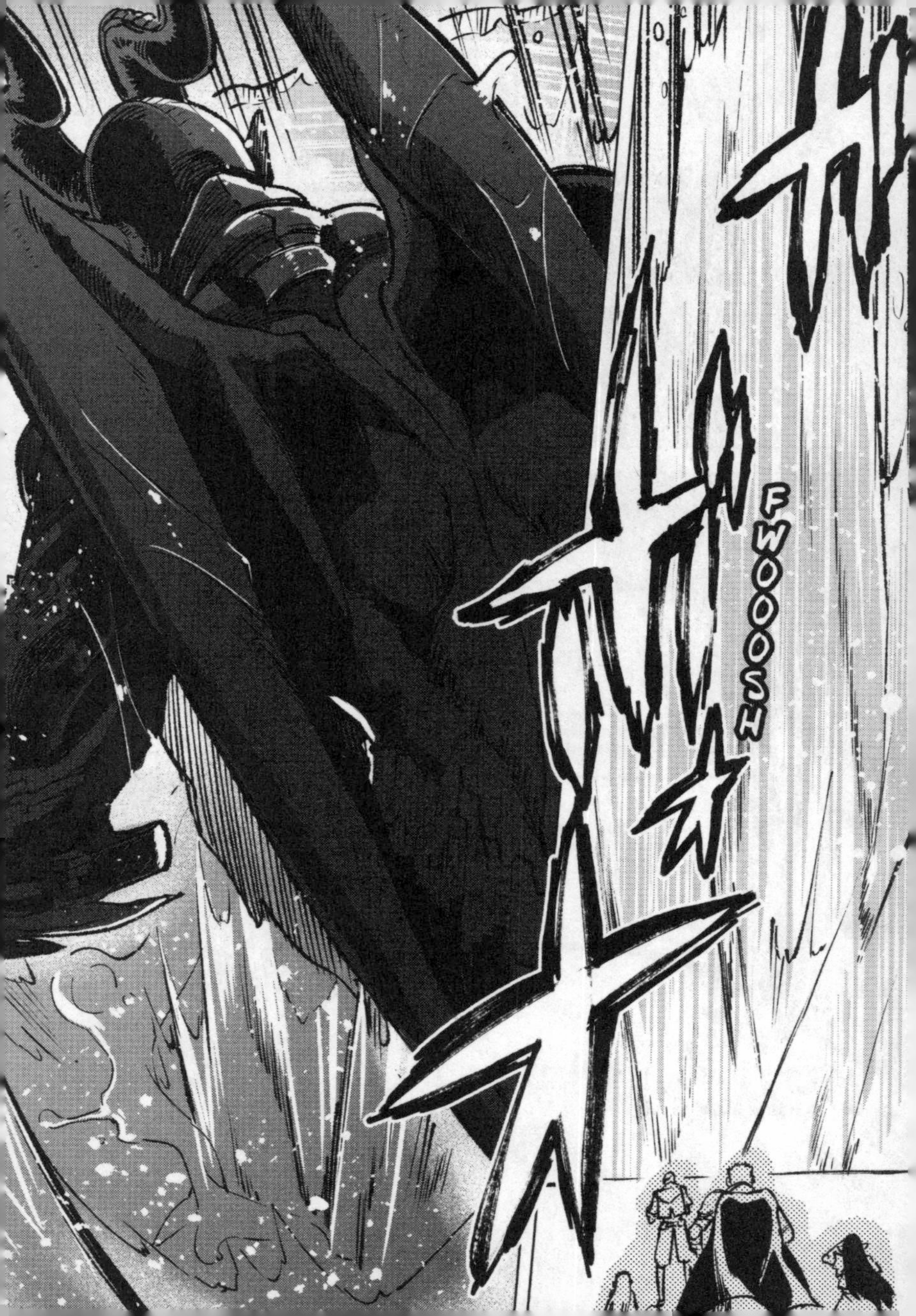
FWOOOSH

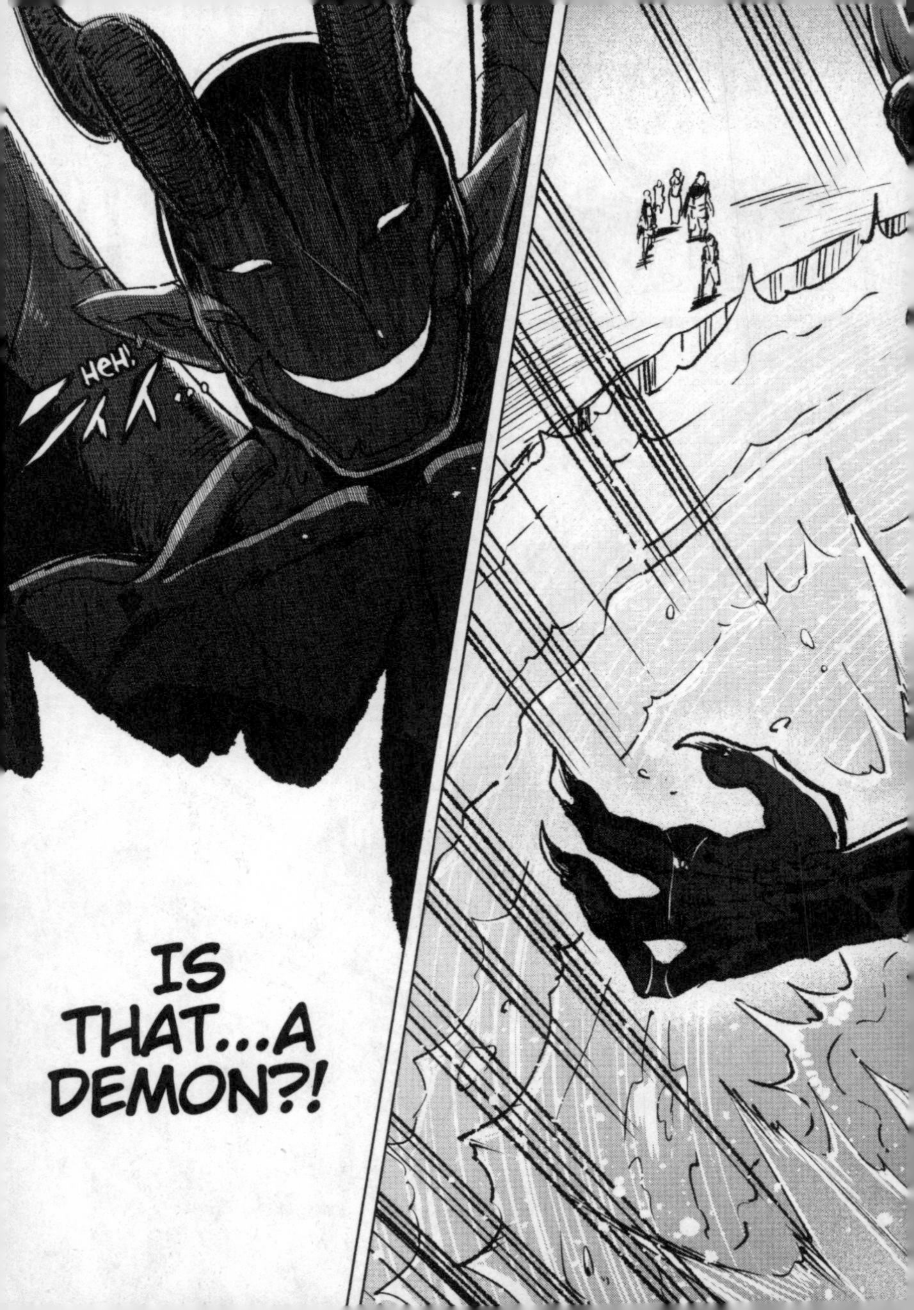
HEH!
IS THAT...A DEMON?!

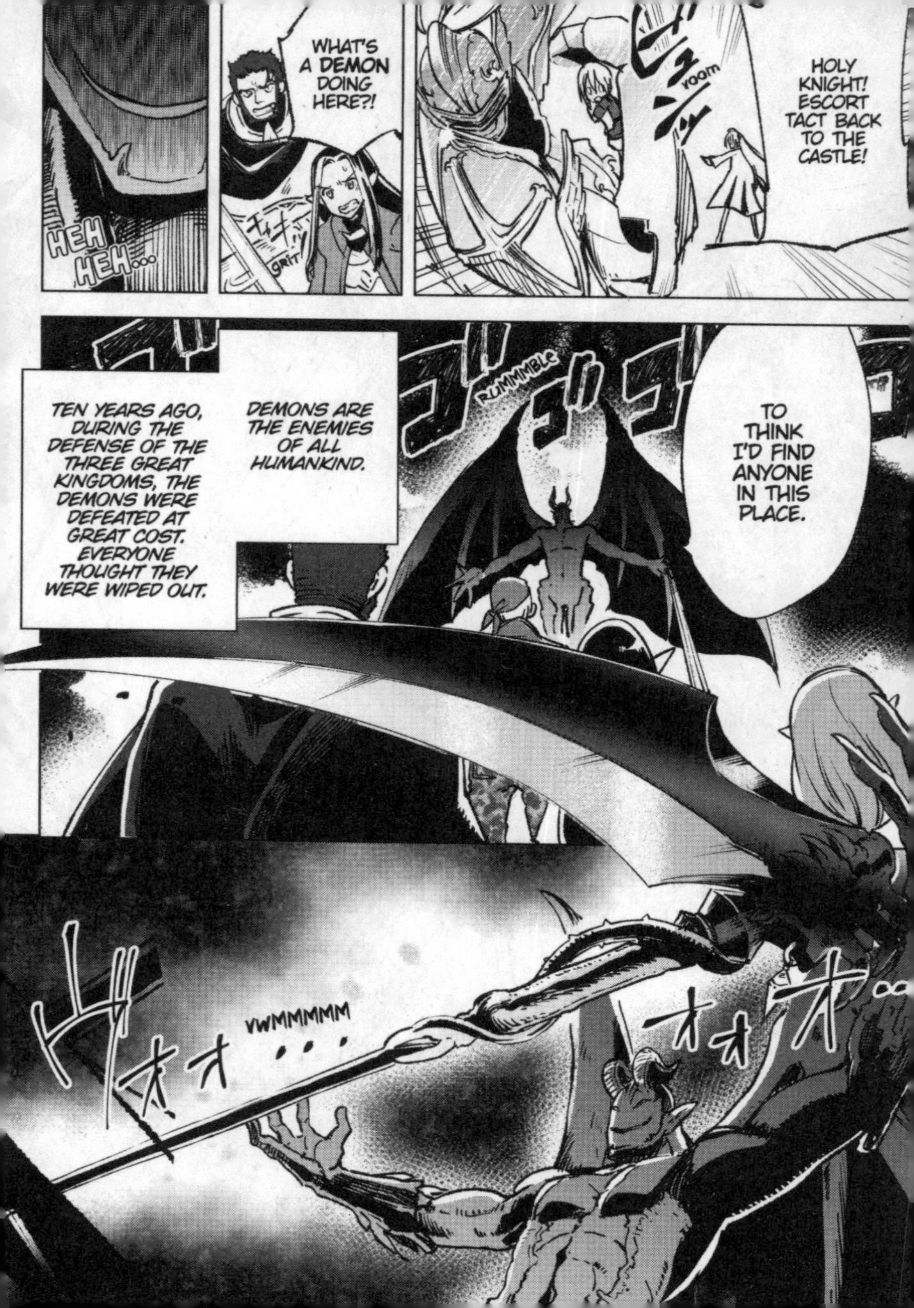

HOLY KNIGHT! ESCORT TACT BACK TO THE CASTLE!
VOOM
WHAT'S A DEMON DOING HERE?!
GRIT
HEH HEH...
TO THINK I'D FIND ANYONE IN THIS PLACE.
RUMMMBLE
DEMONS ARE THE ENEMIES OF ALL HUMANKIND.
TEN YEARS AGO, DURING THE DEFENSE OF THE THREE GREAT KINGDOMS, THE DEMONS WERE DEFEATED AT GREAT COST. EVERYONE THOUGHT THEY WERE WIPED OUT.
VWMMMMMM

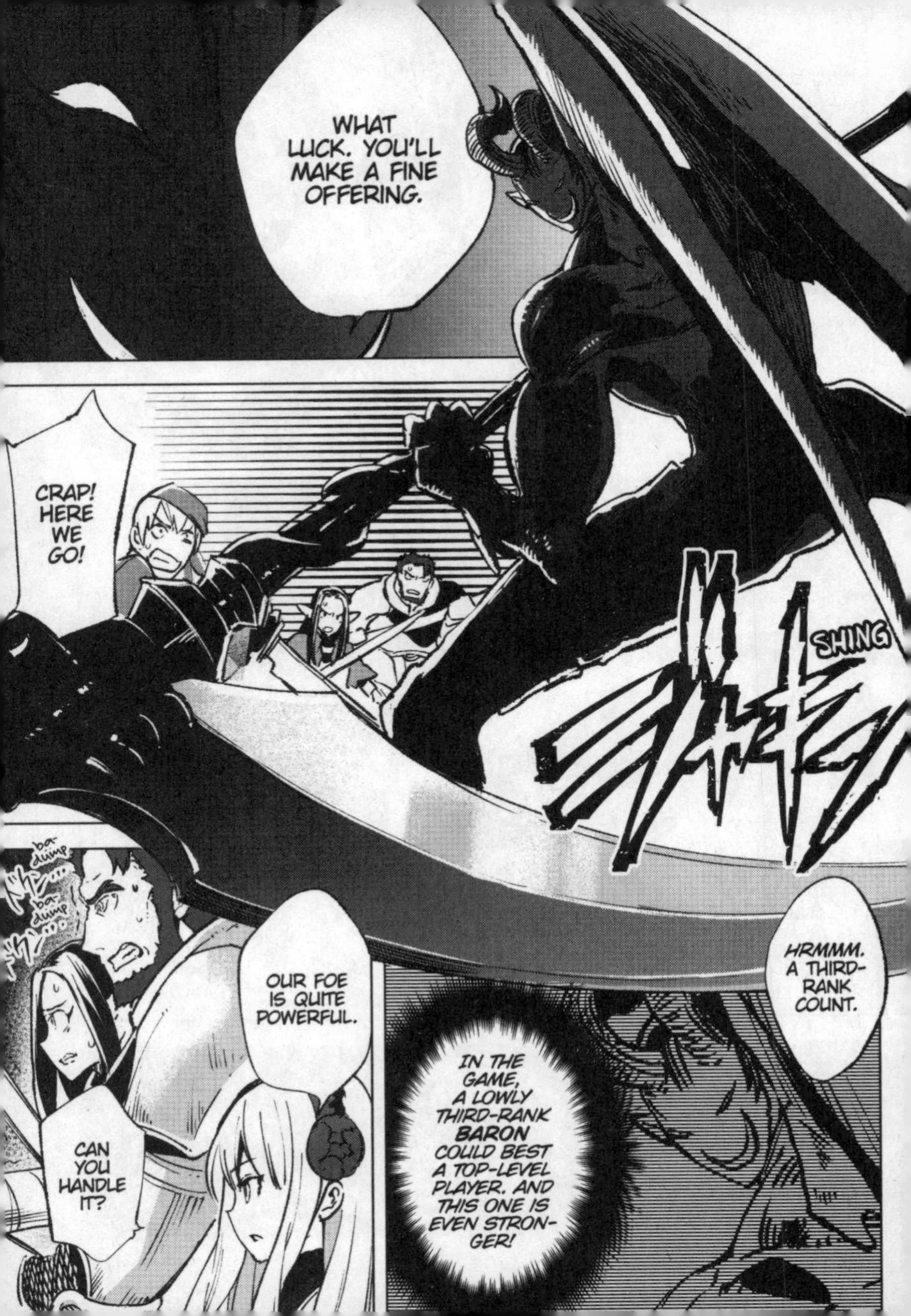
WHAT LUCK. YOU'LL MAKE A FINE OFFERING.
CRAP! HERE WE GO!
SHING
HRMMM. A THIRD-RANK COUNT.
IN THE GAME, A LOWLY THIRD-RANK BARON COULD BEST A TOP-LEVEL PLAYER. AND THIS ONE IS EVEN STRONGER!
ba-dump... ba-dump...
OUR FOE IS QUITE POWERFUL.
CAN YOU HANDLE IT?

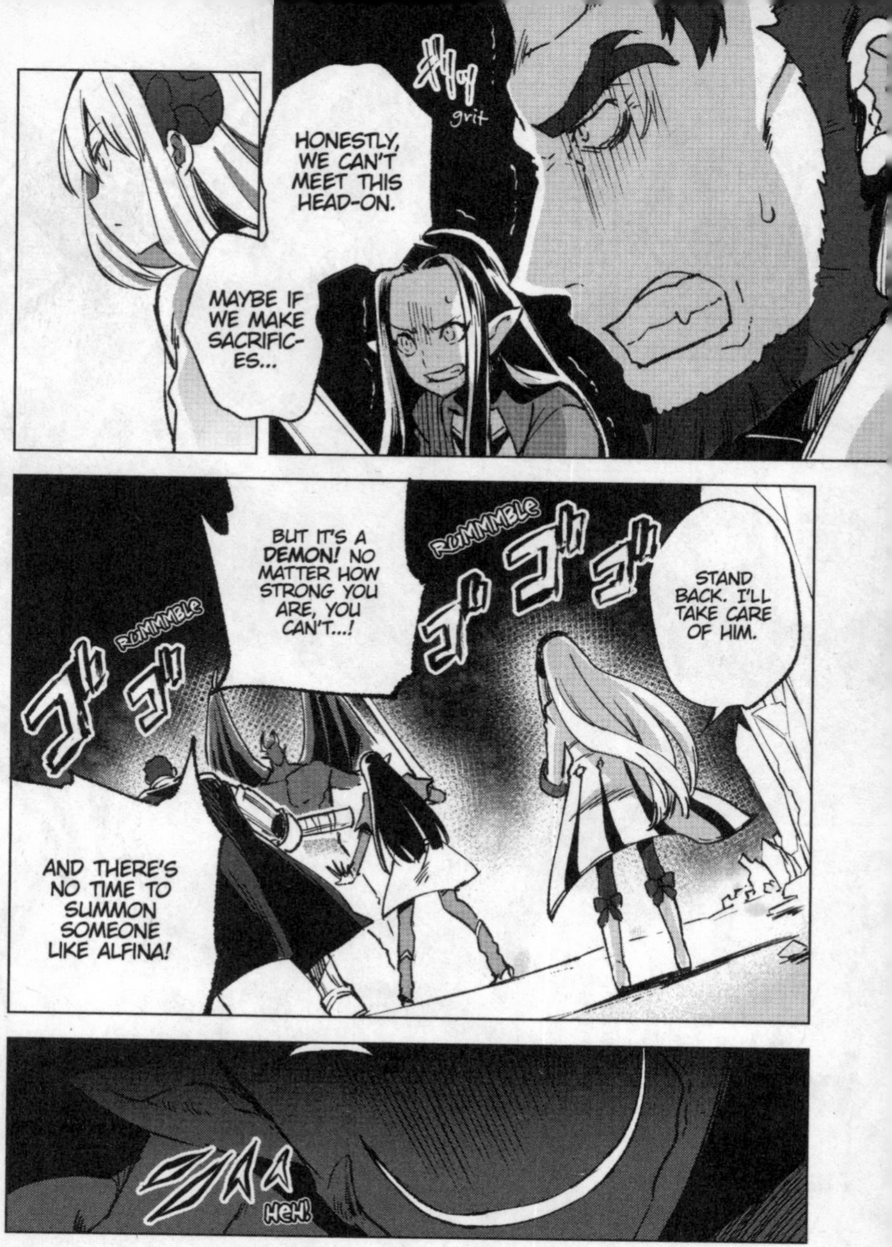
grit
HONESTLY, WE CAN'T MEET THIS HEAD-ON.
MAYBE IF WE MAKE SACRIFIC-ES...
STAND BACK. I'LL TAKE CARE OF HIM.
RUMMMBLE
BUT IT'S A DEMON! NO MATTER HOW STRONG YOU ARE, YOU CAN'T...!
RUMMMBLE
AND THERE'S NO TIME TO SUMMON SOMEONE LIKE ALFINA!
HEH!

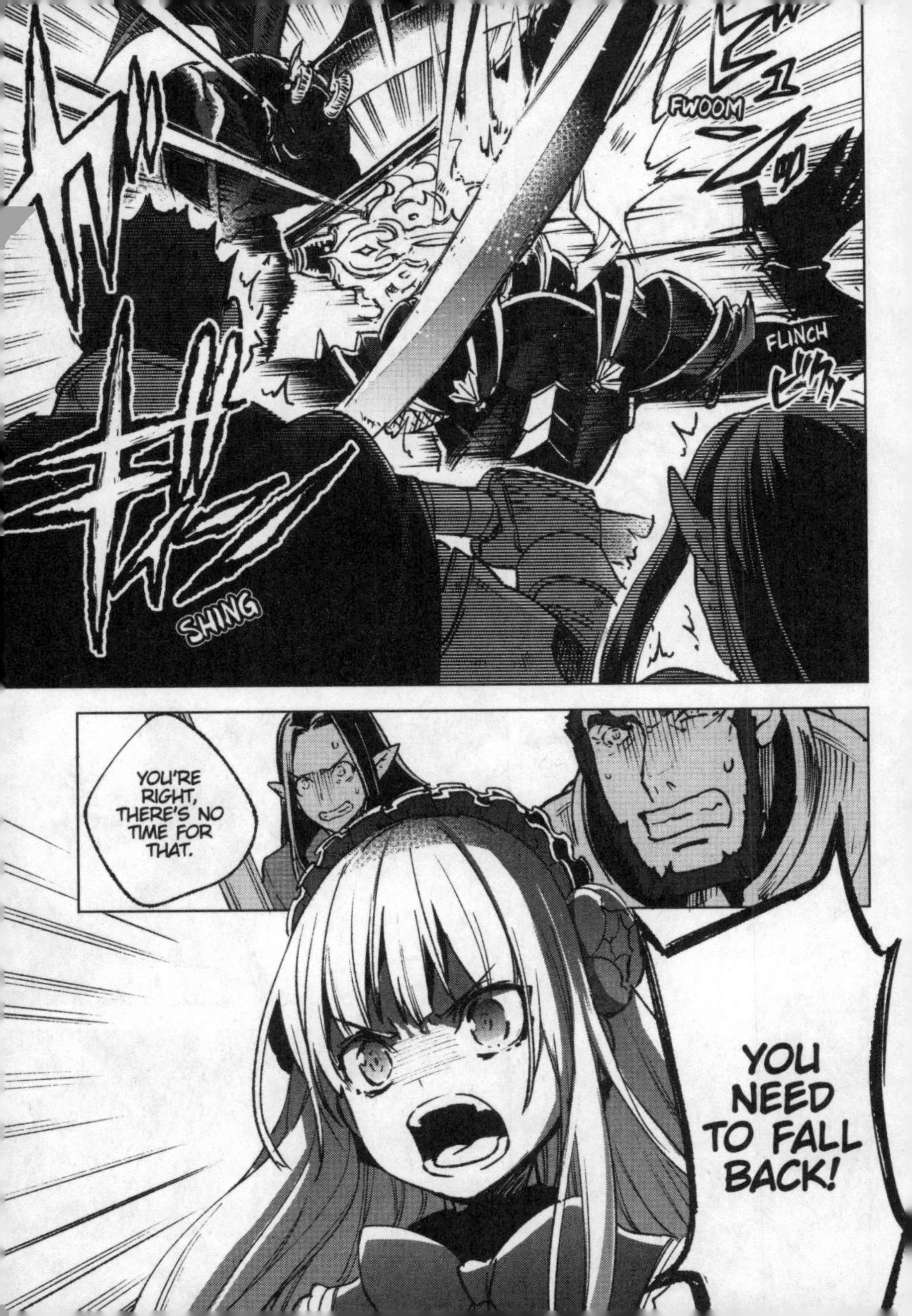
FWOOM
FLINCH
SHING
YOU NEED TO FALL BACK!
YOU'RE RIGHT, THERE'S NO TIME FOR THAT.

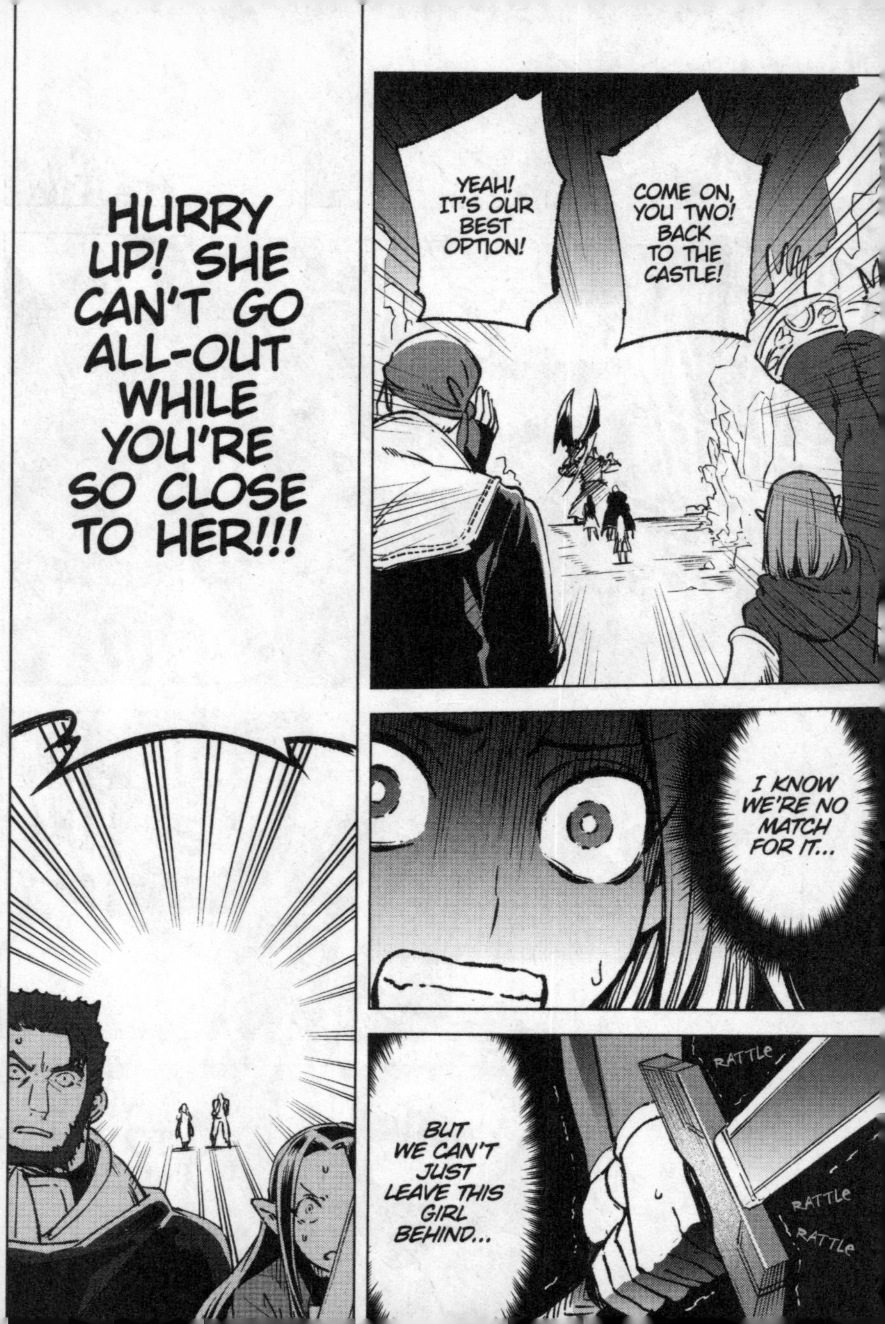
COME ON, YOU TWO! BACK TO THE CASTLE!
YEAH! IT'S OUR BEST OPTION!
I KNOW WE'RE NO MATCH FOR IT...
RATTLE
RATTLE
RATTLE
BUT WE CAN'T JUST LEAVE THIS GIRL BEHIND...
HURRY UP! SHE CAN'T GO ALL-OUT WHILE YOU'RE SO CLOSE TO HER!!!

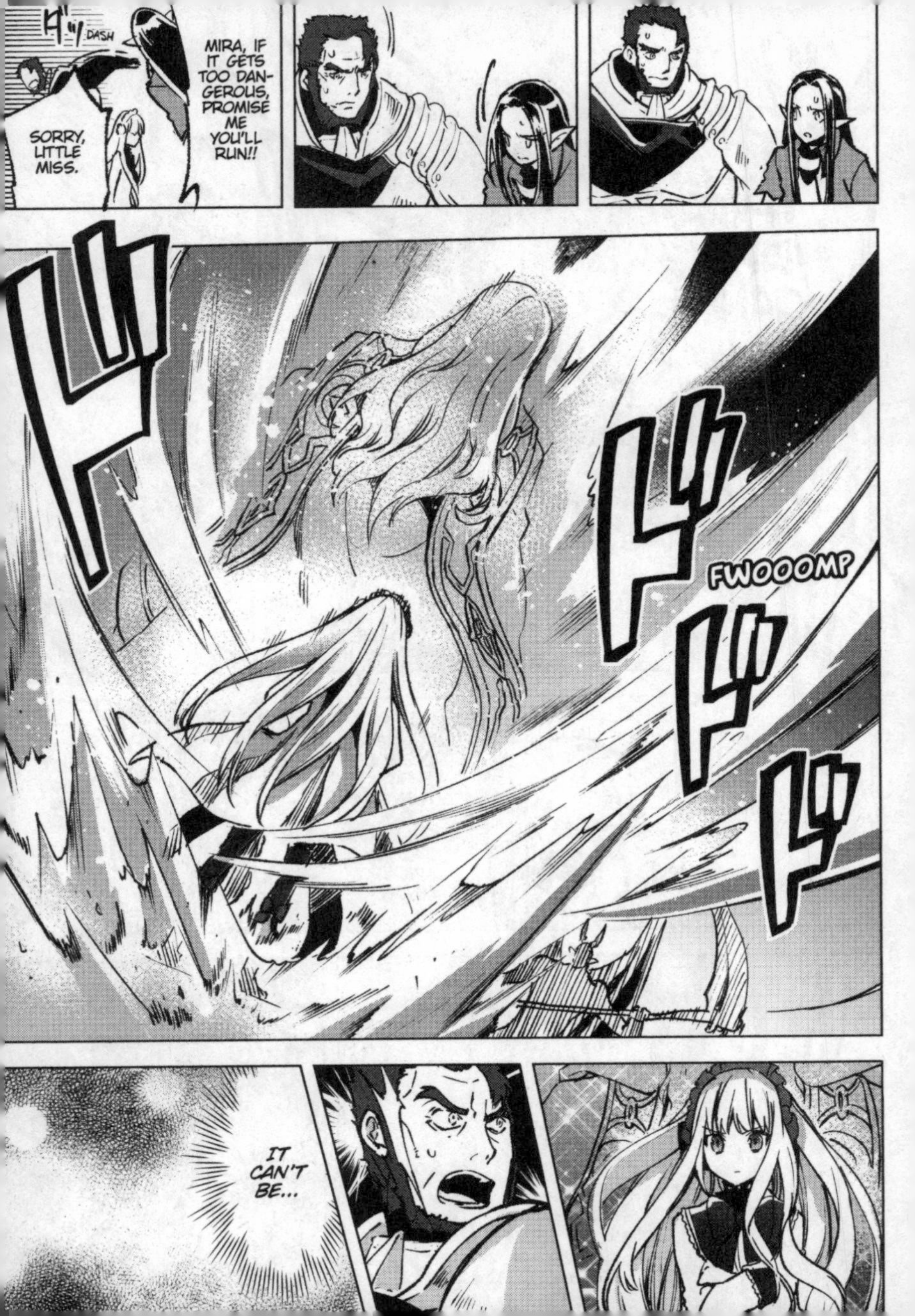
MIRA, IF IT GETS TOO DAN-GEROUS, PROMISE ME YOU'LL RUN!!
DASH
SORRY, LITTLE MISS.
FWOOOMP
IT CAN'T BE...

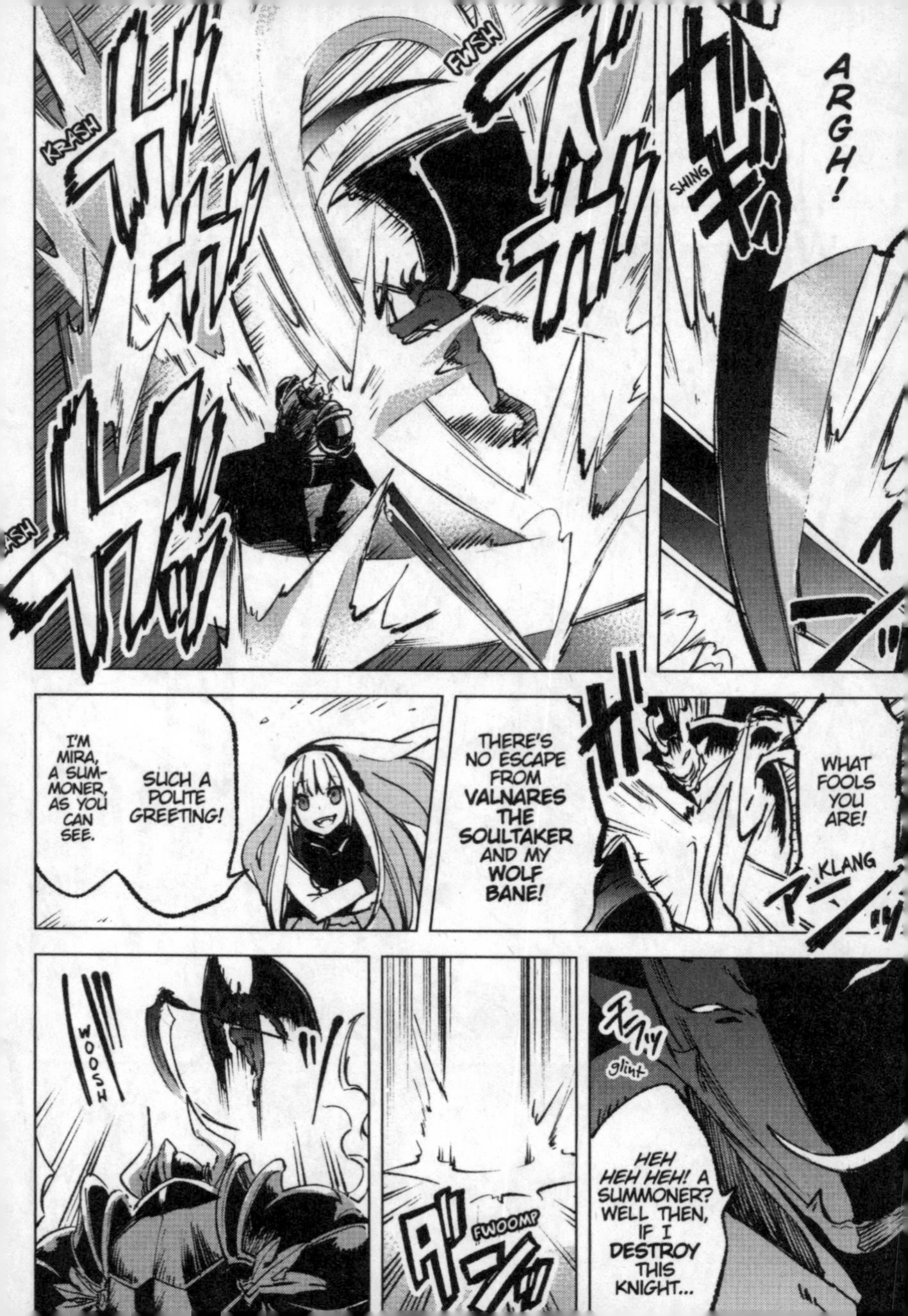
ARGH!
SHING
FWSH
KRASH
ASH
WHAT FOOLS YOU ARE!
THERE'S NO ESCAPE FROM VALNARES THE SOULTAKER AND MY WOLF BANE!
KLANG
SUCH A POLITE GREETING!
I'M MIRA, A SUMMONER, AS YOU CAN SEE.
glint
HEH HEH HEH! A SUMMONER? WELL THEN, IF I DESTROY THIS KNIGHT...
FWOOMP
WOOSH

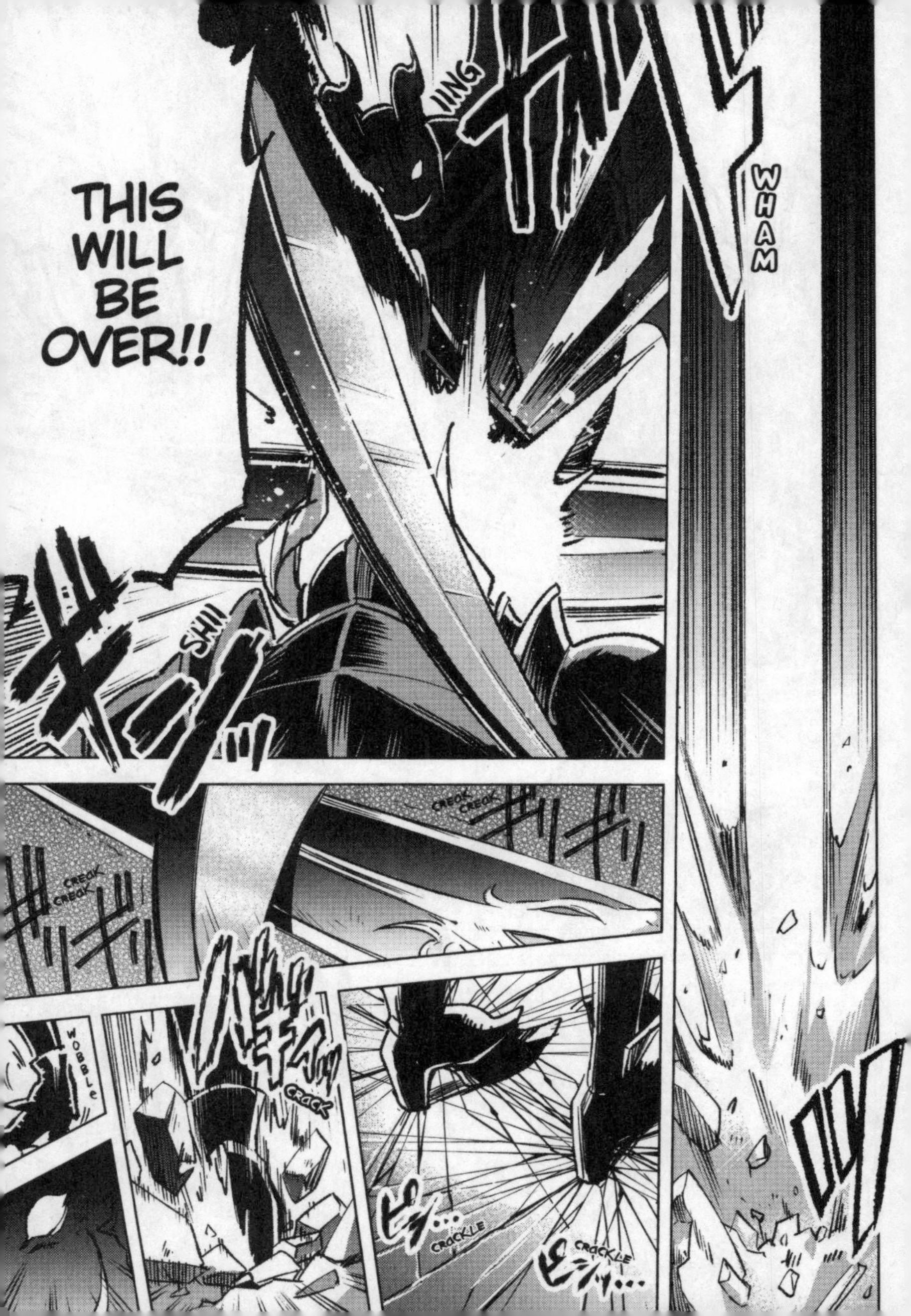
WHAM
JING
THIS WILL BE OVER!!
SHII
CREAK CREAK
CREAK CREAK
CRACKLE
CRACKLE
CRACK
WOBBLE

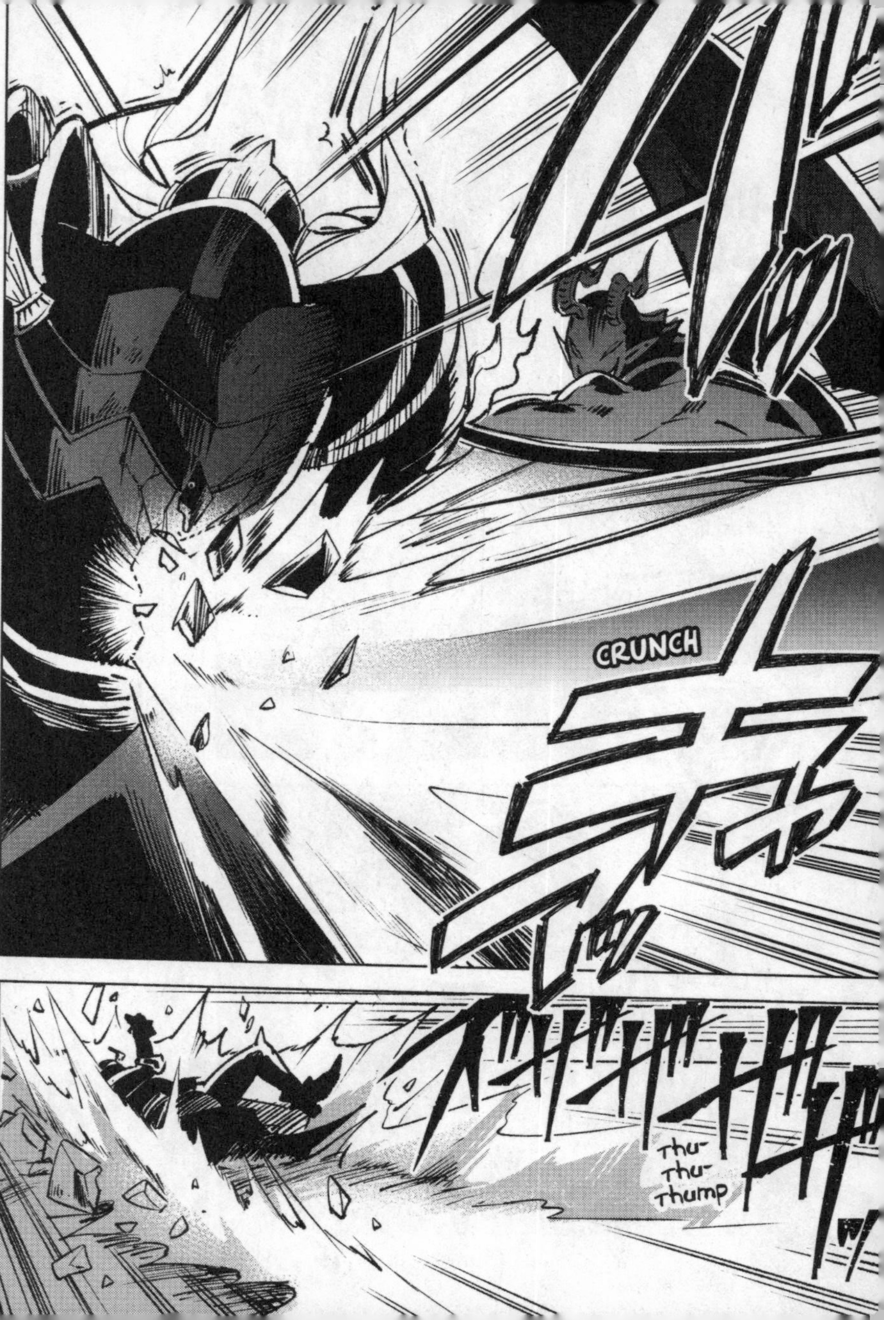
CRUNCH
Thu-
Thu-
Thump

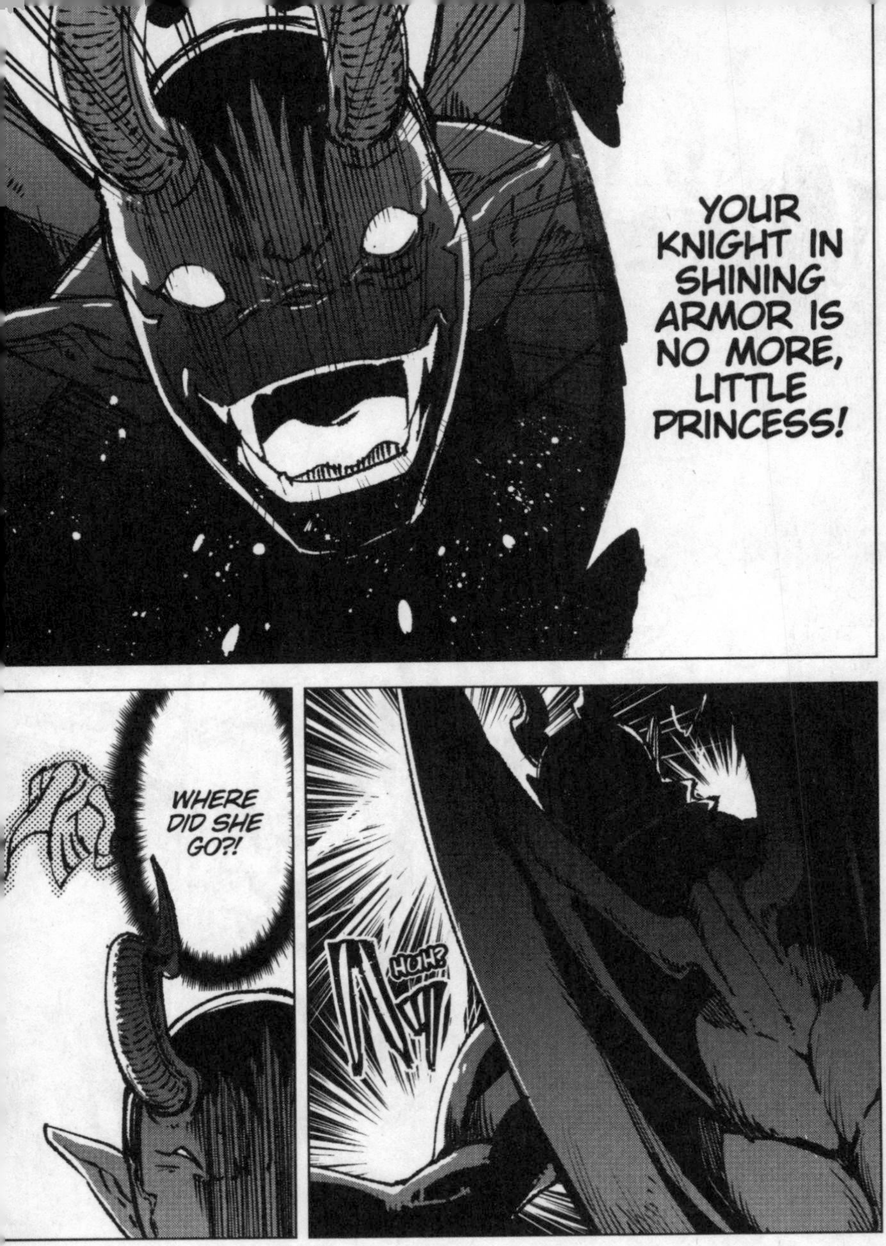
YOUR KNIGHT IN SHINING ARMOR IS NO MORE, LITTLE PRINCESS!
HUH?
WHERE DID SHE GO?!

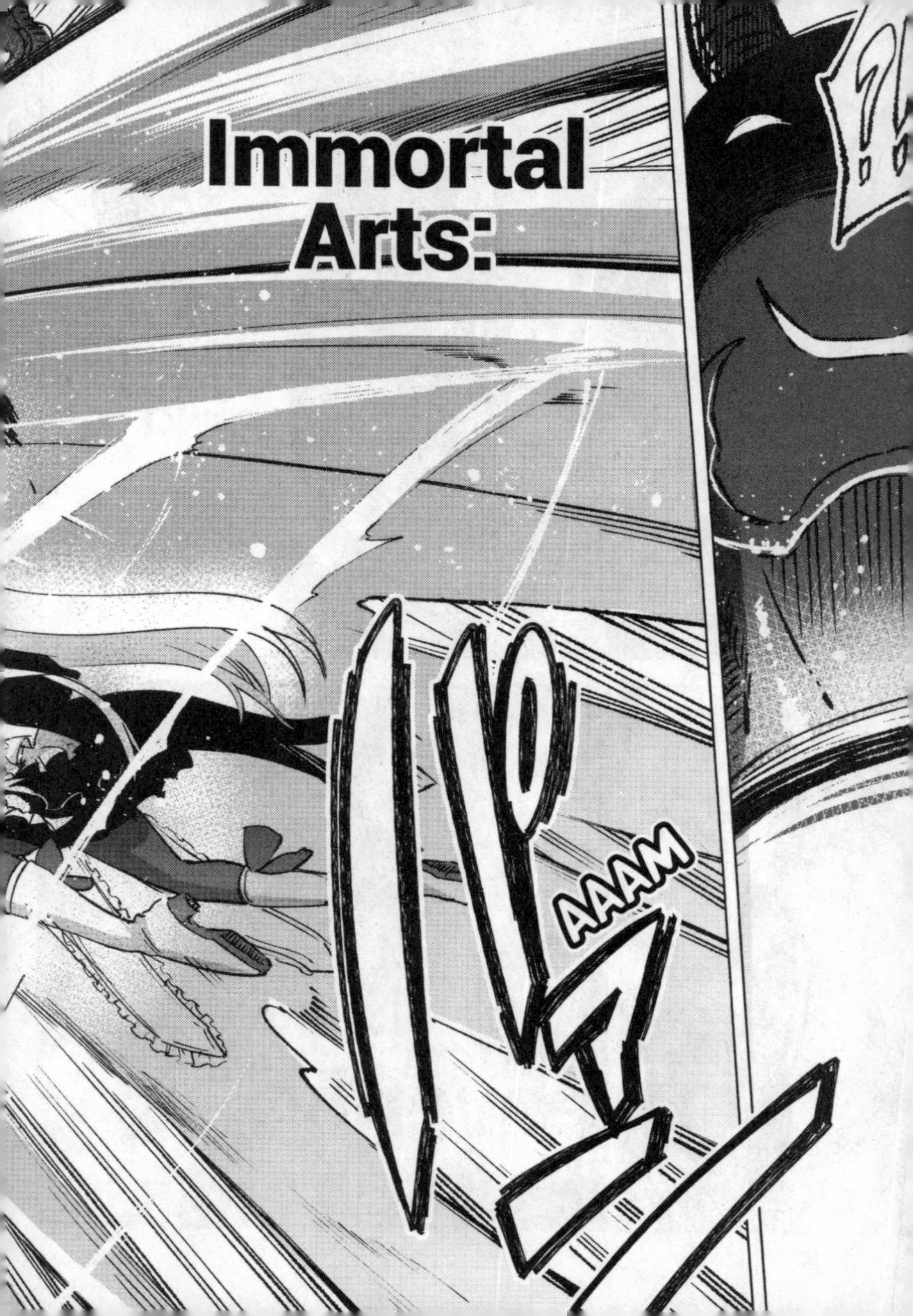
?!
Immortal Arts:
AAAM

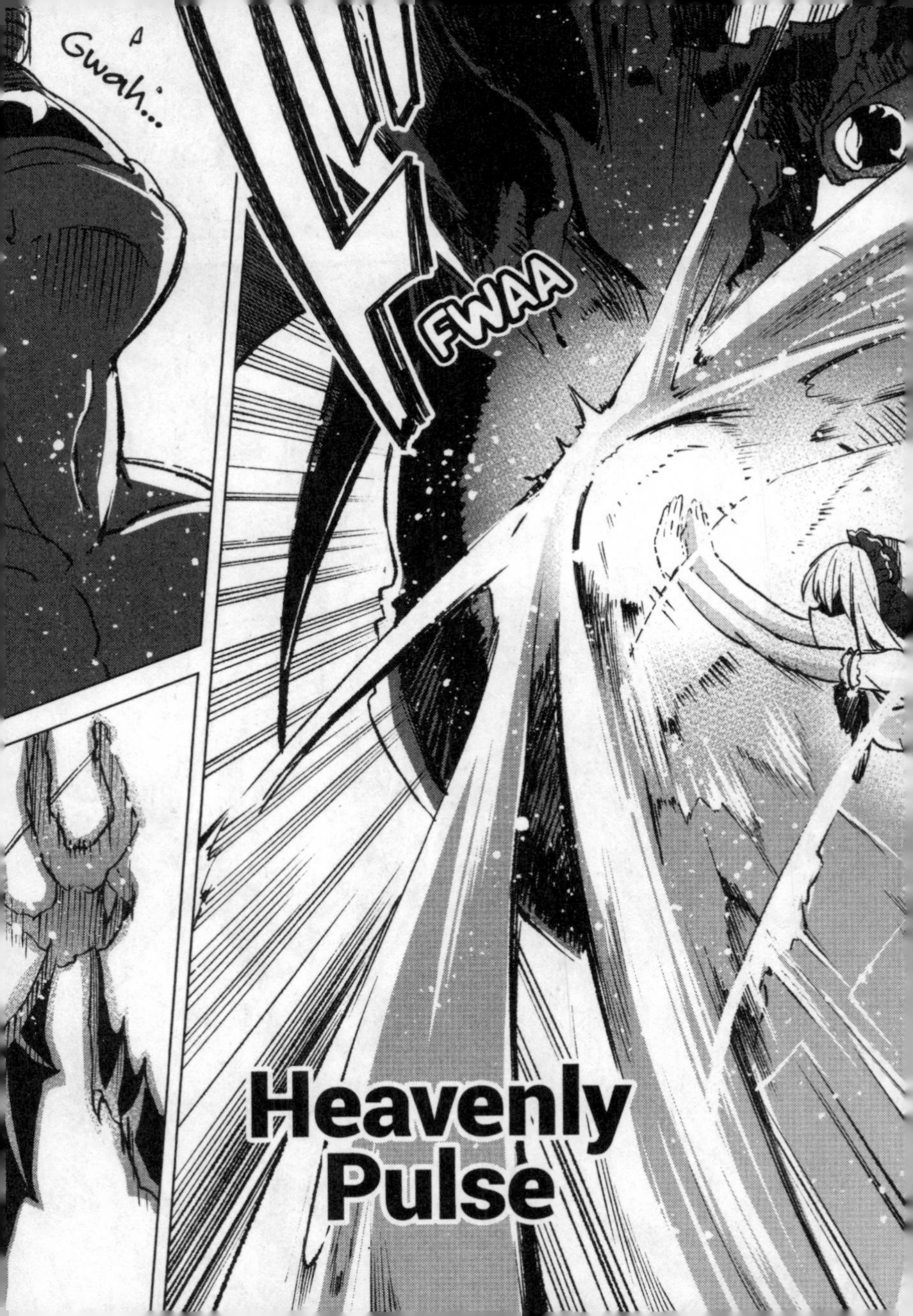

FWAA
Gwah...
Heavenly Pulse

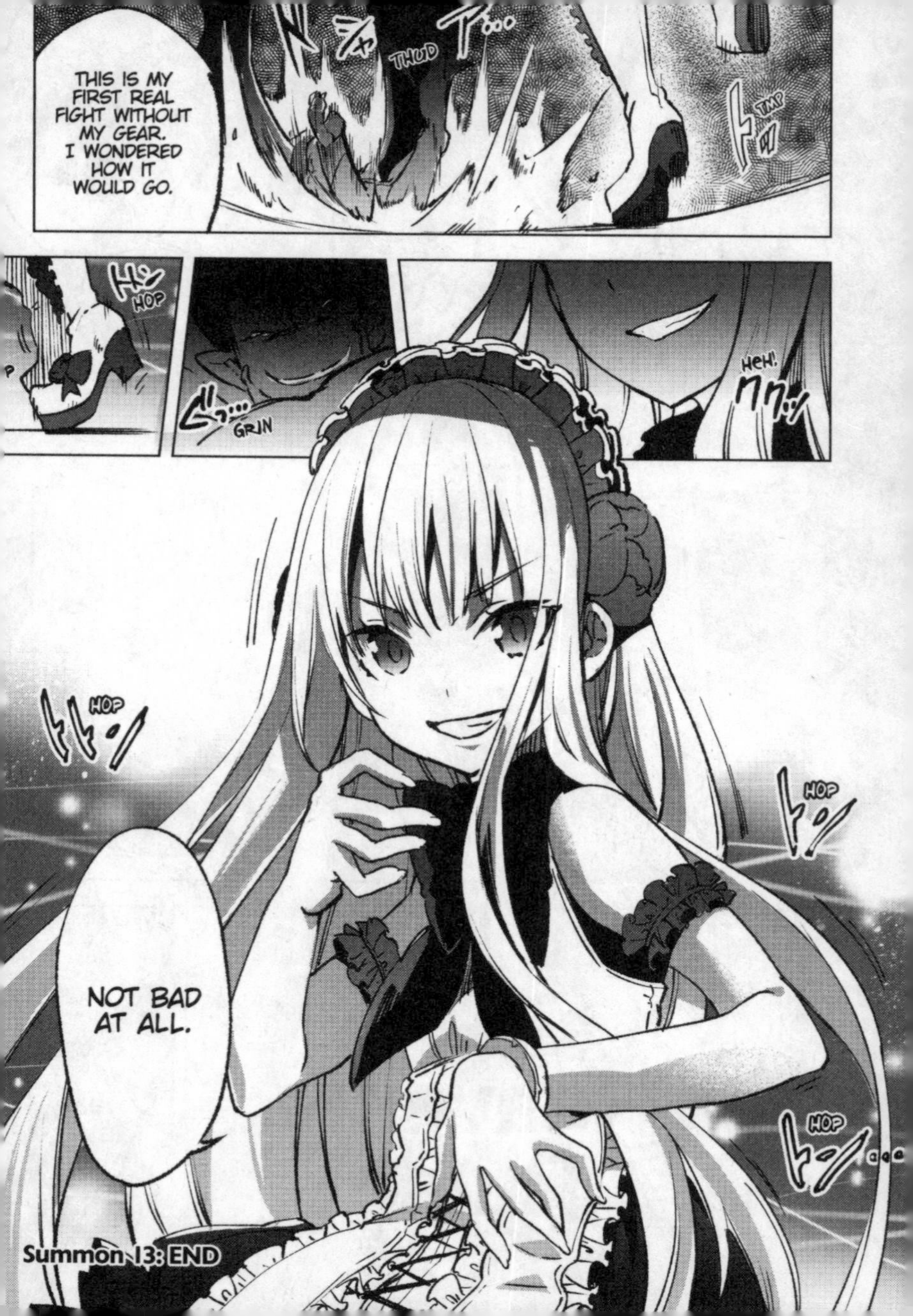
TMP
THUD
THIS IS MY FIRST REAL FIGHT WITHOUT MY GEAR. I WONDERED HOW IT WOULD GO.
HEH!
GRIN
HOP
HOP
HOP
HOP
NOT BAD AT ALL.
Summon 13: END

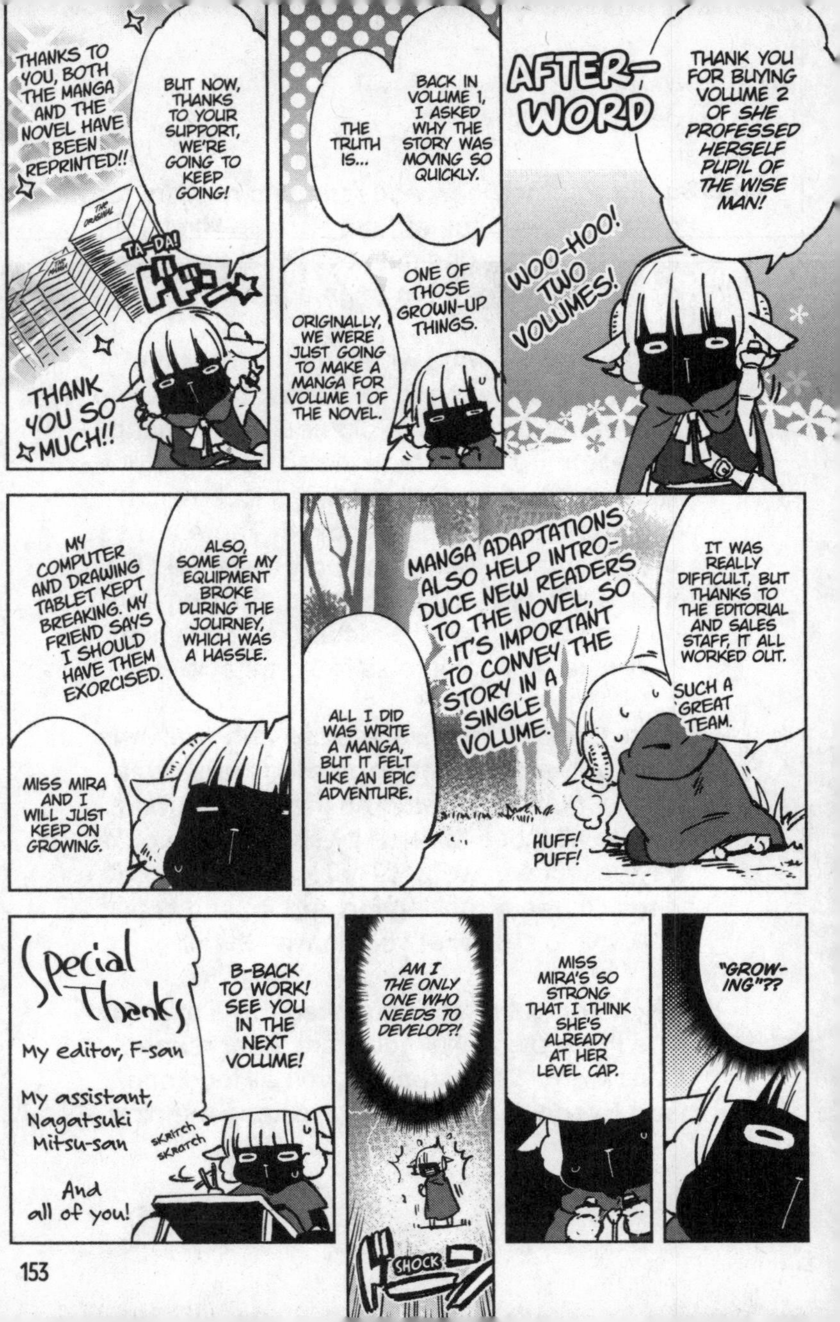
AFTER-WORD
THANK YOU FOR BUYING VOLUME 2 OF SHE PROFESSED HERSELF PUPIL OF THE WISE MAN!
WOO-HOO! TWO VOLUMES!
BACK IN VOLUME 1, I ASKED WHY THE STORY WAS MOVING SO QUICKLY.
THE TRUTH IS...
ONE OF THOSE GROWN-UP THINGS.
ORIGINALLY, WE WERE JUST GOING TO MAKE A MANGA FOR VOLUME 1 OF THE NOVEL.
BUT NOW, THANKS TO YOUR SUPPORT, WE'RE GOING TO KEEP GOING!
THANKS TO YOU, BOTH THE MANGA AND THE NOVEL HAVE BEEN REPRINTED!!
THE ORIGINAL
THE MANGA
TA-DA!
THANK YOU SO MUCH!!
IT WAS REALLY DIFFICULT, BUT THANKS TO THE EDITORIAL AND SALES STAFF, IT ALL WORKED OUT.
SUCH A GREAT TEAM.
MANGA ADAPTATIONS ALSO HELP INTRO-DUCE NEW READERS TO THE NOVEL, SO IT'S IMPORTANT TO CONVEY THE STORY IN A SINGLE VOLUME.
ALL I DID WAS WRITE A MANGA, BUT IT FELT LIKE AN EPIC ADVENTURE.
HUFF! PUFF!
ALSO, SOME OF MY EQUIPMENT BROKE DURING THE JOURNEY, WHICH WAS A HASSLE.
MY COMPUTER AND DRAWING TABLET KEPT BREAKING. MY FRIEND SAYS I SHOULD HAVE THEM EXORCISED.
MISS MIRA AND I WILL JUST KEEP ON GROWING.
"GROW-ING"??
MISS MIRA'S SO STRONG THAT I THINK SHE'S ALREADY AT HER LEVEL CAP.
AM I THE ONLY ONE WHO NEEDS TO DEVELOP?!
SHOCK
B-BACK TO WORK! SEE YOU IN THE NEXT VOLUME!
Special Thanks
My editor, F-san
My assistant, Nagatsuki Mitsu-san
And all of you!
SKRITCH SKRATCH

Thanks to all my new and returning readers for purchasing this volume! I am Ryusen Hirotsugu, the author of the original novel, and this is my postscript for the manga adaptation.

In the novel, I write whatever I want at the end, but I'm going to try to be a bit more serious here. So here is Volume 2 of the manga adaptation! It's very emotional to see my story turned into manga. I've always loved this medium, so I'm incredibly moved. There are so many manga out there. And now there's a story that I created with my own hands. For someone who can't draw a simple picture, much less an entire manga, it feels like a miracle.

Thanks to dicca*suemitsu-sensei and everyone else involved with *She Professed Herself the Pupil of the Wise Man*. And thanks for giving shape to all those Mira panty shots that I could only describe in words! There are a lot more scenes I'm really looking forward to, and I can't wait to see what you do with them.

Oops, sorry, got a bit sidetracked. But I'm pretty sure that's also what you want, dear reader. Don't worry. We're reading you all loud and clear! Everything's just going to keep ramping up… *Heh heh heh.*

Getting back to the second volume, it covers exactly half of Volume 2 of the novel. How many years has it been since I wrote this part of the story? Back then, I had no idea how far this story would take me. I could only dream it would become a manga one day. I never thought it would actually happen. I guess you never know what life will bring.

Volume 2 marks the first appearance of Écarlate Carillon, who definitely have more of a role to play in the future. I'm so grateful to dicca*suemitsu-sensei for bringing them to life so vividly. You created such a fine portrayal of Zef's past, which I didn't fully explore in the novel. It brought me to tears. You made everyone so much more fascinating than I imagined, and Emella's still the wonderful caring older sister, quickly and efficiently keeping Flicker in line.

Oh, right. Flicker. She's just so...Flicker, right? Now that it's a manga, it all flares so violently to life. I can't wait for the next chapter. Thank you for all of your continued hard work. Oh, and if you can, please also read the novel!

Ryusen Hirotsugu

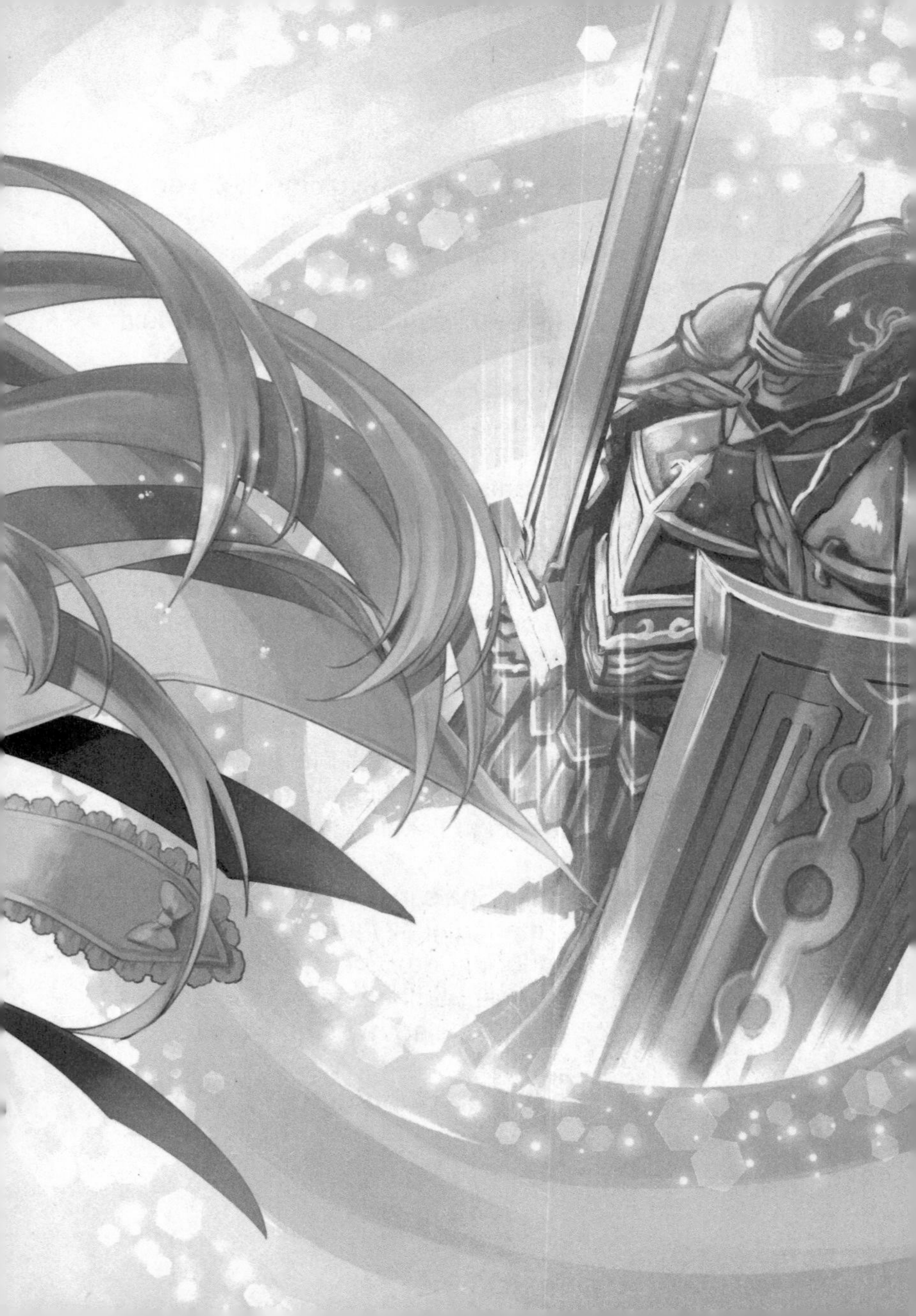

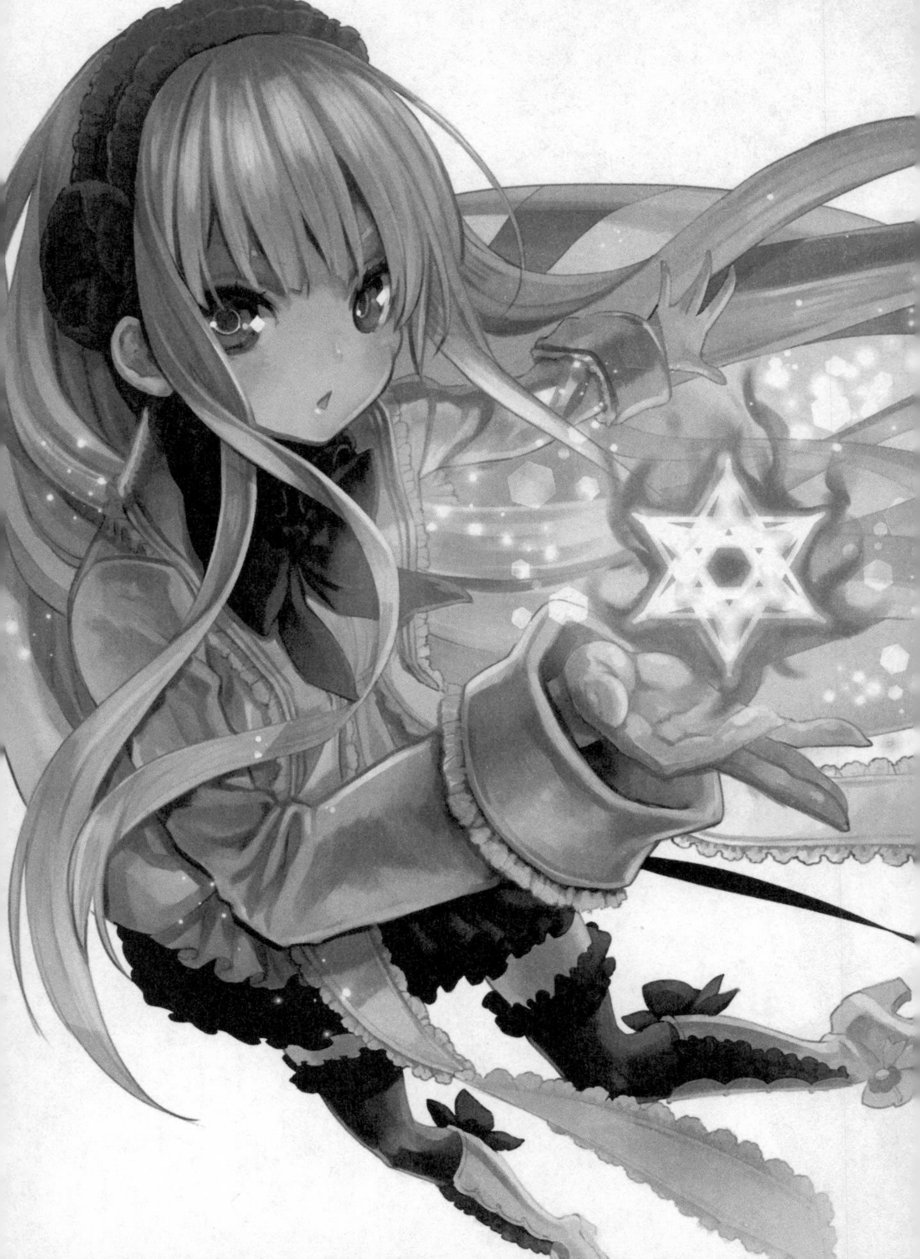

She
Professed
Herself
Pupil of the
Wise Man

SEVEN SEAS ENTERTAINMENT PRESENTS

She Professed Herself Pupil of the Wise Man

Vol. 2

story by RYUSEN HIROTSUGU   art by DICCA*SUEMITSU   character design by FUZICHOCO

TRANSLATION
Wesley O'Donnell

ADAPTATION
C.A. Hawksmoor

LETTERING
Carl Vanstiphout

COVER DESIGN
Nicky Lim

LOGO DESIGN
George Panella

PROOFREADER
Danielle King

EDITOR
Peter Adrian Behravesh

PREPRESS TECHNICIAN
Rhiannon Rasmussen-Silverstein

PRODUCTION ASSOCIATE
Christa Miesner

PRODUCTION MANAGER
Lissa Pattillo

MANAGING EDITOR
Julie Davis

ASSOCIATE PUBLISHER
Adam Arnold

PUBLISHER
Jason DeAngelis

Kenja no deshi wo nanoru kenja
©dicca*suemitsu (Art) ©Ryusen Hirotsugu (Original Story)
This edition originally published in Japan in 2017 by
MICRO MAGAZINE, INC., Tokyo.
English translation rights arranged with MICRO MAGAZINE, INC., Tokyo.

No portion of this book may be reproduced or transmitted in any form without written
permission from the copyright holders. This is a work of fiction. Names, characters,
places, and incidents are the products of the author's imagination or are used
fictitiously. Any resemblance to actual events, locales, or persons, living or dead,
is entirely coincidental. Any information or opinions expressed by the creators of this
book belong to those individual creators and do not necessarily reflect the views of
Seven Seas Entertainment or its employees.

Seven Seas press and purchase enquiries can be sent to Marketing Manager Lianne
Sentar at press@gomanga.com. Information regarding the distribution and purchase of
digital editions is available from Digital Manager CK Russell at digital@gomanga.com.

Seven Seas and the Seven Seas logo are trademarks of
Seven Seas Entertainment. All rights reserved.

ISBN:978-1-64827-442-8
Printed in Canada
First Printing: September 2021
10 9 8 7 6 5 4 3 2 1

//// READING DIRECTIONS ////

This book reads from *right to left*,
Japanese style. If this is your first time
reading manga, you start reading from
the top right panel on each page and
take it from there. If you get lost, just
follow the numbered diagram here.
It may seem backwards at first,
but you'll get the hang of it! Have fun!!

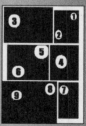

She Professed Herself Pupil of the Wise Man

STREAM THE ANIME
NOW ON FUNIMATION

funimation.com/sheprofessedherself

funimation ©2021 Hirotsugu Ryusen,Fuzichoco/MICRO MAGAZINE/I'm cute Project